ETHEREGE & WYCHERLEY

ENGLISH DRAMATISTS
Series Editor: Bruce King

Published titles

Susan Bassnett, *Shakespeare: The Elizabethan Plays*
John Bull, *Vanbrugh and Farquhar*
Richard Allen Cave, *Ben Jonson*
B. A. Kachur, *Etherege and Wycherley*
Philip C. McGuire, *Shakespeare: The Jacobean Plays*
Kate McLuskie, *Dekker and Heywood*
Christine Richardson and Jackie Johnston, *Medieval Drama*
Margarete Rubik, *Early Women Dramatists 1550–1800*
Roger Sales, *Christopher Marlowe*
David Thomas, *William Congreve*
Martin White, *Middleton and Tourneur*
Katharine Worth, *Sheridan and Goldsmith*
Rowland Wymer, *Webster and Ford*

ENGLISH DRAMATISTS

ETHEREGE
&
WYCHERLEY

B. A. Kachur

Department of English
University of Missouri–St. Louis

First published 2004 by
PALGRAVE MACMILLAN
Houndmills, Basingstoke, Hampshire RG21 6XS and
175 Fifth Avenue, New York, N.Y. 10010
Companies and representatives throughout the world

PALGRAVE MACMILLAN is the global academic imprint of the Palgrave
Macmillan division of St. Martin's Press, LLC and of Palgrave Macmillan Ltd.
Macmillan® is a registered trademark in the United States, United Kingdom
and other countries. Palgrave is a registered trademark in the European
Union and other countries.

ISBN 0–333–57540–7 hardback
ISBN 0–333–57541–5 paperback

This book is printed on paper suitable for recycling and made from fully
managed and sustained forest sources.

A catalogue record for this book is available from the British Library.

Library of Congress Cataloging-in-Publication Data
Kachur, B. A. (Barbara A.), 1950–
    Etherege & Wycherley/B. A. Kachur.
    p. cm. – (English dramatists)
    Includes bibliographical references (p.) and index.
    ISBN 0–333–57540–7 (cloth) – ISBN 0–333–57541–5 (pbk.)
        1. Etherege, George, Sir, 1635?–1691–Criticism and interpretation.
2. Wycherley, William, 1640–1716–Criticism and interpretation. 3. English
drama–Restoration, 1660–1700–History and criticism. 4. Comedy. I. Title:
Etherege and Wycherley. II. Title. III. English dramatists (Palgrave Macmillan
(Firm))

PR3432.K33 2004
822'.05230904–dc22

                                                                        2003067561

10   9   8   7   6   5   4   3   2   1
13   12   11   10   09   08   07   06   05   04

Transferred to digital printing 2005

Contents

Editor's Preface

Each generation needs to be introduced to the culture and great works of the past and to reinterpret them in its own ways. This series re-examines the important English dramatists of earlier centuries in the light of new information, new interests and new attitudes. The books are written for students, theatre-goers and general readers who want an up-to-date view of the plays and dramatists, with emphasis on drama as theatre and on stage, social and political history. Attention is given to what is known about performance, acting styles, changing interpretations, the stages and theatres of the time and theatre economics. The books will be relevant to those interested in studying literature, theatre and cultural history.

BRUCE KING

Acknowledgements and Textual Notes

First, thanks to Bruce King for his invitation to write this book, which I hope makes a modest contribution to the study of Etherege's and Wycherley's comedies. To all of those who aided me in my research abroad – Christopher Robinson for his assistance in guiding me through the wealth of primary documents in the Old Vic Archives at the University of Bristol, the helpful and attentive staff at the British Library's Manuscript and Reading Room, and the patient and friendly assistants at London's Theatre Museum who retrieved the myriad documents I requested faster than I could pore over them – a special thanks not only for their help in giving me access to materials crucial to this study but also for their genuine kindness that made my research trek all the more enjoyable and memorable. To those at the University of Missouri–St. Louis who helped lighten my burden during the preparation of this manuscript – in particular the library staff for their quick responses to my many interlibrary-loan requests, the research board that generously funded my trip to England, my colleague James Tierney for his helpful suggestions regarding non-dramatic Carolean literature, the English department's inimitable administrative team, Jessie Bridges and Gloria Henderson, for their loyalty in all things related to department chairpersons, and Dean Mark A. Burkholder for his unflagging support and encouragement – my sincerest thanks.

My gratitude to a group of very special colleagues – Ruth Bohan, Kathy Justice Gentile, Stephanie Ross and Jeanne Morgan Zarucchi – whose graciousness in allowing Etherege and Wycherley to dominate many hours of conversations about research projects deserves far more than an appreciatory remark; their sound suggestions during the manuscript's various incarnations helped me to proceed with enhanced clarity of purpose. And finally, to Joann Lindsey, whose friendship and sense of humour enable me always to put everything meaningful in its proper perspective.

Space restrictions preclude a study of all seven plays by Etherege and Wycherley, and thus three comedies – *The Comical Revenge*, *Love in a Wood* and *The Gentleman Dancing-Master* – have been omitted to allow more in-depth coverage of the remaining four plays which are the most frequently studied and performed, particularly *The Country Wife*. All quotes and lineation from the plays are taken from Michael Cordner (ed.), *The Plays of George Etherege* (Cambridge University Press, 1982), and Peter Holland (ed.), *The Plays of William Wycherley* (Cambridge University Press, 1981).

To J. T.

'Thanks, and thanks, and ever thanks.'
(Shakespeare)

1
Carolean Context

The yoking of George Etherege and William Wycherley in this study of early English drama proves both apposite and instructive. Although they wrote a combined total of only seven comedies, some of these remain among the most studied and performed in the Restoration canon, and both playwrights – though markedly different in their dramaturgical style, tone, and intent – have garnered a significant place in the history of dramatic literature by virtue of not only their masterpieces but also the extent to which they exerted influence on contemporary and future playwrights of this period. The importance of Etherege and Wycherley, however, lies equally outside the parameters of dramaturgy, for as playwrights during the early years of the Restoration – writing roughly coterminously between 1664 and 1676 – Etherege and Wycherley reveal similar preoccupations with the radical social, political and cultural changes effected by the dissolution of the 18-year Puritan regime and the restoration of Charles II to the throne. With Charles's return as England's king came the revocation of an austere life and Puritan constraints and in their place the tacit promise of national stability, individual liberty, personal prosperity, and ultimately the reinstatement of both a 'natural order' of things and a traditional hierarchy of classes.

Although the restoration of Charles to the throne established a new court as well as new social and cultural forms that presaged regeneration, his monarchy could not, of course, actually 'restore' those pre-revolutionary conditions – political, social, cultural and ideological – that had formed England's previous national identity. In reality, at the Restoration's outset, the English found themselves with no immediate past to reclaim (Charles would demand they disavow the Cromwellian years) and a future not as yet identified, and this initial uncertainty and disconnexion gave rise to a palpable admixture of optimism, anxiety, and confusion – contradictory impulses born out of polarised views as to precisely what conditions should constitute the new epoch. Poised at the threshold of this era, many people glanced back at the most recent object of nostalgia in the pre-war reign of Charles I and hoped for its mythic 'eternal return', while others looked forward to a radically new era divorced from the historical past. But neither the Restoration itself nor the period of Charles's monarchy offered people either option exclusively, and emerging from this conflicted and unsettled climate were tensions and cross-currents in cultural, social, political and ideological longings. Etherege and Wycherley, each in his own unique way, reflect in their plays these conditions that characterised the Carolean years.

This reflection on the part of Etherege and Wycherley of a very specific moment in English history – Charles's reign, 1660–85 – marks them out as distinctly 'Carolean' rather than 'Restoration' dramatists. Of course, the latter term has been applied regularly to them, but 'Restoration' actually proves an inaccurate label because it positions Etherege and Wycherley in too broad a context, both temporally and dramaturgically, to allow for their particular historical connectedness. Typically, the term Restoration drama has come to denote a 40-year span of performance history bracketed by the inception of Charles's monarchy in 1660 and the beginning of Queen Anne's reign in 1702, a temporal block which extends well beyond Charles's reign to include that of his brother, James II (1685–8), as well as William and Mary (1689–1702).[1] While this conventional periodisation has the singular advantage of providing a relatively neat and tidy historical unit – the reinstatement of the Stuart monarchial line with Charles up to the *fin de siècle* – its application to Etherege and Wycherley has the distinct disadvantage of incorrectly suggesting that their works likewise belong to some discrete, organic whole: a monolithic literary movement which began in 1660 and ended at the turn of the century. As a result, classifying Etherege and Wycherley as Restoration playwrights ineluctably locates them primarily in the trajectory of British drama over the course of four decades, and, by extension, fosters an assessment of their works within the larger corpus of later seventeenth-century drama. Indeed, most studies on 'Restoration' drama typically position Etherege and Wycherley in this manner, ferreting out in their plays those dramaturgical or characterological details that were incorporated, modified or perfected by playwrights such as Congreve, Farquhar, and Vanbrugh, writers whose works commonly denote the apogee and culmination of Restoration comedy. While such studies do afford important insight into the development of Restoration drama, such analyses of the quasi-evolutionary effects of Etherege's and Wycherley's plays must necessarily limit discussion to trends and developments in those dramatic details that can be traced over the course of 40 years of drama (e.g., the progression of the rake hero) and, therefore, must necessarily elide analysis of their plays' contents relative to topical issues (e.g., the 'myth' of the Restoration) unique to the Carolean period. As 'Restoration' playwrights, Etherege and Wycherley are positioned in an expansive chronology that obscures the special topicality of their plays, but as 'Carolean' dramatists they are foregrounded as mediators of their own historical moment.

Suggesting that Etherege and Wycherley reflected in their plays the historical conditions of Charles's reign does not imply that they wrote overtly political comedies per se. Of course, their plays – like those by other Carolean playwrights, such as Aphra Behn, whose Tory comedies proffered her royalist inclinations – could comment patently on topical issues and sentiments, such as the anti-Puritan attitudes espoused in Etherege's *The Comical Revenge* or Wycherley's *Love in a Wood*. Most typically, however, they finessed their comedies with subtlety and complexity, so much so, in fact, that in some cases their characters and themes defy critical consensus. As a case in point, the appetitive lead males in Etherege's *The Man of Mode* and Wycherley's *The Country Wife* (Dorimant and Horner, respectively) have been characterised in disparate terms ranging from contemptible libertines emulative of Charles II's debauched court, embodiments of prevailing debates about rationalistic and naturalistic human behaviour, to heroes representative of their age's liberation from Puritan oppression, while the plays themselves have in turn been analysed variously as pure entertainments offering realistic and non-didactic reflections of seventeenth-century London life, endorsements – or, contrarily, indictments – of the radical new theories in philosophy and ontology, farces that reflect transhistorical truths about human appetites and motives, or satiric tracts aimed at a code of ethics and morality rooted in Christian humanism that was now regarded by some as suspect and specious. These are just a few interpretations, but the wealth and variety of these and other critical approaches to the plays by Etherege and Wycherley suggest not only that their works possess a depth and intricacy that preclude univocal readings but also that their comedies manifest the prevailing as well as the conflicting forces and beliefs – both positive and negative – that mark the years of Charles II's reign as anything but cohesive and recuperative. Etherege's and Wycherley's comedies – like much of the literature from the Carolean period – resonate, sometimes stridently and other times obliquely, with social commentary on an era that witnessed a newly restored monarch who brought about positive changes in the social, cultural and intellectual fabric of England but whose indolence, profligacy and maladministration rent tears of disenchantment, dissension, and anxiety across that very fabric.

On 25 May 1660, Charles Stuart disembarked from the Admiral's barge and stepped ashore on the beaches of Dover to reclaim the monarchy that had been vacated by his father, Charles I, at the start of England's Civil War in 1642. After enduring years of isolation, poverty, and starvation while a nomadic fugitive in exile (Cromwell had put a hefty price on his head), Charles II returned to England and stood ready to govern a country that he had tried to recapture militarily on several occasions. Four days later, on 29 May, the king's thirtieth birthday, Charles II began his journey from Canterbury to Whitehall Palace accompanied by his two brothers (James, Duke of York and Henry, Duke of Gloucester) as well as other royalists, and hours later when he made his regal entrance on horseback in London, he was greeted by exultant throngs cheering loudly in the streets and at every window, accompanied by music playing gaily, bells ringing joyously, trumpets blaring triumphantly, and wine flowing freely from fountains – clearly the Interregnum had ended and with it the Puritan laws against all forms of civic merrymaking and pageantry.[2] The royal procession's passage through the flower-strewn streets of London – with a cortège of some 20,000 loyal supporters carried on horseback and myriad others on foot – lasted seven hours, but London's celebratory fervour did not end when Charles arrived at his palace, for the festivities continued non-stop for days after and took on carnival proportions reminiscent of the rites of spring and likening Charles's return to the worship of something as inherently divine as it was divinely ordained. Surely no one in attendance misunderstood that he was witnessing anything short of an historic and momentous event: the reinstatement of a monarchial line in a country previously embroiled in national wars and most recently ruled under the military regime of a usurper.

Without question, Charles II's restoration to the English throne had mythic significance, and in the months preceding the king's restoration as well as in the wake of it, writers crafted panegyrics that sought to glorify his return and to engender similar elation among citizens – not all of whom, particularly the Puritans, welcomed Charles's return – by casting light on the 'restoration' within a requisite religious context, one congenial with those supernatural views through which English society habitually interpreted all events: their poems rhapsodised on the 'second coming' of the English monarchy as a miraculous act of providence. Positioning Charles's return within such positive religious-cum-political propaganda to valorise and authenticate it, however, required that panegyrists focus beyond God's agency in the matter, for they likewise needed to rewrite the recent history of those past atrocities – the regicide of Charles I and Cromwell's usurpation – to which the public had acquiesced on similar grounds. To gloss over the contradiction that providence had also been invoked earlier to justify the inception, existence and survival of Cromwell's commonwealth just as it was now being wielded again to validate Charles's restoration, poets implied that providence and history did not always work in tandem and that God's hand had finally set the world right by effecting the reinstatement of the divinely sanctioned Stuart monarchy – a feudal system of royal, hereditary birthright to which Charles himself subscribed and took great pleasure to foster immediately: within a month of his restoration, the king had spent two days verifying to all his semi-divine status by lending his 'healing' touch to some 1000 people afflicted with scrofula.[3]

Panegyrists, thus having handily dismissed the past, next set about the equally important task of framing the future in a way that mollified the average Englishman's acute fears about his uncertain fate, the possibility of Charles's wholesale retaliation against the country for its treason against his father and its passive support of Cromwell, and, equally disturbing, the very real potential for a resurgence of national strife leading to another civil war, particularly one arising from religious sects. Culling imagery from history, mythology, and religion, poets drew laudatory analogues between powerful figures and the 'resurrected' Charles, using references to such figures as Constantine or Christ. Most often, they relied on allusions to the classical past when forecasting the future of Charles's reign, intimating that England's restored king would not only govern with the compassion and strength of the great Roman leaders such as Augustus, he would stabilise the country and lead it to greatness in all things – from its military strength and world dominance to its cultural, intellectual and artistic enterprises – that would not only mirror the great empires of the past but would also eclipse them in power and glory.[4] Such were the expectations held by royalist poets and much of the country at the beginning of Charles's monarchy, but such hope for either an empire to challenge that of Rome's or a return to a mythic past of peace and concord eroded early within the first decade of the Restoration.

Prior to that erosion of confidence, however, Charles demonstrated that he could be an able and clement leader. In the early years of his administration, he dispatched his royal duties with great energy and political acumen. And as he promised in his Restoration Settlement – the Declaration of Breda, presented to Parliament on 1 May just prior to his return – Charles remained merciful toward his father's traitors, granting a full pardon to anyone who appealed for forgiveness within 40 days, the sole exceptions being the 41 regicides who had signed Charles I's death warrant. After 14 were executed, Charles, 'weary of the hanging',[5] halted the killings and spared the others. In one last act of revenge, Charles sent a chilling message to those covert dissenters rumoured to be plotting against him: the bodies of Oliver Cromwell and two others who presided over Charles I's trial were exhumed and, after being hung publicly from gibbets for a few weeks, the corpses were taken down and beheaded. With the past thus put to rest symbolically, Charles next turned his attention toward his vision of England's 'restoration'.

Although Charles had hoped to repair a good deal of the damage done by the civil wars and Cromwell's regime, such a complete recovery was not possible, for the various terms of the Declaration of Breda left unresolved numerous issues relating to religious affiliation and property rights which created residual dissension and rifts that lasted throughout his reign and beyond. Charles, having the prescience to envisage continual conflict between England's restored Anglican Church and various religious sects (Roman Catholics and other protestant nonconformists such as the Quakers, Baptists, and Presbyterians), made provisions in the Declaration for a future Act of Parliament that would sanction religious toleration. Unfortunately, neither the Convention Parliament that approved Charles's return (composed of Anglicans and Presbyterians) nor its successor, the Cavalier Parliament, which stood from 1661 to 1678 (composed of Cavaliers and Anglicans), would allow for legislation granting such unilateral tolerance. In fact, over the course of a number of years, Parliament issued laws that placed greater hardships and restrictions on non-Anglicans, imprisoning many, like the Quaker John Bunyan, who penned *Pilgrim's Progress* during his 12-year stay in Bedford Goal.[6] Such short-sightedness on the part of Parliament only served to feed the constant tension and divisiveness over religious factions, nurturing a sustained atmosphere of persecution, distrust and fear that finally crescendoed in 1678, when Titus Oates, an Anglican cleric who capitalised on the most intense paranoia shared by all religious groups that Rome's pope would once again control England and her subjects, concocted a colossal lie about a Jesuit plot to murder the king in order to put his brother, the Catholic James, on the throne and thereby re-establish Roman Catholicism as the country's sole religion. Public hysteria over this 'Popish Plot' was acute, ridiculous stories spread that the Jesuits planned to burn the city, witch-hunts ensued, thousands of Catholics were imprisoned while all others were ordered to leave London, and many were executed, on the basis of the perjured testimony of Oates. All the panic led precisely to where Oates and his political conspirators had hoped: to the 'Exclusion Crisis' – Parliament's effort to exclude James from succession, a movement that Charles defeated summarily by dissolving Parliament in 1681, ruling without it until the end of his reign in 1685. The Exclusion Crisis provides an excellent barometer for measuring the palpable degree of fear over religious sects that pervaded this era as well as the hostility that could erupt so fiercely in this climate of intolerance and ignorance, and during the nearly four-year battle over James's exclusion from the throne during which every Englishman lived in constant panic and apprehension over internal warfare, poems and plays (see Chapter 2) addressed issues of rightful succession and revisited the past horrors of civil war in an attempt to assuage the madness.

Just as Charles's steps toward religious toleration proved fruitless, so, too, did his plans for an equitable land settlement fall markedly short with the failure of the Restoration Settlement to return to royalists the estates they had to forfeit to Cromwell's government, and their plight as displaced aristocrats, a plight which generated their feelings of resentment toward the king that never wholly attenuated, proved such a significant loss relative to the anticipated restoration of the natural (i.e., hierarchal) order of society that playwrights addressed its implications in their dramas. The gentry's dilemma was relatively simple and completely insurmountable: while the Declaration of Breda contained provisions for the return of all confiscated Crown and Church property, it stipulated that royalists who likewise had their estates seized outright could legally petition for the return of their property, but many of these aristocrats were locked in a 'catch-22' – without their income-producing land, they lacked the financial means to pursue the costly litigation that was required to reclaim it. In addition, those royalists who had to sell their lands (or mortgage them) in order to pay punitive penalties or exorbitant taxes imposed by the Interregnum government received no compensation and were left without legal recourse. Although recent scholarship suggests that little property belonging to the greater gentry actually changed hands, those owning smaller estates no doubt suffered most, and this group of royalists who had supported the Stuart cause (some even accompanying Charles into exile) felt betrayed and deprived, in large part because those who profited, and continued to profit, from their loss were those who had served the republican regime – lawyers, politicians, generals and other officials – and who now had the means and wealth to eclipse them.

Compounding the lesser gentry's feelings of unfair deprivation was the rapidly rising middle class who had also benefited substantially during the 18-year-long Interregnum: merchants, industrialists, financiers – those whose wealth was not tied solely to their property and the revenues it generated and whose business enterprises garnered them fortunes that not only threatened to challenge the traditional and hierarchal class structure which ideologically conflated land and title to birth and worth, but also threatened to infringe the gentry's perceived right of ownership in a large share of the country's governance. This erosion of the gentry's prestige and power as well as the threat of the ascendancy of the lesser classes was played out in the dramas of the period: from the exiled Cavalier who returns to reclaim his possessions (Bruce in Etherege's *The Comical Revenge*), the businessman consumed by his lust for money and prestige at Whitehall (Sir Jaspar Fidget in Wycherley's *The Country Wife*), the country fool of quite humble parentage who gains property and knighthood from Cromwell (Sir Nicholas in *The Comical Revenge*), to the aristocratic or upper-class libertine who, by marrying a wealthy heroine, garners an estate that symbolises the 'restoration' of his heritage, status, and power (Dorimant in Etherege's *The Man of Mode*), such characters convey the deep-seated resentment that survived the Interregnum and plagued England well after the Carolean era.

Although Parliament would offer no concessions to a Restoration Settlement that left many feeling marginalised, victimised and persecuted under the new Stuart regime, Charles did hit on a partial remedy for the land settlement's failure to reward those who had been loyal to both him and his father: he granted some royalists political appointments – such as Thomas Killigrew and Sir William Davenant, recipients of the two patents on London's newly restored theatrical productions – while others received positions or sinecures within his new court at Whitehall, giving many of them membership in an elite circle that recuperated their sense of entitlement and privilege by placing them at the centre of a royal court which set the tone for the country and which proved strikingly different from any in British history. To punctuate the permanent return of the Stuarts, Charles established a resplendent court modelled in part on that of his 21-year-old cousin and king of France, Louis XIV, whom he visited at Versailles during his exile in Paris. Particularly impressed by the French court's culture and elegance, Charles ordered Whitehall Palace, which had suffered severe neglect during the Interregnum, to be remodelled and outfitted with the finest French imports – from furniture to paintings to wine and food.

The extravagance and ostentation of Charles's court drew condemnation from many, particularly from London's 'citizens', those sober merchants and businessmen, who were mostly Puritans, residing within the ancient walls of the old City of London, the stronghold of mercantile England. But such was not the case with the inhabitants of the 'town', that affluent area around Covent Garden and St James's Square which stood between the city limits and Westminster. Here, with its fashionable shops, restaurants, coffee houses and playhouses all just a stone's throw from the court, London's upper class lived in luxury and possessed the wealth, education, culture and *savoir-faire* to emulate the manners and style of Whitehall Palace. Modelling themselves on Charles's dazzling court, the town's denizens – as well as any who had the means and desire to copy them – adopted not only the manners and culture of the court, but its fashion as well, which likewise followed French tastes and announced boldly that the austerity of Puritan life had ended: in lieu of the drab and dark Puritan gaberdine clothes were the resplendently colourful silk dresses for women, while the men – more spectacularly outfitted than the women – wore ruffled shirts with lace cuffs under a brocade doublet and knee-length waistcoats heavily trimmed with silver and gold, close-fitting silk hose with ankle-high shoes ornamented with ribbons or ornate buckles, a periwig made of luxurious shoulder-length curls, a large hat adorned with plumes, and, at the waist, a sword encased in an intricately embossed sheath. From the arts to fashion, Charles's court set the standard which many embraced as a rejection of Puritan sobriety.

While Charles's court had the external trappings of French culture, all similarities ended there. Unlike the formal ceremoniousness of Versailles, Whitehall was, simply put, a pleasure-palace where the 'Merry Monarch' established a gay and voluptuous court that was the most openly lascivious one in England's history, with the king himself setting the tone through a series of affairs that he never attempted to hide: from the night of his return to London with Barbara Villiers, his long-term mistress and wife to Roger Palmer, accompanying him to his royal bed, to a seemingly endless parade of actresses (including the popular Nell Gwyn), maids of honour, and other willing ladies, the priapic Charles carried on multiple seductions that fostered a permissive climate open to similarly lewd conduct from his courtiers who regarded female court attendants as fair game. Equal to its salaciousness, Whitehall also mirrored Charles's gaiety, congeniality, frivolity and charm, which made for a relaxed and informal court where the king always had time to visit with the string of artists, poets, scientists and scholars whose efforts he encouraged and patronised. The king particularly enjoyed the convivial company of a group of 14 clever and intelligent young men – including George Villiers (Duke of Buckingham and cousin to Barbara Palmer), Charles Sackville (Lord Buckhurst and Earl of Dorset), John Wilmot (Earl of Rochester), and the playwrights Etherege and Wycherley – who formed the nucleus of his favoured companions from 1665 to 1680. Known as the 'Court Wits', these mostly wealthy, well-educated aristocrats and gentry devoted their lives, like the king to whom they gravitated, to self-amusement and pleasure: they dabbled in poetry, plays, and songs not as a professional enterprise for money but rather to demonstrate their keen intellect, sprightly imaginations and creative energies through poetry and prose that would earn them acclaim, which many did achieve.

Notwithstanding their literary interests and fame, the Court Wits' favourite pastimes typically involved gambling, drinking, carousing, wenching and other forms of dissipation that brought at least one – Rochester – to an early death at 33. Emblematic of the new Stuart *élan* and ethos – free-spirited, witty, urbane, and self-possessed – these youthful iconoclasts set the style in everything fashionable: from the elegant and graceful manners of the day to all of the arts, and they wielded considerable influence over the public's acceptance of literature and, more importantly, plays, for they not only helped to cultivate the public's taste for theatre by their own loyal patronage, they could also be found regularly ensconced in theatres' pits (known as the 'wits' circle') surrounded by aspiring young wits who quickly spread the news of their extemporaneous critiques of the performance at hand to the general audience. Their greatest influence, however, was their dedication to libertinism, which infiltrated much of the literature of the period (some of which they wrote) and embodied not only a deliberate break from the past age's repressive Puritanism but also an 'in-your-face' counter-culture that many young aristocrats embraced with enthusiasm as a decisive split from all the failed beliefs and values of the broken world they inherited.[7]

Libertinism, broadly speaking, was a revolt against society's customs, conventions and institutions in favour of a more naturalistic state which allowed an individual free and uncensored expression of desires and drives. Familiar to French and English society prior to the Restoration, libertinism was not a philosophy per se, but rather a body of thought assimilated from various philosophies which its proponents borrowed and tailored to fit their views and way of life. Rejecting many orthodox, Christian views, libertines embraced three major lines of thinking: naturalism, based on the rise in scientific discoveries, posited that the universe is a vast mechanism without any inherent purpose and, as such, remains indifferent to human desires and events, and moreover, since the universe is nothing more than a machine, all explanations for every phenomenon must be examined and verified through empirical evidence rather than rooted in the supernatural; scepticism, a philosophical attitude devoted to challenging the limitations of all epistemological arguments, held that complete and definitive truth and knowledge were doubtful given the questionable and varied approaches on which such inquiries could be based; and Epicureanism, loosely understood by libertines to mean sensuality and hedonism, claimed that man, not bound to a mortal soul, was free to shape his life as he pleased and that his pursuit of pleasure was good and thus inherently moral.

Armed with these tenets, libertines argued that man, albeit a rational creature, is nonetheless an animal within nature who rightly seeks first and foremost to satisfy those impulses to which he is naturally inclined. Furthermore, given that all institutions with which one is forced to comply in the social world are man-made constructs and not those natural laws to which he is bound, man has no obligation to such orthodoxies as religion, morality and laws. In a universe indifferent to his fate and happiness, man is the sole architect of his nature and life, free to shape them according to his own will and how he (and only he) thinks best. With all knowledge based on empirical evidence confined to the natural world only, one is duty bound as a sceptic to rely on no other proofs than one's own senses (the source of empiricism) to ferret out knowledge and truth for oneself, a clear justification for a hedonistic life which encourages one to follow one's nature and give appetite full reign. Thus the libertine, dedicated to the pre-mise that truth resided only in what one could prove by the test of one's senses and that the only good in the world was that which pleased the senses, was an empiricist dedicated to a life of sensual pleasure in his pursuit of all that is good, motivated by self-interest in his rejection of all conventions that sought to inhibit those natural pursuits, who defied all customs – such as marriage and fidelity – that had no place in the natural world, and relied ultimately on only his 'right reason' and free thought for guidance and truth.

Although libertinism never attained widespread endorsement from the public at large, it was a key ingredient in the plays of the period, and whether dramatists endorsed it, problematised it, or satirised it, libertinism stood apart as one of the most subversive threats to the foundations of society. The libertine, who, model-ling himself on the Court Wits, devotes his life to dissipation and thus contributes little to the betterment of society, decries the bonds of marriage and in turn threatens aristocratic patrilineage, dismisses religious dogma and thus undermines the nation's unity as a consequence, and seduces numerous young ladies and thereby deliberately pollutes the well of morality, can be found in almost every dramatic genre of the period, though his icono-clastic and anarchistic strains most suited comedy. And his ubi-quity on the stage was a constant reminder to the audience that though perhaps shorn of his land and heritage, he was a force to contend with. Wielding a youthful counter-culture aimed at antagonising those classes – particularly the bourgeois Puritans – that stood ready to surpass him in wealth and prestige, the

libertine established a code of behaviour that assumed aristocratic privilege, education, and wit, an elitist culture to which only
the equally worthy and qualified need apply.

Just as libertinism was being hotly debated both on and off the
stage, the philosophy of one of the era's most influential theorists,
Thomas Hobbes, was generating considerable controversy. In his
book *Leviathan* (1651), which attempts to pre-empt another civil
war by convincing society of the need to relinquish its thirst for
personal power and instead entrust its welfare to governance by
a sovereign body who could ensure peace and stability, Hobbes
describes the corrosive effects of naturalistic behaviour on the
health of society. Like the scientists and materialists of his era,
Hobbes argued that man, like all other natural phenomena in the
universe which are entirely composed of atoms, is nothing more
than 'matter in motion', and though he possesses rational
thought, his life at the most primal level is spent gravitating
toward those things that satisfy his basic appetites and emotions
(which, to Hobbes, were internal motions of body). In a natural
state without any governing authority to place rules and restrictions on man's quest to satisfy his passions and appetites – envy,
hatred, fear, lust – man has no concept of right or wrong and
justifies his appetitive behaviour by whatever provides physical,
emotional or psychological pleasure or thwarts similar pain.
More importantly, such a pre-social world devoid of moral and
ethical considerations allows man to satisfy freely and with
impunity his most central and passionate desire: power. And it is
this fundamental thirst for power that is most deleterious, for it
positions man in a constant state of warfare with others who
either own the objects that he desires or, more typically, possess
power over him or beyond his reach. Man's drive for such power
derives from his will to survive in the natural world, to satisfy all
his desires, and to secure respect from others because his power
exceeds theirs. Thus, as man gravitates toward all that he desires
and recoils from that which causes discomfort, he is primarily
seeking to assert his power, and in this natural condition of
perpetual war of all against all, man lives in a constant state of
distrust of all others and continual fear of losing his power to
another. To keep such savage instincts in permanent check,
Hobbes argues, man constructs societies as a defence against his
own potential for aggressive and destructive behaviour against

others, thus willingly surrendering his natural right to power to an absolute political authority which, by imposing a 'covenant', agrees to protect him from himself and others so that he and society may thrive.

Leviathan caused quite a stir, for not only did Hobbes imply that man owes allegiance to a mortal sovereign rather than to God if he is to live in civility, his provocative, naturalistic view of man as motivated by appetites in a mechanistic world void of moral imperatives and absolutes likewise afforded no room for Christian dogma. Understandably, Hobbes provoked outrage from many, except, of course, those libertines who – like the king himself and the Court Wits with whom Hobbes visited often – used his theories to buttress their position as naturalists and Epicureans, notwithstanding the fact that Hobbes was advocating social order rather than anarchistic naturalism. Like libertinism, Hobbes's theories had a profound influence on literature, particularly in drama, where they provided for a new type of libertine – the Hobbesian rake – who represented something far more dangerous than the average libertine seeking to assert his power by living his life as he saw fit and to satisfy his appetites by drinking and other forms of dissipation. Such comparatively innocuous libertines in the plays of the period typically surrendered their freedom in the fifth act when they opted for social harmony by accepting the commitment and responsibility of marriage, like Etherege's Sir Frollick and Wycherley's Ranger. The Hobbesian rake, on the other hand, not only makes no such conversion, he is motivated solely by his lust for power over others in order to assert his superiority in the world he inhabits. And in his quest for power, he is vicious, cunning, and predatory, taking no prisoners and willing to commit any number of atrocities such as rape to satisfy his lust for dominance. His greatest danger, however, is not his Machiavellian aggressiveness nor his brutal behaviour, it is rather his unabashed and clever use of the very social institutions which he denigrates and eschews, those institutions meant to symbolise the harmony to which society aspires. Wycherley's Horner is an excellent case in point: he uses the institution of marriage to seduce wives and cuckold husbands, garnering power over everyone who has conformed to social convention. In effect, the Hobbesian rake deliberately brings the naturalistic world into the civilised one where most people are ill prepared for such types of animalistic warfare, believing as they do that they inhabit a civil society, and he is guaranteed to succeed not merely because his will to power is stronger than that of his victims but also because he is clever enough to engage his opponents in a battle (that he instigates) in which he controls the rules and in which he is the only one constitutionally prepared to fight and win.[8]

The radical shift in the nature of the libertine from gentlemanly rake to Hobbesian predator reflects more than just the playwrights' and public's reaction to Hobbes's controversial political theories, for it signals a marked change in the nation's collective response to Charles's 'restoration'. During the 1660s when public euphoria over Charles's return ran high, dramas depicted all conflicts happily resolved, fools and villains duly punished, and, more importantly, clear-cut heroes receiving their just rewards and facilitating peace and stability, thus suggesting that any national crisis or turmoil that erupts will be similarly neutralised by the hero's curative actions. By the 1670s, however, with the appearance of the Hobbesian figure who blurs distinctions between hero and villain and whose self-interest and disregard for social welfare in fact generates a state of crisis that he is content to leave unresolved at the end of the fifth act, the message is strikingly different: chaos dominates for the lack of heroes to set things right. This marked change in the characters, tone and denouement between the early Carolean dramas and those of the 1670s mediated the general public's disillusionment in Charles, whom they no longer perceived as the panegyrists had portrayed him: a resurrected Stuart monarch and hero capable of protecting the country from turmoil, establishing national well-being, and leading England to its former greatness. This erosion of confidence in Charles's monarchy can be attributed to numerous sources, with some of the fault going to Parliament for its refusal to sanction religious toleration, which kept the country in a state of perpetual unease, and its intentional underfunding of the government in order to prevent Charles from proroguing it, which forced the king to make covert agreements with Louis XIV, who provided him with money in return for his support in France's battles to strengthen its empire. The bulk of the blame, however, falls to Charles.

Although Charles initially demonstrated aptitude as a monarch, his self-indulgence and congenital laziness conspired against any sustained application of his abilities. Certainly his years of exile cultivated his 'noble laziness of the mind', as it was characterised by his contemporaries, an idleness induced by wandering the Continent with no other purpose than escaping Cromwell's assassins, and when he returned to London, he was more than content to accept whatever was offered to him so long as he could remain England's king. Committed to no solid political strategy or agenda other than retaining the throne, Charles took no authoritative stance about any issue unless it promised to fall in his favour. Although he could make bold and incisive incursions into policy, his initial energy and enthusiasm often dissipated quickly, especially if failure seemed imminent or another project sparked his interest or amusement. Charles was a charming and genial opportunist whose lack of commitment, indolence, and profligacy engendered pervasive disapproval and disappointment over the restoration that he was shaping.

Of all Charles's negative qualities, his libertine behaviour, particularly his inveterate lechery, proved the most damaging to his monarchy, for the public perceived it as the primary source of his failure to provide strong leadership. As early as 1661, complaints arose as to the high incidence of syphilis at court, and on 27 July 1667, Samuel Pepys noted in his diary: 'the King and Court were never in the world so bad as they are now for gaming, swearing, whoring, and drinking; and the most abominable vices that ever were in the world; so much so that all must come to nought.'[9] Unsurprisingly, Charles's profligate behaviour was blamed for the Great Plague of 1665 (killing 68,000) and the Great Fire of 1666 (destroying most of the old City of London), seen as God's justice for the king's dissipation which was spreading through the country. Indeed, not since the days of Henry VIII had England seen such a flagrant adulterer, but the Tudor monarch's lechery paled by comparison to Charles with his many mistresses and 14 known illegitimate children. And the price tag, paid by the public, was high: once he tired of his mistresses, he pensioned them off, and some, like Barbara Villiers to whom in 1670 he awarded the title Duchess of Cleveland and a palace, received hefty annuities to support themselves and the king's progeny. In particular, Charles's new mistress, Louise de Kéroualle (whom he made

Duchess of Portsmouth in 1673) was widely hated by the British for being both French and Catholic, and the public feared that she could induce the king, whom they rightly suspected was a crypto-Catholic, to convert and to press Parliament (as he had done on a number of occasions) for religious toleration of Catholicism. Charles's lechery, however, did more than exacerbate Anglicans' constant fears of popery or outrage their Christian morality, for it greatly injured his royal dignity at home and in the world: Charles was characterised as effeminate, mocked in satirical verses as a monarch preoccupied solely with his carnal pursuits and a slave to women who could control and manipulate him at will by the sheer force of their feminine sexuality.

Other factors relating to Charles's domestic and foreign policies contributed to the decline of public confidence in his monarchy. His restored court was inordinately extravagant, and to help pay for it, Charles cavalierly entered into agreements without any concern about the country's sentiments: his sale of Dunkirk, Cromwell's most significant and hard-earned acquisition, to France for £300,000 aroused considerable anger over the king's flagrant self-interest and exorbitant expenditures. Charles, underfunded by Parliament and unwilling to hold spending in check, kept the country in a constant state of debt, reporting to Parliament in 1670 that he had spent £1.3 million beyond what they had appropriated. Hope for military gains that would surpass those under Cromwell's reign and recapture England's world prestige fizzled out with Charles's lack of a foreign policy that would enable the country to expand its borders, as was happening in France under Louis' reign. The British navy's debacles in the country's two wars (1664–7; 1672–4) against the Dutch, who were threatening England's mercantile status, proved embarrassing and demoralising, especially in the spring of 1667 when a Dutch fleet sailed up the Medway and, after burning a number of anchored warships, towed away the *Royal Charles*, the English flagship. Not only had Britain suffered international humiliation, it would clearly never achieve the imperial status predicted in May 1660. Moreover, the Restoration Settlement's failure to provide equitable rewards for royalists continued to plague the country with factionalism, while the king's inability or lack of interest in settling the land disputes engendered feelings that Charles could not be trusted to keep his promises, which, of course, he could not. Charles's inability to remain faithful to his oaths, specifically his vacillation between different policies – committing himself to one initiative publicly yet secretly engaging in another that benefited him – provoked the correct impression that Charles was duplicitous and unscrupulous. As a case in point, although he had signed the Triple Alliance (1668) with Holland and Sweden to halt Louis XIV's plan to spread France's natural boundaries, Charles entered into an covert agreement with Louis (the Treaty of Dover, 1670) in which he agreed to provide France with military support in its expansionist efforts in return for an annual pension of £230,000 that would allow him to create an absolutist government independent of Parliament and to establish Catholicism in England. Although the precise details of the Treaty of Dover were not known until 1830, Charles's subjects had accurately long surmised that their king was Louis' secret partner, willing to compromise Anglicanism, and this collusion with France's Catholic king was deemed his most damaging and notorious betrayal against his country.

Ultimately, by the 1670s, Charles's profligacy, duplicity, and reversals of domestic and foreign policy eroded the public's confidence in his ability to restore any aspect of Britain's previous glory. The English came to distrust Charles, the monarch who relied on secrecy and cabals (a neologism of the period[10]) and kept his subjects – and even some of his closest advisers – in the dark as to the initiatives he was pursuing and the true motives for those initiatives. Eventually, the public viewed Charles – indeed, the king and his entire court and government composed of competitive individuals jockeying for position – as self-serving opportunists guided not by the country's welfare but by their own interests, greed and quest for power: Hobbes's natural man in a world desperately needing an absolute sovereign power whose covenant he could trust.

Although Charles initiated various enterprises that presaged England's future greatness – the establishment of the Royal Society in 1662 which included such distinguished scientists as Robert Boyle and Isaac Newton, and after the Great Fire he rebuilt the city of London with the help of Christopher Wren's magnificent architecture – the glorious restoration envisaged by panegyrists in 1660 never materialised, leaving Britons to wait until the nineteenth century for a monarch who could build an empire which eclipsed that of Rome. Of course, during Charles's reign, people could, if they so wished, glimpse such an imposing empire, but to do so they had to look south across the English Channel.

2
Carolean Theatre and Drama

One of the first changes Charles II made shortly after reclaiming
the English throne in May 1660 was to reopen the public theatres,
closed in 1642 by Puritan edict. Although plays were performed
surreptitiously during the Interregnum by a few severely impoverished and poorly patronised companies that stood in continual
fear of arrest and imprisonment, as well as by William Davenant,
who cleverly billed his operatic productions as 'musical entertainments' aimed at 'instruction' and produced them at his residence (Rutland House) to subvert Puritan objection to regular
plays and public playhouses,[1] Charles's restoration signalled
London's liberation from the longstanding and repressive laws
that had forbidden all forms of public entertainment, from plays
and music to dancing and outdoor games. On 9 July 1660, less
than two months after his return, Charles, eager to revive and
personally sanction cultural activities as emblematic of a complete 'restoration' and shrewd enough to appreciate how his
imprimatur on theatre could shape and effect public approval of
him, granted two personal friends and courtiers – Sir William
Davenant (Poet Laureate to Charles I) and Thomas Killigrew –
hereditary patents which gave them equal and sole control of
London's theatrical productions, effectively instituting a system
of stage monopoly that would last for 182 years. These royal

charters gave the patentees exclusive rights to the formation of acting companies and the construction of theatres, and after months of quashing opposition to their control, battling independent acting companies, recruiting stage performers, and securing theatres in which to perform, Davenant and Killigrew finally asserted their exclusive control of theatrical production and stood poised to present performances to the public.[2]

Thomas Killigrew, an amateur Caroline playwright and both a court jester and a groom of Charles I, probably used his connexions with the court and favour with Charles II to finagle the upper hand over Davenant by receiving proprietary rights to a large number of pre-Commonwealth plays and also first choice from a corps of actors that included London's most experienced and popular Caroline performers. Having secured an immediate advantage over his competitor, and being eager to precede Davenant in production in order to establish his niche among London patrons, Killigrew immediately set up temporary quarters for his new acting troupe, the King's Company, in the old Red Bull Theatre, the only playhouse not completely demolished or partially dismantled by the Puritans. Shortly after, Killigrew commissioned the conversion of Gibbon's Tennis Court into a workable performance space, one that his company would use for the next three years. This indoor tennis-court theatre, measuring 70 by 25 feet externally, was an intimate playhouse, similar to an Elizabethan private theatre, with a seating capacity for only 400 spectators and a platform-stage area approximately 14 feet wide and 22 feet deep. Although the theatre lacked scenery – the wings and shutters characteristic of Continental theatres that would be incorporated in future Restoration playhouses – Samuel Pepys, writing on 20 November 1660 shortly after the inaugural production, remarked that Killgrew's makeshift theatre was 'the finest playhouse, I believe, that ever was in England'.[3]

By the end of June 1661, some eight months after Killigrew's start, William Davenant and his troupe, the Duke's Company (under the livery of the king's brother, James, Duke of York), which had been performing occasionally at the refurbished Salisbury Court theatre, moved to another renovated space. Like Killigrew, Davenant also chose to convert an indoor tennis court into his Theatre Royal, Lisle's Tennis Court in Portugal Street near Lincoln's Inn Fields,[4] but unlike Killigrew, Davenant, whose pre-

Commonwealth masques and operatic productions as well as his Rutland House performances relied heavily on scenery and scenic spectacle based on the Italianate model, transformed the tennis-court space into a proscenium theatre with changeable scenery, thus making it the first public theatre in the country to be so outfitted. In addition to installing scenic apparatus, Davenant also reconfigured the acting area to include doors built into the walls flanking a proscenium opening; these proscenium doors (probably two on each side) were used by actors during performance for entrances and exits, and surmounting these proscenium doors were balconies which could be used by performers or spectators. Davenant's theatre, referred to variously as the first Lincoln's Inn Fields (LIF) and the Duke's Playhouse, likewise provided Londoners with another intimate performance space, accommodating some 400 patrons, and, more relevant to this study, it also served as the venue for Etherege's first two comedies, *The Comical Revenge* (1664) and *She Would If She Could* (1668).

Davenant's introduction of changeable scenery may well have been predicated on his desire to attract London's upper-class playgoers, many of whom had been in exile on the Continent and had enjoyed the productions in Paris and elsewhere that used movable, perspective scenery. Additionally, of course, Davenant, disadvantaged by a group of inexperienced actors and a limited number of available plays, had to devise a viable tactic that would help him compete against Killigrew's veteran acting company and established repertoire. Clearly, Davenant's strategy to siphon spectators from his rival's playhouse by use of scenery and scenic changes worked exceptionally well, for by 4 July 1661 Pepys, after attending Killigrew's theatre, reported that it seemed 'strange to see this house, that used to be so thronged, now empty since the Opera [Davenant's playhouse] begun – and so will continue for a while I believe'.[5] In response to Davenant's success and the loss of patrons at his theatre, Killigrew set about immediately to build a new playhouse, and as early as 7 May 1663 his Theatre Royal opened in Bridges Street, Drury Lane.[6] Built on the plot of ground of the modern Drury Lane, this new facility boasted the latest inventions in scenes and machines, and thereafter both companies could compete equally in luring spectators with scenic display. Eight years after the theatre opened, Wycherley's first comedy, *Love in a Wood*, had its première there in 1671.

Unfortunately, in the year following Wycherley's debut – on 25 January 1672 – Killigrew's Theatre Royal burned to the ground with all its costumes and scenery, forcing the King's Company to relocate temporarily to Lincoln's Inn Fields, recently vacated by the Duke's Company when it moved to its new Dorset Garden facility.

The Duke's Company's new playhouse in Dorset Garden, ostensibly designed by Christopher Wren and ready for performances in November 1671, was the most magnificent of all Restoration theatres. Facing the river Thames and decorated with the Duke of York's coat-of-arms, the Dorset Garden Theatre accommodated an estimated 1200 spectators in its U-shaped auditorium and boxes, had a stage 51 by 30 feet, and was richly decorated and equipped with the most modern and expensive scenic machinery,[7] making this playhouse the ideal venue for those types of entertainments Davenant had most enjoyed staging: opera and spectacular tragedies. In fact, when the two companies merged in 1682 to form the United Company, the new troupe used Dorset Garden mainly for spectacles and operas. Wycherley's second play, *The Gentleman Dancing-Master* (1672) and Etherege's final comedy, *Man of Mode* (1676), opened at this ornate playhouse.

While the Duke's Company gained the competitive edge with its spectacular new playhouse, Killigrew spent his two-year tenure at Lincoln's Inn Fields raising money to erect a theatre to replace the demolished Bridges Street playhouse. Built on the site of the old, incinerated theatre, Killigrew's new facility, the Theatre Royal, Drury Lane, opened in March 1674. Designed by Christopher Wren, this new playhouse, the last completely new theatre construction in the seventeenth century, lacked the ornateness and capaciousness of Dorset Garden (a seating capacity of some 800 in its fan-shaped auditorium), but it did have the scenic machinery and changeable scenery now expected by theatregoers.[8] Wycherley's two final plays, *The Country Wife* (1675) and *The Plain Dealer* (1676), were performed by the King's Company at Drury Lane.

These Restoration theatres, with the exception of Killigrew's first two playhouses, offered audiences a new theatrical experience that had heretofore never been available to the general theatregoing public. The earlier Elizabethan open-air public playhouse with minimal, emblematic set pieces and a benchless pit gave way to a new performance edifice, an enclosed building with seating in the pit, a proscenium arch, and, most importantly, perspective scenery. Indeed, Davenant's pioneering introduction of the proscenium performance space and changeable scenery painted in perspective proved the most significant scenographic development in the public theatres – the precursor of the modern stage – and although he did not invent anything new but rather combined elements from earlier British public and private theatres (the platform stage and stage doors of the Elizabethan theatres with the proscenium arch and scenic devices of the Jacobean and Caroline court masques), the stage configuration he introduced at his first theatre, Lisle's Tennis Court, was adopted by Killigrew and all subsequent theatre managers. While some of the precise details in each playhouse varied (e.g., the number of proscenium doors and balconies), each Restoration theatre's performance space, modelled on Davenant's design, had the same basic components: a scenic area behind the proscenium arch with side wings and shutters painted in perspective, and a forestage area in front of the proscenium arch with at least a pair of doors and balconies at both sides of the stage walls.

The scenic area, twice as deep as the forestage, was composed of sets of wings – three or four sets of painted flats running in grooves on each side of the stage with each set fixed behind the other and positioned parallel to the proscenium line; these wings were backed by several shutters – two halves of a painted scene mounted on wooden frames, sliding in grooves and joining at centre stage behind the last set of wings, thereby closing off the stage a number of feet in front of the theatre's back wall. Thus, one set of wings in each of the stage positions with its correspondingly painted back shutter depicted a scene in perspective, and this perspective view was enhanced further by the raked stage (pitched from the front edge of the forestage to the back shutters, levelling off from behind the shutters to the back wall) and the progressively decreasing height of the wings from downstage to upstage. The scenic area extended also to the space between the last cluster of shutters and the back wall – referred to as 'the discovery area' – where actors and furniture could be positioned for special 'discoveries'. In these instances, all shutters were opened fully (masked by the side-wings) to reveal this upstage scenic area with actors already in position. One of the most well-known discoveries in Carolean drama occurs in

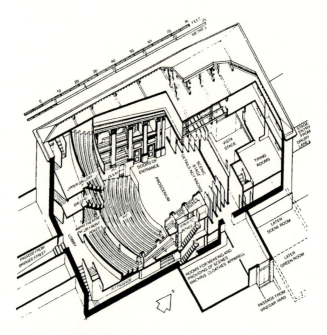

Figure 1   The Restoration stage
Source: Richard Leacroft, *The Development of the English Playhouse: An Illustrated Survey of Theatre Building in England from Medieval to Modern Times* (London: Methuen, 1973). Reproduced courtesy of Methuen Publishing Limited.

Etherege's *The Man of Mode* where the opening stage directions for Act IV, scene ii call for *'Dorimant's lodging, a table, a candle, a toilet, &c. Handy tying up linen.'* Here the shutters would open to reveal Handy upstage while Dorimant and Bellinda enter downstage through a proscenium door. Variations on the exact workings of this scenic area have been posited by theatre historians, some suggesting that sufficient room existed between each of the shutters to allow for discoveries within this scenic space: one set of shutters opened to reveal the characters in front of the next shutter scene. The frequent use of successive discoveries in many plays indicates that this staging method may also have been used to accommodate the need for multiple discoveries and rapid shifts of scenes. Others opine that shutters could have been placed behind any of the wing positions, though this development would probably not have occurred until mid-eighteenth century.[9]

Regardless of the various ways in which scenic areas could accommodate discoveries and action (and it no doubt varied in each theatre according to specific stage configurations), certain characteristics of the types of scenery and scene changes do apply to Carolean stage practice in general. The proscenium arch which separated the scenic area from the forestage was intended to mask the sides of the stage from the auditorium and to hide any scenic machinery or stagehand from audience view. All scene changes, conducted by backstage machinists who (out of the audience's sight) simultaneously either pushed on a new set of wings and a shutter or drew off a set of wings and shutter (to reveal a new vista behind it), were made in full view of the audience and intended to be watched as part of the performance's entertainment. The alacrity with which scenes could be changed (quite literally in just a few seconds) enhanced the performance's visual energy, an especial benefit in comedy and farce, which required rapid shifts between scenes to keep the fast-paced action moving.[10] In addition, the scenery (wings and shutters) used in each performance was neither created anew nor intended to replicate specific locales. Dramatists repeatedly set their plays in the same general locales (chambers, gardens, taverns, prisons, palaces, streets, etc.), thus enabling the reuse of generic scenery that depicted not a specific indoor or outdoor scene but rather a representative one. Noting that the scenery did not attempt realistic illusion, Richard Southern described it as 'scenery in the stage sense of the decking of a stage, but not scenery in the landscape sense of a background seen behind people', while more recently J. L. Styan, referring to the lack of stage directions indicating scenic locales, summed that the 'texts carry only general suggestions about place, and are at best a loose guide, not for painting, but acting'.[11] In those instances where action is set in a very specific and familiar location – for example, Etherege's *She Would If She Could*, which places much of the action in actual places quite popular with theatregoers (the New Exchange, the Mulberry Garden, Vauxhall), and Wycherley's *Love in a Wood*, set partially in London's fashionable St James's Park – scenery may well have been specially painted to replicate these well-known places.

While the scenic area was used primarily for perspective scenery, the forestage area served as the actor's performance space. Although action could occur upstage, this practice seldom occurred, and even when characters were 'discovered', they most usually moved downstage to the apron to begin their dialogue. With all action occurring on the forestage, proscenium doors and balconies became pivotal as permanent stage props that helped suggest locales. These doors and balconies could be used in many ways. They could represent interiors or exteriors, with the doors serving as exits and entrances, and thus, as in the case of the Elizabethan stage where the two tiring-house doors were used to signal a character's remove from one locale to another, the Restoration proscenium doors (at least two at each side of the apron, built into the proscenium wall) could indicate a character's departure from an interior or exterior locale or his arrival at another interior or exterior location. To achieve these effects, a character need only, for example, exit from an interior room by leaving through one door and suggest his arrival outside by re-entering immediately through either the same or the adjacent door (the proscenium area would then represent an exterior façade, and the wings and shutters could also be changed from the previous interior scene to the new exterior location), or he could exit through one door, quickly move behind the wings and shutters unnoticed by the spectators (who were probably focusing on the fast scene change), and enter through a door on the opposite side of the stage. In those single scenes requiring a juxtaposition of both exterior and interior locales, the wings and backshutter could depict an exterior space while the proscenium wall and doors represented an interior one (or vice versa with the painted scenery representing the interior and the proscenium doors suggesting an exterior façade). For interior scenes, doors could also represent closets or access to another interior room; and for exterior scenes, doors could represent access to various houses, shops or taverns on a street. The placement of action on the forestage mandated (and no doubt encouraged) imaginative use of the doors, as in the case of Etherege's *She Would If She Could* (II,i) where both pairs of proscenium doors are put to brilliant use for visually comedic effect as Courtall and Freeman chase Ariana and Gatty about the Mulberry Garden: the stage direction notes, *'The Women go out, and go about behind the scenes to the other door'*, Courtall and Freeman exit after them, and moments later *'Enter the Women, and after 'em Courtall at the lower door, and Freeman at the upper door on the contrary side'*. Also, the balconies above each proscenium door served as windows, balconies, or entrances to second storeys, and once again Etherege uses the forestage to good advantage in his first comedy, *Comical Revenge*, in which a side balcony is used when Sir Frederick's commotion on the street below a window at Widow Rich's house in Covent Garden brings Betty *'to the window unlaced, holding her petticoats in her hand'* followed seconds later by Widow Rich's appearance at the window as well (III,ii).[12]

These innovations in the staging of plays during the Carolean era – the actors positioned on the forestage proximate to the audience and performing in front of perspective scenery – fostered a new scopic experience for theatregoers. From a performance standpoint, the placement of actors on the forestage not only enabled the audience to hear dialogue from any seat in the auditorium and to see an actor's slightest gesture or facial expression, it also created a very intimate audience–performer dynamic. And given that both the auditorium and stage remained lit throughout the performance (by chandeliers over the stage and the auditorium, as well as the natural light through the theatre's windows), the actors' and spectators' visibility of one another enhanced the performance's level of intimacy, an atmosphere that Jocelyn Powell likened to that of a 'sophisticated cabaret'[13] – a performance event in which the mutual propinquity and visibility of spectator and performer encouraged a unique reciprocity between both, a shared activity in which the actor was continually cognisant of the viewer's noticeable gaze and the spectator was likewise aware of the actor's recognition of his presence. Unlike most proscenium performances today with a darkened auditorium that fosters 'fourth-wall' realism in which the spectator is lulled into passive viewing and the actor is withdrawn behind the proscenium arch and absorbed in his character's interactions with other characters on stage, the Carolean proscenium theatres allowed for no such distancing between actor and viewer: the spectator knows always that he is watching a performance enacted for him and for the other spectators whose reactions are constantly observable to him, while the actor never forgets that he is enacting a role in front of a watchful and responsive audience. It's a performance without privacy, and one that lends itself to considerable pandering to the viewer.

Equally significant in the actor–audience dynamic, the perspective scenery's illusion of three-dimensional locales enabled
the spectators to concentrate on the action and characters without
having to direct any of their imaginative energy to visualising
scenic locations described by the dialogue but not visible on
stage, as audiences did at Shakespeare's Globe with its paucity of
emblematic set pieces and absence of painted scenery. For the first
time on London's public stages, representational scenery was
used, and while this realistic scenery pinioned the action in
locales that could be immediately read by spectators at its most
basic level as an index of place, it is certainly probable, as Peter
Holland suggests, that it fostered another level of performance
semiotics heretofore not possible: as heuristically charged locations that aided spectator comprehension, commented (perhaps
ironically) on the play's characters and dramatic action, and gave
the play a structural design (by virtue of the placement of specific
types of action within particular locales, as well as the juxtaposition of these locales) that could reveal thematic implications or
even clarify denouement.[14] More than just *trompe-l'oeil* back-
grounds, the perspective scenery introduced in theatre performances another level of visual semantics.

The proscenium-arch stage with its changeable scenery painted in perspective was the most significant innovation in the
scenographic practices of the period, but the introduction of
actresses to the stage was unquestionably its most radical contribution. Although women had appeared in the private court
masques of Charles I and had been featured regularly on French,
Spanish and Italian stages since the mid-sixteenth century, the
English custom of males playing female roles in public performances continued until 1660 when Killigrew and Davenant, aware
of the casting arrangements for both the Caroline masques and
the Continental public playhouses, recognised the commercial
advantage of featuring actresses – that is, they would certainly
lure paying customers, who were mostly men, into their theatres.
The identity of the first English actress is not certain, though most
scholars speculate that it was Anne Marshall, who played
Desdemona in Killigrew's 8 December 1660 production of *Othello*,
just one month after the manager opened the doors to the Red
Bull Theatre. Notwithstanding this actress's early appearance on
the Carolean stage, the use of female performers in all women's

roles was neither instantaneous nor routine: Samuel Pepys, an inveterate theatregoer, recounts having first witnessed an actress at Killigrew's revival of Fletcher's *Beggar's Bush* as late as 3 January 1661, but only four days later, he records his attendance at the same playhouse to watch a performance of Ben Jonson's *The Silent Women* featuring Edward Kynaston (an outstanding female impersonator) in three different roles, one of which was a woman. This continued use of men in female roles eventually engendered outrage from the Puritans, who objected to the lewd, homosexual overtones inherent in these transvestite performances, which they insisted sanctioned homosexual proclivities and encouraged such behaviour at large, and they exerted pressure on the government to rectify these moral dangers to social welfare. Within two years of issuing the royal patents, on 25 April 1662, Charles II amended the charters, making it mandatory that only women enact female characters in all stage performances. Ironically, while the use of actresses on stage was allegedly intended to help rid drama of its putative obscenity, it actually had the opposite effect, for Carolean drama grew increasingly prurient, sexually explicit, and violent – passionate sex scenes, nudity, rape, and attempted rape – because of their very presence.[15]

Female performers and spectacular scenic displays were not, of course, the only inducements that lured audiences to the newly opened playhouses, for the regular patronage of Charles II and his court – many of whom, along with the king in exile, enjoyed the productions in Paris – helped to cultivate audiences' tastes for theatrical entertainment as part of the newly restored Stuart culture. Without question, no other period in British theatre history can boast of such close ties between dramatic performances and sovereign patronage. In fact, Charles II's habitual attendance at both playhouses accompanied by his courtiers had initially fostered the assumption among modern scholars that Carolean theatres catered strictly to an aristocratic audience and that dramatists crafted their plays with the sole intent of pleasing the king and his acolytes by creating characters that reflected the elegance, spirit and sensuality of the new Carolean court. More recent scholarship has debunked this theory. Evidence from primary documents, including diaries (such as Samuel Pepys's), letters and other sources reveal that in addition to the king and other

court satellites and luminaries, the actors catered to a cross-section of patrons: lawyers, wealthy merchants, members of
Parliament, civil servants, foreign visitors, apprentices, journey-
men, soldiers, as well as a few pickpockets, prostitutes and
orange sellers. This cross-section applied to women as well, as
David Roberts shows in his impressive study of female patrons,
previously believed to be comparatively unrepresented: the wide
array of female spectators included ladies in the exclusive and
private box seats, women with vizards (masks) in the fashionable
area of the pit, wives of city merchants and prostitutes in the less
expensive gallery seats, as well as a host of other women:

> Duchesses, royal mistresses, the wives of the aristocracy, and
> members of their households; the wives, daughters, sisters,
> and nieces of Members of Parliament, playwrights, profes-
> sional men, craftsmen, merchants, and shopkeepers; a large
> contingent of lady's companions and maidservants; as well
> as that conspicuous minority of women of all classes who,
> whether to trick a lord, tout for custom, or simply appear
> fashionable, disguised themselves at the theatre.[16]

While the evidence suggests that audiences were far more heterogeneous than once believed, it does not, however, denote that
these divers patrons attended the playhouses regularly. Two factors in particular argue against such a conclusion: the performances' curtain-time and the cost of admission. Performances
began in the afternoon at 3:30 p.m. – after the customary midday
meal – a time that accommodated the schedules of the leisure
class but conflicted with the work hours of the gainfully
employed, and while some had freer control of their work schedules (as did Pepys), allowing them to dash to a performance or
two during the week, all would not have been so fortunate.
Similarly, the admission prices prohibited many from attending
the theatres routinely: the least expensive seats in the upper or
middle galleries cost, respectively, one shilling (i.e., 12 pennies) or
one shilling and sixpence (i.e., 18 pennies), while the most sought
after seats in the lower gallery, boxes and pit ran to two shillings
and sixpence (i.e., 30 pennies). The latter amount, as Jocelyn
Powell notes, equalled a farmworker's average weekly income,
and one could hire a cook, as did Pepys in 1663, for an annual

salary of £4.[17] In all likelihood, this wide spectrum of theatregoers attended performances only on special occasions or when finances and time permitted, and it did not constitute the audience's makeup on a daily basis. There was, however, a significant proportion of playgoers who did patronise the theatres regularly, at least once a week but typically more often, and managers came to depend heavily on them to support the playhouses. To be sure, although London had a population of approximately 400,000, the playhouses attracted probably no more than an average of 500 spectators daily – relatively unimpressive and low numbers compared to the earlier decades of the seventeenth century and insufficient to sustain both playhouses by 1682 when the insolvent King's Company merged with the Duke's to form the United Company.[18] Thus, the faithful patronage of this *de facto* coterie – one not strictly court-based – helped to keep the theatres open. And certainly these avid patrons, who knew one another, befriended the actors and managers of both companies, whiled away the hours at the popular eateries discussing the current productions, and, by their approval or disapproval of a performance, could secure the success or demise of a new play as well as influence the opinions of the general theatregoing public, had cultivated a preference for particular types of dramas to which playwrights eagerly catered.[19]

The core Carolean audience was clearly not as heterogeneous as those who attended Shakespeare's Globe, but it did possess a catholicity of taste in drama that posed for Davenant and Killigrew the immediate challenge of finding new plays that would appeal to its diversity and diverse preferences. The 18-year ban on performances had interrupted the continuous tradition of playwrighting, leaving both managers with a marked scarcity not just of performers but also of dramatists,[20] and to fill the serious shortage of new scripts both companies initially had to rely primarily on pre-Commonwealth dramas to build an immediate repertoire and attract audiences, staging plays by Jonson, Heywood, Ford, Middleton, Brome and numerous others including Shakespeare and Fletcher, who proved the most popular. Shortly after the theatres reopened, new plays slowly trickled in, but without any recent models as a guide, aspiring new playwrights ransacked, borrowed (sometimes verbatim) and blended many segments from discrete and numerous sources, culling from Elizabethan, Jacobean and Caroline plays, adapting contemporary Continental dramas, and imitating the successful new plays at both patent houses. The early years of Carolean drama witnessed a high level of experimentation as amateur playwrights tried to find new dramatic forms that would appeal to an audience that had not attended the professional theatre in 18 years or had never seen any performances at all, and while much of the experimentation resulted in inchoate and unproducible dramas that defied generic classification as well as straining credulity and comprehension, occasionally it did lead to exceedingly popular plays, as with Etherege's *The Comical Revenge* (1664), a multiplot comedy with four different plot lines and an admixture of various genres. By the mid-1660s, however, all the experimentation eventually led to distinct play types that endured in popularity throughout the Carolean era and, in the case of some genres, until the end of the century.

Carolean drama – and Restoration drama at large – is often misunderstood as synonymous with comedy of manners only, for no other genre from this period has enjoyed as many professional and amateur productions or has secured such a solid niche in the curriculum of English drama as this one has. However, comedy of manners actually represents a small percentage of approximately 400 plays written between 1660 and 1700 by some 180 playwrights, and while it may have been the darling of Carolean theatre – the comic genre emblematic of the new Stuart ethos and *élan* – it alone could not satisfy the diverse taste of an audience that had demonstrated to managers early on its preference for exciting plots, exotic locations, spectacle, music, heroic action, and compelling, dashing characters. Carolean theatre was eclectic: new plays running in repertory with pre-Commonwealth plays, adaptations of Shakespeare, operas, burlesques, farces, and a host of other types of dramas – much like contemporary television or film – and no one type of theatrical entertainment appealed equally to every spectator, just as all the different types of performances did not please a given ideal spectator. To satisfy audience demand for variety, dramatists offered up different genres which, though significantly eclipsed today by the popularity of manners comedy, served the needs of an audience that, having endured the crucibles of regicide, Civil War and

Puritanism, preferred lighter fare void of tragic endings with the deaths of noble kings.

The first entirely new dramatic form to gain audiences' widespread approval was the comedy of intrigue, which derived from the popular, contemporary Spanish romances. First appearing in 1663 with Sir Samuel Tuke's *The Adventure of Five Hours* (adapted, at Charles II's suggestion, from a play of unknown authorship, *Los Empeños de Seis Horas*), intrigue comedies focused solely on erotic love plots and featured mismatched lovers, rival lovers, mistaken identities, kidnappings, duels of honour, misdirected letters, eavesdropping, serenades, disguises, and obstructive parents or guardians, subordinating character to plot, emphasising local colour, and highlighting exaggerated sentiments and violence. Jam-packed with action and complex plots that pile one complication and confusion atop another to thwart the union of the young lovers, intrigue comedies underscored the conflict between the rigid code of Spanish honour and equally strong emotional desires, but the denouement was guaranteed to present the destined couple happily joined. Although normally set in foreign exotic locales – for example, Aphra Behn, the first professional female dramatist and a prolific writer of intrigues, set *The Amorous Prince* (1671) in Florence, *The Rover* (1677) in Naples, and *The Dutch Lover* (1673) in Madrid – the English intrigues typically had an unmistakably British flavour, featuring familiar characters such as Behn's libertine rover, Willmore, and plots redolent with a quasi-London atmosphere and contemporary urban themes. The enormous popularity of the intrigues encouraged Carolean dramatists to incorporate some of their characteristics into other dramatic genres.

Tragicomedy and heroic drama accommodated audience tastes for more serious plot lines without tragic consequences, and though lacking the highly complicated plots of the intrigues, both genres placed a similar emphasis on honour and passion while concomitantly foregrounding character over plot. Tragicomedy proves an illusive term in the Carolean period, for many dramatists applied it to any play that wanted deaths but ended happily – Tuke, for example, described his intrigue as a tragicomedy – while others labelled their tragicomedies as comedies. Likewise, modern scholars deploy the term differently, some classifying heroic dramas as heroic tragicomedies, and others identifying

various subgenres such as domestic tragicomedies, political tragicomedies, romantic tragicomedies, and court tragicomedies.[21] All
of these generic distinctions – each equally valid – speak to the
impossibility of reducing tragicomedy to a neat and all-inclusive
definition that conveys the remarkable variety of character types
and plot lines that dramatists crafted within this genre. For the
sake of simplicity, however, tragicomedy can be defined general-
ly as a play whose inexorable movement toward tragic consequences is averted in the fifth act by some intervening force
(another character, providence, fate) that allows the action to end
without catastrophe. Like some of the earlier models by Fletcher,
Carolean tragicomedies featured two plot lines, one an heroic
'high' plot and the other a comic 'low' plot, which could either
run parallel as split or divided plots without the characters from
both lines of action sharing scenes (except, perhaps, in the
denouement), or they could be unified with characters from the
two plot lines intermingling in various segments throughout
the play. The serious high plots typically concentrated on the
heroic or unheroic actions of rulers who grapple with issues of
power and sovereignty while the lower comic plots often focused
on the romantic entanglements and pursuits of courtiers or the
upper class. Whether running in parallel or joining throughout
the action, each plot provided comment on the other relative to
themes of constancy, loyalty and trust. Although many Carolean
dramatists tried their hand at this genre, the tragicomedies by
John Dryden (e.g., *Secret Love; or, The Maiden Queen* [1667] and
Marriage à-la-Mode [1671]) and James Howard (e.g., *All Mistaken;
or, The Mad Couple* [1665]) are considered the most representative.

As tragicomedy was flourishing between 1660 and 1671, heroic
plays answered the need for dramatic representations of extraor-
dinarily noble characters of great stature. Conceived as a dramatic counterpart to the epic poem – Dryden, one of the most prolific
writers in the genre, defined it in his *Essays of Heroic Plays* (1672)
as 'an imitation, in little, of an heroic poem' – heroic drama featured grandiose love-and-honour plots with an idealised hero of
illustrious birth and a chaste heroine whose mutually intense and
noble love is sure to precipitate their own ruin as well as that of
their country. Like an epic poem, heroic drama was intended to
arouse admiration for the hero who embodies superhuman qualities – a valiant warrior, a noble creature with extraordinary loy-

alty to his lover for whom his pure devotion transcends carnal lust and possesses his soul and for whom he will sacrifice all. His conflict against a formidable antagonist bent on destroying him plays out against a martial background set in exotic locales (e.g., Morocco, Granada) with heavy doses of elaborate spectacle, violence and physical action that include ships sailing across the stage in fake seas, clashes of armies firing hordes of arrows or battling with swords, deaths by torture, apparitions, rapes (off stage), drums beating and trumpets blaring – and a wealth of other horrifying and visually compelling elements that moved spectators to shock and awe. Written entirely in rhymed couplets and replete with ranting speeches, high-flown sentiments, and bombastic monologues, heroic dramas depicted larger-than-life characters and conflicts demonstrating that the noble qualities of love and honour were worth aspiring to as ends in and of themselves, and although heroic dramas ended happily with the lovers retaining their honour, thwarting danger to their nation, and uniting in spiritual love, the sheer epic scope of these dramas has garnered them the alternative labels of epic tragedy and heroic tragedy. First produced in 1664 with John Dryden's and John Howard's *The Indian Queen*, heroic drama – best exemplified in Roger Boyle's (the Earl of Orrery) *Mutaspha, Son of Solyman the Magnificent* (1665), Dryden's *The Conquest of Granada* (1670), and Elkanah Settle's *The Empress of Morocco* (1673) – flourished until 1676.

By the mid-1670s, many dramatists, including Dryden, began to repudiate heroic drama for its overall remoteness to audiences – the stilted language, artificial rhyme scheme, inordinately elevated emotions, formulaic plots, and implausibly perfect superhuman heroes – and they turned to tragic plot lines that explored more complex human passions and suffering rather than heroic stoicism. Different from their one-dimensional, god-like counterparts in heroic dramas who emerge the victor in their battles against nefarious external forces and enemies, Carolean tragic heroes – like protagonists in classical tragedy – are flawed, imperfect individuals who engineer their own inevitable doom because of such universal motives as revenge, ambition and lust, motives which in turn drive the heroes to act on blind impulse and irrational passion rather than intellect or reason and thus lead them to an irreconcilable conflict between two courses of action that ensures their own tragic end. Written in blank verse and adhering loosely to the French neoclassical unities of time, place, and action, tragedies explored the less heroic side of human nature by exposing weaknesses and psychological distress that rendered heroes infinitely more sympathetic and lifelike. Tragic heroes such as Dryden's Antony in *All for Love* (1677) – considered the finest Restoration tragedy – who struggles (as the title suggests) between his love for his wife and his mistress Cleopatra rather than, as depicted in Shakespeare's original, his conflict between his passion for Cleopatra and his loyalty to Rome, and Thomas Otway's Don Carlos (*Don Carlos, Prince of Spain* [1676]) whose love for his father's wife kindles an uncontrollable jealousy in the King that leads to the deaths of both Don Carlos and the Queen, convey the types of complex characters that now appealed to spectators who had, by the 1670s, come to regard heroics as wholly removed from everyday reality and as a thoroughly unattainable fiction.

Of all the dramatic genres, comedy far outpaced the others in popularity, taking the form of farces, burlesques, satires, comedy of humours, and comedy of manners, all of which displayed a marked difference from pre-Commonwealth comedies. Prior to the Restoration, dramatists held to the theory (based on Aristotle's *Poetics*) that while tragedy is the domain of noble and aristocratic characters, comedy should be reserved for middle- and lower-class characters whose punishments for their vices and follies (e.g., greed, hypocrisy) provide humorous, dramatic caveats against such behaviour inimical to social harmony. Carolean playwrights, however, in response to their more aristocratic patrons – influential patrons who expected plays to reflect their lives and society – rejected this view of 'corrective' comedy with its restriction of only lower-class characters and instead agreed with Dryden, who, in his *Essay of Dramatic Poesy* (1668), insisted that comedies should deal with gentlemen and ladies of fashion in order to make the plays 'suitable to the Audience, which most considerably doth consist of these'. While not every Carolean comedy demonstrates this practice – farces, for example, showed such typical comic inversions as prostitutes acquiring peerages and knaves successfully impersonating their betters – for the most part, the various comic forms, ranging from Wycherley's and Durfey's satires, Ravenscroft's farces, to

Shadwell's comedies of humours and Etherege's comedies of manners, featured upper-class characters as rogues and fools who provided fodder for ridicule and laughter.

The Carolean theatre's most popular forms of comedy – divided roughly into two types, humours and manners – dominated the stage throughout the Restoration period and generated considerable debate among playwrights as to which proved the most suitable for contemporary audiences and their moral instruction. Neither subgenre, of course, was necessarily pure, for dramatists mingled elements from both, as well as from other comic forms including farce, to forge unique blends of comic characters and plots that catered to the tastes and addressed the desires of Carolean theatregoers.

Carolean comedy of humours diverges significantly from its Caroline source in the plays of Ben Jonson, who created a wide range of eccentric character types based on the quasi-medical theory that an imbalance of four bodily 'humours' (blood, phlegm, and yellow and black bile) predisposed one to antisocial, ridiculous or destructive behaviour. Although this belief that humours determined one's temperament and behaviour no longer held sway in the late seventeenth century, Jonson's fusion of eccentric characters and contemporary subject matter into energetic and vigorously satirical and realistic plays appealed to various Carolean playwrights such as Thomas Shadwell, who reworked Jonson's 'humours' theory and characters into ones more congenial with Carolean attitudes and expectations. Humours were now equated with psychological pathologies and penchants rather than bodily fluids: 'a byas of the mind', wrote Shadwell in his Epilogue to *The Humourists* (1670), which makes one emotionally and constitutionally powerless to remedy one's imperfections and to change one's ridiculous, self-destructive, or antisocial conduct. Finding abundant 'humours' in the real world filled with individuals who manufacture their own pride, greed, villainy and fears which generate conflict with others and make their lives miserable but from which they cannot extricate themselves, dramatists like Shadwell capitalised on the comic material readily discernible in a rich variety of characters with whom Carolean audiences could identify – for example, libertines, bourgeois merchants, aristocrats, fops, gentry, clergymen – intentionally eliding class distinctions and showing that all individuals have a common bond in their predilection toward folly and vice. Humours comedies were not without sexual intrigue, of course, for dramatists also included the inordinately popular 'gay couple' – gay not in its current usage but meaning merry or care-free – those fashionable and witty lovers of manners comedy who provided the requisite dose of sexual energy for which spectators clamoured. Relying on common Carolean themes such as youth versus age, appearance versus reality, dupe versus villain, and liberty versus restraint, humours comedy sought by negative example to expose the absurdities of human behaviour, holding up a mirror for the spectator to recognise his own deficiencies and to purge himself of his ridiculous and offensive conduct.

The influence of humours characters on other comic subgenres was far-reaching, for comic playwrights not only gave their characters individuating traits that afforded them a degree of realism as actual people, notwithstanding their exaggerated behaviour, they also used allusive names that corresponded to a character's nature and personality. Descriptive names such as Lady Cockwood or Lady Wishfort telegraphed these women's lascivious drives before they spoke their first lines of dialogue; Freeman, a name used in numerous Restoration comedies, signalled the character's preference for an unshackled life of libertinism; Pinchwife conveys the physical abuse enjoyed by its bearer; while Horner indicates a sexual pun on cuckoldry (horns) and sexual appetite (horny). Through these and other names such as Petulant, Sparkish, Fopling, Courtall, and Fidget, playwrights gave ready clues as to the psychological traits of each caricature, traits that inexorably propelled these characters toward their risible behaviour or discomfiture.

Exceeding either humours plays or any other comic genre in popularity was a new form adapted in part from earlier sources (including John Fletcher), modified to suit the disposition of the coterie Carolean audience, introduced in the mid-1660s and perfected by the mid-1670s: comedy of manners. Labelled 'genteel comedy' in its own day, manners comedy depicted the coruscant world of London's *beau monde*, the glamorous, sophisticated and urbane aristocracy whose elegant dress, graceful carriage, keen intellect and witty language provided them with a code of manners that bespoke their eminence, setting them apart from the vulgar classes below them in society's hierarchy and proving the maxim that birth equals worth. The members of this leisure class from the fashionable area of the town, for whom money holds no reverence, devote their endless free time and boundless energy to pleasure-seeking – drinking, theatregoing, gossiping, card playing – finding countless diversions, preferably sexual ones, to fill their lives with purpose, excitement and intrigue. Central to manners comedy is the feisty and antagonist courtship between a lively and attractive young couple whose union was typically thwarted by a parent or guardian who had other matrimonial plans for them and threatened disinheritance should they not comply. Dubbed the 'gay couple' by John Harrington Smith,[22] this duo bears no resemblance to those romantic lovers of earlier comedies who spew cloying, platonic sentiments. In fact, the gay couple are pragmatic, antiplatonic individuals who reject and mock the previous generation's subscription to the fiction of courtly love – or the school of *préciosité* – which proffered that beautiful and chaste women possess a semi-divine status and an irresistible ocular power to which men immediately succumb, falling in love and revering them as objects of worship.[23] Instead, they adhered to the current philosophies which challenged all orthodox views and dogmas and which tacitly espoused the impermanence of love, the unlikelihood of constancy, and the transitoriness of all things human. Fuelled by a pragmatic view of love, the gay couple, though mutually attracted to one another, play out their courtship in a series of witty verbal skirmishes during which both, according to current fashion and custom, conceal their feelings under a mask of indifference and scepticism while trying to trick each other into dropping their façade and thereby gaining the upper-hand over one's opponent in the battle of the sexes. The palpable comic energy of these two youthful combatants desperately in love but refusing to admit it, especially according to the conventional platonic mode, escalates into a provocatively erotic, sexual tension as both try to contain their passion within the confines of contemporary modes and manners that demand they eschew sentimentality and maintain their emotional control and self-possession.

The gay couple of manners comedy represented the new vitality and spirit of Charles's restored court: the libertine hero, a handsome gallant devoted to freedom and pleasure, who railed against all forms of custom, commitment, and convention (especially marriage), and sought to satisfy his appetitive and aggressive nature,[24] while the attractive and chaste female escorting this heretofore reluctant rake to matrimony offered a new type of heroine who likewise reflected the new Stuart *élan*. Possessing greater freedom than her dramatic predecessors, the Carolean heroine has the sparkling wit and keen intelligence of her male counterpart; she is her own woman who refuses to capitulate to any master and who also demonstrates an indomitable will to power that guarantees her a degree of autonomy in a world which denies freedom to women. Although never allowed the sexual licence of the libertine, the heroine, forced to ratify the double standard by remaining virtuous, nonetheless negotiates deftly in a society that would curb her spirit, ultimately securing happiness on her own terms.[25] Diametrically opposed to the gay couple who embody the new Stuart ethos stand the laughable fools, dupes, and social pretenders – the frenchified fops, country visitors, rich merchants, cuckolds, rapacious women, hypocritical Puritans, and adulterous wives – a host of outsiders who symbolise either the repressive ideas and stifling conventions of the past age or the current phenomenon of lesser individuals attempting to emulate their betters even though these laughable imitators sorely lack the intelligence, wit, sophistication and *savoir-faire* to succeed. Driven by familiar Carolean themes (e.g., old versus new, age versus youth, country versus town, convention versus freedom) that addressed the concerns of the upper class regarding the potential erosion of its pre-eminent status at the hands of the rising merchant class and similar social climbers who were acquiring sufficient wealth and status to threaten their elite social rank, comedy of manners reinscribes the myth of aristocratic privilege – particularly the privilege to rule – by portraying the upper class as superior in every way, from their style, breeding and wit, to those interlopers and pretenders whose birthright, stupidity, or folly precludes them from joining the *beau monde*'s exclusive club.

Labelled variously as 'sex comedies' – for their prurient language and rampant sexual escapades, particularly during the 1670s – and as 'wit comedies' – for their display of witty characters with facile, lively and penetrating intellects that bespoke their wit, the single most important barometer of one's social em-

inence[26] – comedy of manners reached its apogee in 1676 with
Etherege's *The Man of Mode* and Thomas Shadwell's *The Virtuoso*,
and after a hiatus during the Glorious Revolution, it experienced
a resurgence in the 1690s, particularly with the comedies of
Thomas Southerne, Susanna Centlivre, Colley Cibber, Sir John
Vanbrugh and William Congreve, a resurgence which lasted until
the end of the seventeenth century with the latter's masterpiece,
The Way of the World (1700). Comedy of manners' enormous
popularity quickly declined in the the first decade of the eighteenth
century, for with the changing audience composition – the
wealthy, influential and comparatively conservative merchant
class – spectators preferred the sentimental comedies of Richard
Steele and George Farquhar, which offered them middle-class
characters and a more conventional morality that echoed their
own. And for the next 200 years, comedy of manners – indeed,
much of Carolean and Restoration comedy altogether – would
suffer oblivion until early twentieth-century scholars and directors finally took them off the shelves, dusted them down, and
rediscovered them as stageworthy, literary treasures.

Carolean drama, often misread as the coterie, royalist enterprise of Cavalier managers and dramatists devoted principally to
flattering Charles and his court by depicting heroic and glamorous characters who reified the philosophies, behaviour and
spirit of Whitehall (i.e., the overall image that Whitehall had of
itself), has often been dismissed as trite, dull, and escapist.
Recently, however, scholars have engaged in historicist studies
which reveal that these plays, typically deemed mere reflections
of a court-based audience, actually spoke to their historical
moment in a different and unique manner, sharing a far more
important common thread that has heretofore gone unexplored:
specifically, each major genre – comedies, tragicomedies,
tragedies, heroic dramas – contains a strong political subtext
which Carolean audiences, acutely sensitised to national climer-
actics, would have gleaned immediately and found compelling.[27]
Indeed, post-Interregnum theatregoers, as Michael Neill put it,
'were more extensively politicised than at any other time in
English history',[28] and these spectators were highly primed to
detect in the plays those subtle political nuances that addressed
the range of their emotions, expectations and reactions attendant
to Charles's restoration and monarchy.

From its very inception, Carolean drama showed its political inclinations, beginning with the unsurprising issues of rebellious usurpers and restored monarchs depicted in dozens of plays written within the first few years, including John Tatham's *The Rump* (the first new Carolean comedy,1660), which satirises the Puritans and celebrates the historical General Monck's success in effecting the restoration, Orrery's heroic drama, *The General* (written in 1661, performed 1664), featuring another loyal general defying a usurper and helping to reinstate the rightful ruler, and Dryden's *The Indian Queen* (1664) showing an insurrection followed by the return of Montezuma to the throne of Mexico. And throughout the Carolean era, the new Stuart monarchy was played out in some fashion in every major genre, each one probing a particular political perspective. In very general terms, tragicomedy explored the realities of regicide and restoration by typically dramatising the movement from a volatile environment to a stabilising one, thereby exorcising the past atrocities while auguring national harmony through the regenerative effects of the rightful king; heroic drama examined the nature of the restorative hero whose qualities as a worthy ruler and valiant warrior affected the well-being of an entire nation; and comedy showed the clash between the flawed, older generation who supported regicide and the new generation of youthful and anarchistic aristocrats whose marriages signalled the recuperation of civil order and their rightful rule over their domain.

Such political underpinnings in the plays – and there were many – did not, however, remain static throughout the period, for as the country's initial, twinned states of euphoria and optimism over the king's return regressed to an inevitable condition of disenchantment and anxiety over Charles's personal and political missteps, dramas followed suit in their overall themes and tones. During the 1660s when sanguinity ran high, plays, in the main, glorified and mythologised the Restoration by providing definitive resolutions in which all ended happily with turmoil quashed and deserving heroes legitimised and rewarded, but by the 1670s, when political tensions escalated due to a series of events – including England's alliance with the Catholic Louis XIV in another war with the Protestant Dutch, Charles's continual and numerous sexual debaucheries which seemed to eclipse his interest in England's rule and vitiate his stature among his subjects

and national leaders as well, and James's public admission of his
Catholicism that generated considerable fear that the country's
next monarch would be an absolutist king who would force
popery on the nation – dramas most usually concluded on a note
of irresolution that intimated chaos and uncertainty reigned,
leaving national harmony and unity hanging in the balance.

Consistent with these changes in the nation's sentiments was
the marked decline in popularity of heroic dramas by the early
1670s that coincided with the rising appeal of tragedies which
dramatise capricious leaders flawed by personal desires that
interfere with political needs and jeopardise social welfare.
Equally consistent with this trend was dramatists' use of
tragedies to focus, albeit obliquely by means of exotic and remote
locales, on very specific topical issues. Public concern over
Charles's infatuation with an unpopular French mistress, for
example, prompted a horde of tragic characters such as Dryden's
Antony who gives all for love, and Thomas Otway's emperor
Titus who succumbs to Roman law and renounces his foreign
lover, Bernice (*Titus and Bernice*, 1676). Likewise, the nation's
acute fears that the strong division over James's succession would
provoke another civil war sparked a wealth of dramas that either
worked admonishingly by reminding audiences of the devasta-
tion brought on by the earlier national crisis or addressed issues
of succession head on, like Dryden's *Aureng-Zebe* (1676) with two
sons of an emperor battling one another for their father's throne,
Aphra Behn's *Abdelazar* (1676) depicting dissension in a royal
family and the dire consequences of disrupting succession based
on religious convictions, and even an opera, Charles Davenant's
Circe (1677), that portrayed a lustful king whose rapaciousness
causes the destruction of the entire royal family, including the
heir to the throne. Clearly, this hotly volatile climate and overall
darker mood in England during the 1670s explains the marked
increase in violent, horrific and prurient actions depicted in
almost every genre – from the ruler whose rape of a young
maiden bespeaks his thorough tyranny and potential to destroy
the innocent, to the unrepentant rake whose sexual anarchy
engenders disharmony and mirrors a court seemingly bent on
personal pleasure over social concord.

Throughout the Carolean period, dramatists responded to the
changing political, cultural and social tides that swept across the

country, and while at first glance many of the some 400 plays written during the entire period of the Restoration may appear formulaic, irrelevant and unstageworthy today, they are in fact rich cultural documents that flesh out and humanise the dry facts of history that constitute this epoch. And during this 40-year span and its mix of approximately 180 playwrights who reflected the disparate beliefs, anxieties and desires of a country poised at the threshold between the dark ages of Cromwell's republicanism and the Age of Enlightenment, Etherege and Wycherley stand at the top of the pantheon for their masterpieces which capture vivid, comic pictures of Carolean society caught in the ebb and flow of Charles II's reign.

3
Etherege and the Carolean Theatre

George Etherege (*c*1636–92), the second of seven children, was born in Maidenhead, Berkshire, to Captain George and Mary (*nee* Powney) Etherege.[1] The elder George served as purveyor to Queen Henrietta Maria from 1636 until 1642 when the Civil War forced the queen to flee London and seek exile in France. Captain Etherege, who died in France in 1650, probably accompanied the queen, leaving his wife and children in the care of his father, a wealthy London vintner. In 1654, Grandfather Etherege apprenticed young George to the prominent attorney George Gosnold in Beaconsfield, Buckinghamshire, where he served as a clerk until autumn 1658. The following year and perhaps with Gosnold's clout, George gained admittance to Clement's Inn as preparatory study for law at the Inns of Court. How long Etherege remained at Clement's is unknown, and although he probably did not complete his law studies, his tenure there afforded him an advanced education, exposing him to Law-Latin, Law-French, and legal instruction as well as providing him with lodgings proximate to the fashionable London world which was to be both his playground and the fodder for his comedies. At this time Etherege did gain a modest amount of financial independence when in July 1659 a lawsuit over his deceased grandfather's estate netted him a lump settlement of £150 and an annual income of £36 (shared with two siblings). Although not a sizeable fortune, the inheritance and annuity did enable Etherege to enjoy a level of comfort in London and gave him the financial security to pursue his pleasure.

For the next five years until the April 1664 première of his first comedy, *The Comical Revenge*, Etherege's precise activities remain unknown. Given that Etherege leaves no trace in London during this time and that his first comedy as well as his final play, *The Man of Mode*, reveal his personal familiarity with French society and culture,[2] he may have used his inheritance to travel abroad between 1659 and 1663: Edmund Gosse suggests that he spent most of this time residing in Paris, while Oldys remarks that 'it seems he travelled into France, and perhaps Flanders also, in his younger years'.[3] In 1663, Etherege appears to have resurfaced in London where he befriended Lord Buckhurst (Charles Sackville, Earl of Dorset), a fellow patron of the arts who had earned a degree of infamy from a well-publicised brawl at Cock Tavern – an event that included Buckhurst, Sir Thomas Ogle and Sir Charles Sedley and involved bottle throwing and window smashing, a drunken mêlée not unlike Sir Frollick's escapade in *The Comical Revenge*. In late 1663, Etherege and Buckhurst were obviously on close terms, for they exchanged bawdy verses recounting their sexual escapades and months later, in early 1664, Etherege would dedicate his first comedy to his fellow libertine.

If Etherege made slight inroads into the fashionable world of London prior to 1664, his first play, *The Comical Revenge*, gained him immediate prominence with London's *beau monde*. The unprecedented success of this comedy, opening at the Duke's Theatre in Lincoln's Inn Fields in April 1664, running for an entire month (a nine-day run was deemed a smash hit), and earning a staggering profit of £1000, established Etherege as a man of wit and artistry and earned him a place in London's elite social circle that included Charles II, the courtiers, and the Court Wits. In fact, the king (though probably not in attendance at the première of *The Comical Revenge*) ordered performances of the play at Whitehall and four years later sat in his royal box at the Duke's Theatre for the opening of Etherege's next comedy, *She Would If She Could*. Etherege, now a member of the circle of courtiers and wits that included John Wilmont (Earl of Rochester), George Villiers (Duke of Buckingham), and Sir Charles Sedley – young gentlemen who dedicated their lives to pleasurable pursuits – probably spent the next four years enjoying his celebrity and the companionship of his fellow wits and court satellites.

When *She Would If She Could* opened in February 1668 at the Duke's Theatre, Etherege's closest companions, Sedley, Buckhurst, and Buckingham, joined him in the pit (the 'wits' circle' in both playhouses) to watch what they certainly hoped would be a comedy that eclipsed the playwright's first attempt. Spectators no doubt expected the same, for an astonishing number queued at the theatre, forcing some 1000 patrons to be turned away for lack of available seats. Unfortunately, the play fared poorly because of the actors' lack of rehearsals and unfamiliarity with their lines. Although Charles II requested private performances of this comedy at court, the cool reception it received initially plagued its subsequent theatrical success: it enjoyed only a dozen performances during the seventeenth century and had a less than stellar stage history after the eighteenth century. The initial failure of *She Would* no doubt proved disappointing to Etherege, for although he never intended to make a living as a playwright, he certainly expected this second comedy to add to rather than detract from his reputation as a man of keen wit and artistic sensibility. How the failure of *She Would If She Could* affected him personally is unknown, for he nowhere refers to the première in any of his extant letters. His reaction to this public discomfiture, however, may well have been a tacit and deliberate remove from playwrighting altogether: shortly after the première, Etherege accepted two appointments awarded him by Charles II, as a Gentleman of the Privy Chamber, and as the secretary to Sir Daniel Harvey, ambassador to Turkey. Etherege served in the latter position from August 1668 to the spring of 1671, when he vacated his post in Constantinople and travelled first to Paris en route to London.

By November 1671, Etherege had reappeared in London, where he wrote a special prologue to Dryden's *Sir Martin Mar-all*, the inaugural performance at Davenant's new theatre in Dorset Garden. Three days following the première of Dryden's comedy, the Duke's Company revived Etherege's *The Comical Revenge*, which ran for two days to full houses. Although Etherege would have received no remuneration for this revival, both Dryden's invitation to pen his play's prologue and Davenant's willingness to resurrect his first comedy paid the dramatist a considerable compliment, illustrating to both the playwright and the public at large that despite his long absence from Britain, Etherege remained in high regard among London's theatrical world. From this time until the appearance of his last comedy, *The Man of Mode* in 1676, Etherege's exact pursuits cannot be chronicled with any certainty or preciseness. During this period, he wrote a number of songs and poems, nine of the latter subsequently published in 1672 as part of an anthology, Hobart Kemp's *A Collection of Poems*, which included verses by two of his long-time friends, Buckhurst and Sedley.[4] Etherege may well have travelled intermittently, but by March 1676 he was ensconced firmly in London to oversee the première of his final comedy, the play that would revive his fame among his contemporaries as one of London's most brilliant playwrights and ultimately secure his later place in the history of Restoration drama as the reigning Carolean playwright of manners comedy.

For the production of *The Man of Mode*, Etherege took great pains to prevent any repetition of *She Would If She Could*'s first night infelicities by enlisting the best available talent: the Bettertons, who had appeared in *The Comical Revenge* but unfortunately not in *She Would If She Could*, were cast as Dorimant and Bellinda; Henry Harris, who had acted the earlier role of Sir Frollick and was thought by some a superior actor to Betterton, performed Medley; William Smith, who excelled in heroic parts, played Sir Fopling; Elizabeth Barry, an especially powerful tragedienne, enacted Mrs Loveit; Sir Carr Scroope, a fellow Court Wit, wrote the prologue and a song; and Dryden contributed to the epilogue. The care taken in rehearsals and planning to prevent any missteps proved well spent, for *The Man of Mode*, according to Charles Gildon, 'met with extraordinary success; all agreeing it to be a true comedy, and the characters drawn to the life', while John Downes, the stage prompter for the Duke's Company, summed that 'this Comedy being well Cloath'd and well Acted, got a great deal of Money'.[5] In addition to earning Etherege an income, the success of this comedy must have brought him encouragement from his fellow Court Wits and others to write another play, but *The Man of Mode* would be his final dramatic effort.

Between 1676 and 1685, Etherege resided in London, for sporadic accounts of his wild escapades have him consorting with

Sedley and his usual band of cohorts. Sometime around 1680 Etherege was knighted, an honour he ostensibly sought in order to marry a wealthy widow who, according to Oldys, 'would not marry him unless he could make her a Lady'.[6] Shortly after knighthood, Etherege did indeed marry a rich widow, Mary Sheppard Arnold, who was eight years his senior. The nature of their relationship is vague, and it is unclear whether they married for love or some other less romantic convenience: Mary for status and Etherege for money. While contemporary satiric and acrimonious verses portraying Etherege as having wed for financial motives may be inaccurate or exaggerated,[7] not long after the marriage, Etherege did begin spending his wife's money as though it were his (which, of course, it was, legally speaking), squandering it on drinking and gambling. Moreover, during this time when Etherege and Mary would have been newlyweds, Etherege cohabited with Elizabeth Barry, the actress who had been Lord Rochester's mistress until his death in 1680. Etherege's affair with Barry, who bore him a daughter, and his freeness with Mary's money suggest that his marriage gained him little personal happiness and considerable financial benefits. Etherege's notorious behaviour during their early married years may well have strained their relationship, for when he took a post in Bavaria in 1685, Lady Etherege remained in Britain, receiving only a dozen letters from her husband during his four-year absence and most probably never seeing him again.

In 1685, nine years after his most significant comedy, Etherege, at the invitation of the new king, James II, accepted the post of envoy at Ratisbon (Regensburg, Bavaria), the diplomatic capital of the German empire. Of all the events in Etherege's life, his tenure at Ratisbon – the least interesting portion of his life, one unrelated to his playwrighting years – is the most thoroughly documented; excluding a few prurient verses he wrote to fellow Court Wits, his early years come down to us by way of occasional anecdotes written not by Etherege but by others, while his later years in Ratisbon yield some 400 letters (official reports and personal correspondence) he penned, and these provide the bulk of information from which historians and biographers limn Etherege's personal traits.[8] Of course, given that the letters were transcribed as official copies from Etherege's originals by his secretary, Hugo Hughes, who disliked Etherege immensely, the credibility of their contents must be viewed with some caution. Nonetheless, notwithstanding an occasional hyperbole or two, these letters, as well as Hughes's own sent to officials at home, paint a less than flattering portrait of Etherege, one that depicts him, now at the advanced age of 49, conducting himself in ways consistent with the notorious and unsavory behaviour of his younger libertine days in London. Those London escapades – ranging from duels, tavern brawls in which individuals were wounded, to the more notorious nocturnal mêlée in 1676 at Epsom where Etherege and others began a riot by tossing fiddlers in a blanket for refusing to play, a bit of harmless fun that escalated into a fracas with a constable and ended in the death of one of Etherege's companions and the subsequent flight of both Etherege and Lord Rochester – garnered Etherege a reputation as a wild rake and made him fit company for the likes of such men as Rochester and Buckingham. But such behaviour that proved acceptable as a Court Wit in London did not transplant well in Ratisbon, and although Etherege seems to have dispatched his duties effectively and efficiently, any positive service he accomplished for his king as his ambassador was neutralised in Ratisbon by his continual scandalous conduct that earned him disdain from the sober Austrians. Either unable or unwilling to exercise some discretion and temper his behaviour, Etherege lived the libertine life, consorting with gamblers who caroused all day and took their raucous behaviour to the city streets, as well as befriending musicians who spent their nights playing at taverns or carrying their merriment to the town where they fiddled and danced al fresco until early-morning hours, tormenting the citizens with their noise and cavorting. Most notoriously, shortly after he arrived in Ratisbon, he publicly courted a Nuremberg actress named Julia, and his flagrant affair with her so scandalised the town that magistrates exiled Julia from Ratisbon and citizens insulted Etherege wherever he went, engendering Etherege's indignation which never attenuated during his remaining years there. Etherege's last communication from Ratisbon indicates that he left Bavaria quickly, intending 'to be with his Majesty, being resolv'd to live and dy in serving him faithfully';[9] thus in 1689 he followed the deposed James II to Paris, where he remained until his death in May 1692.

Etherege's diplomatic service in staid Ratisbon was certainly a curious appointment for this man who preferred living the fashionable life among the Court Wits, and Etherege himself seems to have mused over those qualifications that recommended him to James; writing to Buckingham in November 1686, Etherege, after confessing that 'Ten years ago I as little thought that my Stars designed to make a Politician of me', admitted that James II had 'the Charity to believe me Master of some Qualities, of which I never suspected my self'.[10] Certainly Etherege's previous experience as secretary to Harvey in Constantinople, his law studies, his indefatigable charm, and his unimpeachable loyalty to the king helped him secure the position as ambassador, one that netted him a handsome income by seventeenth-century standards, £3 per day plus expenses.[11] And Etherege's willingness to accept the post (despite his lack of political ambition) may have, as some biographers suggest, had something to do with escaping both his gambling debts and a strained, loveless marriage.[12] Regrettably, if Etherege sought refuge in Ratisbon, he paid a high price for this freedom, for he quickly came to regard his life as one of exile in a city that paled by comparison to the more refined and cultured London or Paris to which he was accustomed. His personal letters to Lord Middleton, Dryden and others sustain a motif of nostalgia for the gaiety of London, its playhouses, parks and promenades. However, were it not for his post in Ratisbon that left him sufficiently homesick and comparatively idle, he would not have composed those personal correspondences that afford historians not only more information about Etherege than do any other extant documents relating to the lives of any seventeenth-century playwrights – thus providing the best existing portrait of a Restoration dramatist and wit – but also significant first-hand commentaries that help illuminate the thoughts, attitudes and impulses underpinning his comedies.

George Etherege was a figure of his time, and his life not only mirrored that of libertines who populated his plays, it also reflected the era's *zeitgeist*. After spending his youth during the unsettled time of the Civil War, he enjoyed an adulthood that witnessed the restoration of the monarchy and with it the rise of new attitudes and ideas that dominated public thought and cultural modes. As both a young gentleman and a royalist, Etherege understandably gravitated toward the new ethos fostered by

Charles II and his court, a new way of life and outlook that placed a premium on libertinism, cynicism, and rationalism. Like fellow Court Wits who took their cue from the king, Etherege possessed a keen distrust in any absolutes or abstracts of the previous age: traditional morality, orthodox wisdom, romantic love, and selfless motives had become suspect and obsolete values. Typical of the wits of his era, Etherege had little interest in metaphysics, philosophy, religion or epistemology, and his letters reveal a man with few convictions or strong opinions. Regarding religion, for example, Etherege (most likely a deist rather than an atheist) echoed the growing disdain for dogmatic theology after the hypocrisies of repressive Puritanism and he reflected the age's indifference toward proscriptive religious doctrine: 'I have ever enjoyed a liberty of opinion in matters of religion. 'Tis indifferent to me whether there be any other in the world who thinks as I do; this makes me have no temptation to talk of the business.'[13] Living in an age that offered few concrete truths in which to believe, Etherege followed the lead of other contemporary libertines and put his trust in the philosophy of *carpe diem* – the constant pursuit of personal pleasure, a pursuit born out of the reality of life's transitoriness.

Those who knew Etherege described him as courteous and generous, as 'a fair, slender, genteel man' who had 'spoiled his countenance with drinking and other habits of intemperance'.[14] His association with the court and its eccentricities appears to have shaped Etherege into a fop, for acquaintances refer to him 'as thorough a fop as ever I saw' and he was known for his 'foppishness of dress',[15] while Etherege himself offered a similar self-characterisation: 'I must confess I am a Fop in my heart; … I have been so us'd to affectation that without the help of the aer of the Court what is naturall cannot touch me.'[16] In addition to cultivating his status as a fop and courtier, Etherege coveted most his reputation as an idle and lazy gentleman who, like the wits of his day, made their mark and garnered their fame in society not by arduous enterprise but by their innate genius, creativity, and acumen. Writing to Lord Godolphin (February 1687), Etherege declared proudly 'I am too lazy and careless to be ambitious', and in a letter to Dryden (also February 1687), Etherege takes his friend to task for trying to lay claim to a higher degree of idleness, stating adamantly 'I, whose every action of *my* life is a witness of my idleness, little thought that you, who have raised so many immortal monuments of your industry, durst have set up to be my rival. ... [Y]ou have no share in that noble laziness of mind which all I write make[s] out my just title to.'[17] Etherege's carefree temperament and inveterate indolence earned him the alliterative sobriquets 'easy Etherege' and 'gentle George', and the 'noble laziness' in which he prided himself helped to foster the public impression he sought for himself as a typical gentleman of his day, that is, one who eschewed hard work and embraced life with little seriousness. No doubt Etherege, with regard to his playwrighting, preferred that others view his comedies as products of his inspired genius and facile intellect, evidence of the superior literary and creative abilities of a contemporary gentlemen of letters and wit. His plays, however, do reveal that writing was a serious matter to him, for his plotting of scenes and dialogue show not first draft efforts but rather great care and craft. And although he wrote only three plays – which has stood as evidence for some critics that he took this creative pastime lightly – the brilliance and vitality of his comparatively small oeuvre had a marked influence on other Restoration dramatists.

Etherege was not a professional playwright, depending, like John Dryden, on box-office successes for a portion of his income. Why Etherege began playwrighting is not clear, but his attraction to the theatre most likely began during his early visits to Paris, where performances (tragedy, comedy – especially Molière's) flourished under the reign of Louis XIV. Etherege, after settling in London, surely continued to attend theatrical performances not only at the Inns of Court while studying law but also at the two patent theatres. Perhaps Etherege, like Wycherley and others after him, was drawn to theatre's vitality as a literary medium, its ability – unlike any other art form – to recreate and display human action in lifelike detail through a live enactment, a three-dimensional performance experience offered to a collective audience that gives the playwright immediate feedback as to success or failure. Theatre is, after all, a social art not a solitary one, and it can reward a dramatist, through audience approval and celebration, in personal ways not achievable for a poet or a novelist. Theatre's popularity in London – especially with the king, members of the court, and the upper class – certainly encouraged Etherege to try his hand at playwrighting, for he knew that any success he could acquire as a dramatist would bring him instant celebrity, praise as a man of wit, and entrée to the court of Charles II – all of which of course did occur with the appearance of his first play.

Although Etherege was neither a student of drama nor a prolific, professional playwright, the three plays he penned – a less-than-modest number compared to the output of other contemporaries such John Dryden or Aphra Behn – earned canonical rights in the corpus of Restoration drama. Writing initially at a time when the theatres had been dominated for the most part by plays either of the Caroline period or contemporary variations of them, Etherege crafted comedies with strikingly different characteristics that appealed greatly to his Carolean audience.

For his first play, *The Comical Revenge; or, Love in a Tub* (1664), Etherege experimented with popular dramatic and theatrical modes of the day to create a multiplot comedy with four distinct threads of action, each providing commentary on the others relative to themes of love and honour. The heroic 'high' plot crafted in rhymed couplets follows the plight of a pair of lovers, Lord Beaufort and Graciana, the latter promised by her father to Colonel Bruce, whom Aurelia, Graciana's sister, secretly loves. After he returns from imprisonment by the corrupt Commonwealth government that falsely accused him of murder, Bruce learns that Graciana loves Beaufort, and he challenges his rival to a duel, but when Beaufort wins, Bruce, out of despair at having lost Graciana, impales himself on his sword. While tending to Bruce during his convalescence, Aurelia confesses her love to him, he immediately reciprocates, and both couples are happily united. The 'low' comedy plot shows the Middletonian cheats and rogues, Palmer and Wheadle, attempting to swindle the Cromwellian knight and fool, Sir Nicholas Cully. After Sir Nicholas loses £1000 to Wheadle at a game of hazard (which, unknown to Cully, has been rigged) and refuses to pay, Wheadle challenges him to a duel, but Sir Nicholas's cowardice on the battle field gets the better of him and he agrees to pay his gambling debt. Wheadle schemes next to rob his cully of his entire estate by convincing Sir Nicholas to impersonate the town gallant, Sir Frederick Frollick, and to wed the wealthy Widow Rich, who is actually Grace, Wheadle's mistress, in disguise. A second 'low' plot centres on Dufoy, the French servant to Sir Frederick, who pretends unrequited love for the maid Betty in order to conceal the real affliction causing his sickly appearance, syphilis; to get her revenge, Betty locks Dufoy in a tub (a 'sweating' tub, used to cure venereal diseases – hence the play's subtitle), forcing the valet to carry himself about in the ludicrous contraption. The 'middle' plot – actually the main plot and the most original in the play – features the roisterous escapades of Sir Frederick Frollick, cousin to Lord Beaufort and a contemporary young libertine who feigns indifference toward the Widow Rich in their mutual tricks and manoeuvres to coerce the other into an admission of love.

Shrewdly catering to the public's taste for disparate forms of theatrical and dramatic entertainment, Etherege fused courtly romance, heroic sentiments, love chases, mistaken identities, duels, disguises, songs, dances, farce and burlesque into an original comic piece that was guaranteed to capture audience appeal by its sheer diversity alone. But the play's originality extends beyond Etherege's successful merging of varied theatrical elements – each with its own distinct style, rhythm, and tone – into a unique and energetic comedy, for audiences especially savoured Sir Frederick Frollick, Etherege's comic hero and the new Stuart cavalier who embodied, unlike any libertine heretofore portrayed in Carolean comedy, the nascent *élan* emblematic of Charles's restored court. Sir Frederick, dedicated to drinking, wenching, carousing, and nocturnal window smashing, is a free spirit – brave, witty, urbane, nonchalant, and self-confident – who dominates the play's action by his inimitable verve and charisma, and although other playwrights (Dryden's *The Wild Gallant* [1663] and James Howard's *The English Mounsieur* [1663]) had depicted this new figure of the rake in London society, their portraits proved comparatively sober and insipid next to Etherege's strikingly realistic and captivating replica of the new seventeenth-century gentleman. In the character of Sir Frederick and the sphere he inhabits, Etherege limned many of those traits consistent with the upper class's view of itself – polished, witty, stylish, resourceful – and the coterie theatregoers (the court, its contingent, and its imitators) regarded his appearance on stage as an image of themselves, a validation and celebration of their carefree and coruscant new world where elegant appearances, sophisticated manners, and witty repartee proved the true distinctions reserved for their social class only.

Yet the appeal of Sir Frederick as a 'restoration' hero to early Carolean audiences may have extended as well to the political connotations of his actions – specifically, his fifth-act orchestration of order out of the chaos that preceded it by unravelling all the confusion in the low plot and doling out the appropriate comic punishment for the dupes and sharpers: he exposes Wheadle and Palmer, returns Sir Nicholas's gambling debt, and he forces all three into marriage – Wheadle gets Grace, Palmer will wed Jenny (Grace's maid), and Sir Nicholas marries Lucy (one of Sir Frederick's previous mistresses). Most notably, however, in his own marriage to Widow Rich, Sir Frederick 'restores' order on a larger scale by taking possession of the Widow's estate, which symbolises the entire 'estate' of England itself, and he embraces the greater good of social welfare by disavowing his anarchic libertinism and opting for marital concord. That Etherege deliberately sets the play's action during the latter years of the Interregnum, pits Sir Frederick against various characters who represent different political attitudes just prior to Charles's return, and ultimately rewards this new cavalier with all the spoils of war (in a play loaded with war imagery), suggests that the playwright wished to have spectators read the action as a quasi-political comedy about the 'restoration' of the Stuart monarch whose rightful reclaiming of English soil and subjects forecasts, at least in the early 1660s, regeneration and harmony.[18]

Despite its few novel features in plotting and characterisation, *The Comical Revenge* did not appreciably effect a revolution in Carolean comic dramaturgy, but with his next play, *She Would If She Could* (1668), Etherege carved out a special form of drama that has become synonymous with the Restoration theatre: comedy of manners. Essentially, in this second play, Etherege jettisons multiple plots, eliminates lower class characters as major figures in the action (they are reduced to functionaries), sets all the action in the fashionable area of the 'town', refines the characters' language and actions to reflect London's *beau monde*, and extends the role of the antagonistic 'gay couple', now a standard component in the comedies, into the dominant portion of the comedy. Specifically, that is, he restricts his comedy to the 'middle' plot of *The Comical Revenge*, the plot that most appealed to audiences; he polished his hero by ridding him of crude behaviour and providing him with a more brilliant level of wit, transformed the heroine into an equally vibrant and self-sufficient young virgin, cranked up the sexual tension and innuendo a notch, and thus introduced a gay couple whose repartee, antagonism and reciprocal attraction would set the standard for playwrights who followed. And Etherege, wishing to capitalise on the enormous popularity of the gay couple, took this characterological device one step further by doubling the formula: he depicts not one couple but two – a pair of libertines, Courtall and Freeman, who pursue two witty and resourceful sisters, Ariana and Gatty, both of whom prove equal combatants in the love chase. Providing satirical commentary on the value of love and honour established through the gay couples are two minor plots that involve the wealthy gentry who have trekked to London in order to enjoy the venal pleasures it offers: Sir Oliver Cockwood, a country knight, hopes to escape the boredom of the rural life and the clutches of his wife by imitating the young rakes and satisfying his lust, while his wife, Lady Cockwood, likewise wishes to evade her impotent husband and secure a sexual liaison with Courtall.

With *She Would If She Could*, Etherege begins to sharpen his singular focus on the manners and mode of an elite society preoccupied solely with its own personal pleasures and cultural signs – an idle and privileged class dedicated to fashionable apparel and graceful deportment, clever aphorisms and linguistic finesse, and emotional control and self-possession, all those attributes that set it apart from the crude and vulgar *hoi polloi* and validated its ostensibly rightful claim to social and cultural superiority. In this comedy, Etherege also begins to explore the discrepancy between inner nature and outer appearances – the difference between the real person and his actual motives and emotions hidden behind the attractive and deceptive exterior mask wrought by the various components of mode and manners. And Etherege likewise shows his incipient thematic interest in the nature of manners as an artificial construct, a false façade that can be readily studied, mastered, and donned as allegedly revelatory of a specific inner state that the individual wishes to portray to the ever-vigilant and watchful eye of the public observer-cum-spectator.

The tangential treatment of the artificial and performative aspects of manners that Etherege depicts in *She Would* burgeons into a full-scale, satiric disquisition in his final comedy, *The Man of Mode* (1676). Recognised by most critics as the finest Carolean manners comedy and the most influential on later Restoration playwrights, especially Congreve, *The Man of Mode* dramatises an entire society – from the libertine hero, his Francophile emulator, to his shoemaker – caught up in an unending game of pretence and affectation, an elaborate masquerade in which individuals derive their greatest pleasure from the myriad performances they enact. In his last play, Etherege narrows his focus particularly to the trope of 'play-acting', the characters' skilful or inept portrayal of the roles they assume, thus striking the apt analogy – one that echoes throughout many Carolean and Restoration plays – between role-playing and manners, between the art of crafting a naturalistic and believable performance within the confines and rules of the acceptable social mode. Through the main characters – Dorimant, the eponymous Sir Fopling, Medley and Harriet, all of whom are singularly dedicated to the display of brilliant external and linguistic forms – Etherege presents an empty and atrophied society in which the 'mask' has replaced interiority and surface appearances are more critical than inner substance: the performance is paramount, and most often the observer – like a spectator in the playhouse – cannot discern the other's real nature from the role he has performed. With everyone performing, donning an artificial veneer in the hope that the true self and desires will not be detected and that the performance will be regarded as a believable substitute for one's identity, Etherege reveals individuals who, in caring more about the efficacy of their performances than the underlying truth in self and others, remain forever precluded from self-cognisance and eternally isolated from each other. Manners, initially intended to enable individuals to negotiate gracefully and interact cordially within society without offending the sensibilities of others while concomitantly allowing one to maintain an open and honest communication with another, have become a barrier to social intercourse, an artificial and frivolous façade that cloaks reality and, more significantly, have been transformed into the most important of all life's games and pursuits.

As the first of the major Restoration playwrights, Etherege has been credited with inventing a form of comedy that most responded to the temperament and spirit of his day, a comedy whose vitality reflected the new and highly energised epoch.

A 'sheer original', as Rochester dubbed him, Etherege was the first to paint an accurate portrait – albeit a polished redaction – of London's fashionable world, presenting true-to-life characters whose attitudes and behaviour embodied the era's new philosophies such as libertinism, materialism, scepticism, as well as using an innovative and elegant prose loaded with witty aphorisms and sparkling banter which ostensibly emulated the conversation of seventeenth-century gentlemen. As suggested above, of course, Etherege's plays are more than slice-of-life comedies that solely foreground the outward display of form and fashion without any critique of his era's desiderata of style and manners, for they do comment satirically and ironically on the *beau monde*'s singular preoccupation with creating its own cultural signs that distinguish it as the privileged class. Unfortunately, however, the plays' wealth of realistic details often suggests to readers, directors and, by extension, spectators that Etherege aimed at merely chronicling with naturalistic, photographic detail the manners of his age, and this misreading of his comedies as mere dramatisations of the superficies and manners of the leisure class elides the intricate depth and rich texture of his unique dramaturgical style. Etherege is actually as much a realist as an impressionist, and like an impressionist who seeks to capture objects under certain lighting conditions in order to create a sensory perception in the viewer rather than to duplicate photographic reality, he sought likewise to invoke in spectators a sensory experience through which they apprehend the characters not as static, one-dimensional individuals, but rather as living and dynamic creatures caught in specific and varied moments of illumination. The end result, as Joycelyn Powell observed, is to kindle in the audience the feeling of 'what it is to be alive in these situations, to communicate the texture of existence'.[19]

To create this heightened sensory reaction in spectators of life's texture unfolding before them and being experienced by the characters as they are living it in the moment, Etherege utilises prismatic scenes which give the impression of life's randomness and he concludes the action on a caesura. Etherege crafts his plays prismatically, using each scene to reveal a different aspect of a main character's personality, but the scenes he depicts typically and intentionally present not a complete and composite picture of a given character but instead a fragmented sketch of the individual, thus intimating that identity and personality are not one-dimensional, fixed and knowable realities. Unlike Wycherley, whose characters behave along predictable lines according to their single-faceted personalities, Etherege captures the complexity of human beings by showing a character's potential for varied behaviour – and sometimes behaviour strikingly contrary to what one would expect – according to the different conditions and circumstances which he or she encounters. Dorimant, for example, exhibits the charming attributes of a witty and affable libertine that make him attractive to audiences one moment, but in the next he shows a dark and malevolent strain that prompts most spectators to recoil and withdraw their approbation, and this absence of a univocal, single personality renders it impossible for spectators to determine unequivocally whether Dorimant will marry Harriet and move to the country.

By constantly shifting the perspective from which audiences view a given character, Etherege forces spectators to direct their concentration on the immediate moment in which one particular facet of the character is being illuminated, and to further his dramatic focus on this immediacy of the moment, these prismatic scenes that he creates foreground action composed of seemingly trivial activities, those prosaic details of day-to-day life which give the impression of both randomness and reality. Again using Dorimant as a case in point, the first act of *The Man of Mode* depicts the hero readying for his day's activities as he entertains friends, and this mundane activity of Dorimant's dressing and conversing conveys the nature of his life and character rather than something momentous. For this reason, Etherege's plays seem to lack well-structured and viable plots – Rochester, for example, characterised his friend's last two comedies, *She Would If She Could* and *The Man of Mode*, as 'two talking plays without one plot'. To be sure, Etherege's plays are 'talking plays', for he wishes to focus not on complicated plots but rather on the ideas and perceptions of reality that characters experience. Thus, Etherege forgoes plot as a source of dramatic tension and instead uses dialogue to generate the underlying conflicts between characters – that is, his prismatic scenes define characters and illustrate the tensions between them based on their differing visions of the world, and this conflict is generated through their conversations rather than the by conventional dramatic use of suspense-building crises which unfold in the denouement. Etherege's dramaturgical style can thus lead to the inference that nothing of importance occurs in his plays other than a recreation of contemporary manners. And Etherege's strategic use of an open-ended resolution likewise solidifies this impression, for readers, left without clear-cut answers, assume the action should be taken as frivolous since it comes to naught. However, by concluding the plays on a caesura, Etherege engineers not only the spectators' re-examination of the characters' actions and attitudes that brought them to a point of stasis or irresolution but also audiences' reflection on the many realities and perceptions that operate upon the characters as they go about their daily lives.

Etherege has been likened to Chekhov: specifically, the latter's use of 'indirect action' which presents a series of seemingly trivial, quotidian or inconsequential activities that add up to no significant changes within the characters nor a definitive denouement. However, life, as Chekhov brilliantly shows, is in the trivial details, and Etherege possessed a similarly keen ability to penetrate human behaviour – the attitudes, ideas, follies and fears – and render them visible with clarity and lifelike detail in common and everyday occurrences. Like Chekhov, Etherege enjoyed a true comic spirit: neither didactic nor judgemental, he was able to laugh at the excesses around him – the fops, the libertines, the fools, the country bumpkins – and treat them with an element of understanding and sympathy but also with the requisite dose of comic detachment that enables spectators to laugh at them as well while also withholding moral judgements. Unlike Wycherley, whose scorn for fools and pretenders hovers over the action, Etherege did not elicit audiences' visceral reactions to his characters. He sought their laughter and their intellectual engagement toward a host of characters who amused him because they internalised a code of manners that had ironically rendered them victims of style rather than liberating them, as they believed, from all the shackles of conformity.

4
She Would If She Could:
Comedy of Manners

The excitement generated by Etherege's first play, *The Comical Revenge* (1664), clearly endured the four-year hiatus until the première of his next comedy, for when *She Would If She Could* opened on 6 February 1668, the Duke of York's Theatre immediately filled to capacity. Regrettably, for those who attended the opening performance, *She Would If She Could* did not meet with the same degree of success accorded his first comedy. The inveterate play-goer Samuel Pepys found 'nothing in the world good in it', adding that patrons in the pit 'blame the play as a silly, dull thing, though there was something very roguish and witty; but the design of the play, and end, mighty insipid'.[1] Etherege attributed the play's failure to the actors' lack of preparation and unfamiliarity with their lines, and his accusations were corroborated a few years later by Thomas Shadwell, who, in his preface to *The Humorists* (1671) – a play also hampered by poor acting on its première – remarked that 'imperfect Action, had like to have destroy'd *She would if she could*'. However, regardless of the reasons for the cool reception at the première, the play's initial failure did not eclipse its dramatic merits: John Dennis, in his Epistle Dedicatory to *The Comical Gallant* (1702), said 'it was esteem'd by the Men of Sense, for the trueness of some of its Characters, and the purity and freeness and easie grace of its dialogue' – distinctive dramatic qualities that earned it performances at Whitehall and praise in Shadwell's preface as 'the best Comedy that has been written since the Restauration of the Stage'.[2]

The originality of *She Would If She Could* that earned Etherege encomiums from his contemporaries has also been remarked on by numerous modern scholars, many of whom debate its status as the first true comedy of manners. Clearly Etherege did not invent this genre with *She Would*, for he borrowed freely from trends in recent Carolean comedies, including his own: prose comedies set in contemporary London and reflecting the romantic escapades of the idle and fashionable *beau monde*, whose intrigues and libertinism are contrasted sharply by satirical social pretenders and country dupes, had surfaced in such plays as James Howard's *The English Mounsieur* (1663) and Dryden's *The Wild Gallant* (1663); the gay couple, also introduced in Howard's comedy, had become staple protagonists in comedies performed at both patent theatres, and the young lovers' badinage that charged their sexual antagonism-cum-attraction had displayed a modicum of polish in Dryden's *The Secret Love* (1667).[3] Similarly, in some respects *She Would* appears modelled on *The Comical Revenge*, with Etherege merely doubling character types: the rake-hero Sir Frederick splits into Courtall and Freeman, the heroine Widow Rich transforms into Ariana and Gatty, and the fool Sir Nicholas bifurcates into Sir Oliver Cockwood and Sir Joslin Jolly. Notwithstanding Etherege's culling from popular scenes and material, as well as his own earlier smash hit, however, *She Would* does demonstrate both a marked departure from any identifiable prototypes and a movement toward a new mode of comedy. And the dramaturgical novelties in *She Would If She Could* that make it a solid contender as the first comedy of manners include Etherege's handling of plot, character, and language.

Atypical of this early stage in Carolean comedy, *She Would* demonstrates a shift in focus toward a central plot exclusively devoted to the love chase of the gay couple – the standard material of manners comedy – and a move away from the popular 1660s multiple-plot comedies, which relied on mixed genres and their stratified character types to provide thematic parallels or counterpoint; there are no Fletcherian verse speakers here, nor

Middletonian cullies (as in *The Comical Revenge* or Sedley's *The Mulberry Garden* [1668]) to afford audiences disparate types of action, amusement via farce, and thematic commentary through class contrasts. Although the play does contain three levels of action (Lady Cockwood's attempts at seduction, Courtall's and Freeman's pursuit of Gatty and Ariana, and Sir Oliver's and Sir Jolly's quest for personal pleasures), Etherege has constructed a taut plot that concentrates essentially on the two witty pairs of lovers – Courtall and Gatty, Freeman and Ariana – and has crafted the other two lines of action relative to how they affect this courtship, thus orchestrating these three lines of action to impinge on each other, with all characters interacting continually and doing so in the same public and private spheres. Equally significant in the play's trajectory toward manners comedy, Etherege privileges characterisations over plot complications, doing so by diminishing the use of popular intrigue devices, that is, those mistaken identities, coincidences, confusions and accidents (as in *The Comical Revenge* and Dryden's *The Rival Ladies* [1664]) used to generate plot entanglements that will be unravelled ultimately in a neat and tidy denouement. Admittedly, there are moments of such comic discomfiture (characters hiding under tables or in closets to avoid detection, Sir Oliver and Sir Joslin carousing at the Bear when Courtall and Lady Cockwood arrive coincidentally), but these devices do not drive the bulk of the plot per se; the major intrigues or embarrassments characters encounter are generated not so much from the playwright's plotting of mechanical complications (which would make them victims of circumstance) but rather from the characters' own ambitions, personalities and motives (which makes *them* the architects of their own dilemmas and fates).[4]

These stylistic changes result in a significant shift in dramatic focus that typifies comedy of manners: specifically, they indicate the reduced importance of plot entanglements and the all-important, rising centrality of character. Thus, by eschewing the multiple-plot formula, jettisoning the heroic lines of action and farcical city comedy (as in *The Comical Revenge*), and focusing on characters in the same social class, Etherege can emphasise his satiric points about the behaviour of London's fashionable society not by conventional comparisons between characters from different genres and their inherently stereotypical and inviolable class hierarchies, but rather by contrasting characters of the same social status based on the acceptable precepts of 'manners' and decorum which, of course, become the cynosural material for scrutiny and commentary in all comedies of manners. And by avoiding intrigue, which places audience interest, as Laura Brown explains, 'toward the untangling of the trivial mistakes of the plot, at the expense of characterization or theme',[5] Etherege can, axiomatically, obviate spectators' misplaced attention on plot trajectory or the denouement and redirect their concentration on characters' behaviour, thus further facilitating his dramatic purpose of highlighting the characters' manners – their language, deportment, and interplay – as a social and stylistic construct, an unstable and arbitrary code of behaviour that forms the fabric of fashionable society.

And it is this fashionable society on which Etherege singularly focuses that also signals *She Would*'s seminal connexion with comedy of manners, for this comic genre revolves dramatically and thematically around the axis of the *beau monde*. Indeed, while Etherege's unique de-emphasis of plot points stylistically toward comedy of manners, his singular depiction of a refined society – its pastimes, preoccupations, milieu, values and, perhaps most notably, its language – points similarly to the very characterological substance of manners comedy. Certainly dramatisations of sophisticated society and its mode of conduct had appeared in earlier plays, but only intermittently; in *She Would*, however, such characters and their actions energise – as they do in subsequent manners comedy – the entire plot of the play. Not only do all major characters belong to the leisure class, but also the dramatic action in which they are engaged centres exclusively on this idle society's indulgence in temporary amusements and pleasures – ranging from playgoing, carousing, courting, mating to wenching – with each character inventing some type of intrigue (usually sexual) in order to inject excitement into an otherwise dull life. In the initial scene, Etherege establishes this motif immediately with Courtall's opening query, 'Well, Frank, what is to be done today?' (I,i,4), and the remaining scenes depict an ostensibly refined group of characters from both town and country attempting to satisfy their natural and personal desires within the boundaries of social custom and current fashion. For the first time on the London stage, audiences glimpsed a play devoted solely to portraying an homogeneous people whose world and lifestyle either mirrored their own or proved readily recognisable. And the recognisability of these Carolean socialites and the deliberate life-like note that Etherege wished to strike were further facilitated for audiences by the topographical exactness of the play's contemporary London setting – the New Exchange, the Mulberry Garden, the Bear, the New Spring Garden (Vauxhall) – an unprecedented saturation of realistic locales (ones certainly frequented by the theatres' patrons) that vivified London in a way not achieved in previous comedies and that served as scenic signs of the action's topicality. To be sure, comedy of manners is, at its simplest, a comedy of contemporary and fashionable London life, and thus the characters, their conduct, and the locales presented in this play gave spectators a degree of verisimilitude heretofore unseen on the London stage, one that Oldys remarked on in his appreciation of the play's importance: 'These applauses arose from our author's changing the study after old copies ... for those taken directly from the freshest practice and experience in original life. He drew his characters from what they called the beau monde; from the manners and modes then prevailing with the gay and voluptuous part of the world.'[6]

The lifelikeness of Etherege's characters derives not merely from their conduct and environs, for, more notably, Etherege introduces here characters with a distinctive language and linguistic strategies that not only vividly concretise this society but also point specifically toward those stylistic discursive modes that would epitomise manners comedy. Typical of Etherege's use of language, on the one hand, characters' dialogue exhibits a degree of spontaneity, naturalness and grace which emulate everyday discourse rather than the artificial and forced conversations of, for example, Dryden's plays to date. However, on the other hand, and without diminishing this appearance of naturalistic conversation, the elegant prose displays a wealth of verbal brilliance and polish that form a high and unprecedented level of 'wit', the quintessence of Restoration comedy.[7] In *She Would*, Etherege deploys with significant artistry many of the basic types of verbal patterns in witty dialogue which have become the trademarks of Restoration manners comedy. Raillery, for example, dominates the courtship scenes, no doubt those scenes Pepys found 'very roguish and witty', and this witty repartee between the two gay couples peppers their very first encounter:

COURTALL: By your leave, ladies –

GATTY: I perceive you can make bold enough without it.

ARIANA: Or any other ladies' that will give themselves the trouble to entertain you.

COURTALL: Can you have so little good nature to dash a couple of bashful young men out of countenance, who came out of pure love to tender you their service?

GATTY: 'Twere a pity to balk 'em, sister.

ARIANA: Indeed methinks they look as if they never had been slipped before.

FREEMAN: Yes faith, we have had many a fair course in this paddock, have been very well fleshed, and dare boldly fasten. (*They kiss their hands with a little force.*)

ARIANA: Well, I am not the first unfortunate woman that has been forced to give her hand, where she never intends to bestow her heart.

(II,i,91–110)

Here the thrust and parry between the two couples show real verve as the females ridicule the men for brash liberties they freely take with them, and the men, in like fashion (but also with an impudent double entendre from Freeman) retaliate with playful quips about female vanity; and their verbal swordplay gains considerable vitality at each encounter, culminating in the most barbed exchange when Ariana and Gatty accuse the libertines of forging the letters (IV,ii). Likewise, Etherege shows increased skill with his use of comparisons and similitudes – those risible, linguistic strategies that echo throughout the plays of Wycherley, Congreve and others – which can enable the speaker to withhold any information that could give another the advantage by disguising inner feelings impersonally and dispassionately, as in the denouement when Courtall, in referring to the month-long probation prior to their nuptials, tells Gatty 'Now shall I sleep as little without you, as I should do with you: madam, expectation makes me almost as restless as jealousy' (V,i,649–51). Through his characters' facile use of such discursive manoeuvring, Etherege foregrounds language as part and parcel of manners, as a gauge of one's social fitness, finesse, and superiority: the ability to display intellectual acumen and astuteness (i.e., wit, raillery), the skill to negotiate through society without offending others and still

attain one's personal agenda, which may be contrary to theirs
(i.e., dissembling and complaisance, as with Courtall making
Lady Cockwood believe that his delays in consummating their
relationship spring from his concern about her honour), and the
capacity to transform vices into positive virtues (i.e., inverting, as
when Courtall tells Freeman that bragging about sexual conquests should never be done at the beginning of an affair 'for fear
of frighting a young lady from her good intentions' [IV,ii,101–2] –
'good' referring not to moral propriety but to the woman's sexual
compliance).[8] These and other rhetorical devices were used extensively throughout Carolean and later Restoration comedy as
dramatists highlighted language as a stylistic ideal, *the* primary
stylistic barometer by which to measure one's social status and
ascendancy. In sum, Etherege's use of language and rhetoric in
this play, as well as his handling of character, plot and setting,
point toward a new direction in comic drama adopted by many
who followed. Although Robert Hume argues that this play's lack
of success and meagre performance record probably precluded
any significant influence on later comedies,[9] *She Would If She
Could* did appear in print in 1668 and 1671, thus making it accessible for detailed study by contemporary playwrights.

In combining all these dramaturgical elements – elements that
make *She Would If She Could* a viable candidate as the first comedy
of manners – Etherege was perfecting his formula for the type of
satire synonymous with this genre. Clearly, manners comedy
does not aim strictly at a naturalistic aesthetic which merely
reflects a shallow society bent on self-indulgence, for its realistic
materials – the genteel society, the witty language, the gay
couples, the social pretenders, the fashionable London locales – are
not the comedy's end in themselves but rather are all naturalistic
ingredients in a recipe that yields this genre's principal aim: social
satire. *She Would* does, true to manners comedy, take a satiric and
ironic look at both the absurdity in subscribing to fashionable
modes as well as the manners themselves, anatomising the affectations, pretences, and deceptions of a sophisticated society
attempting to assert its pre-eminence as the socially elite sect by
redefining their social prerogative through a new mode of mores
and behaviour, those cultured and exquisite traits which clearly
distinguish them as the privileged few and legitimise them as

the aristocracy. Through its depiction of the superficial details of manners and each character's attempt to adhere to these new stylistic imperatives, Etherege's comedy actually problematises the social codes by which his characters live as arbitrary, mediated, and artificial constructs that can be manipulated, donned, and discarded as necessary as they pursue their personal pleasure and fashion their self-identities. Indeed, 'good comedy of manners', as Susan Staves explains, 'often expresses a more basic wonder at the power of social codes, not only to determine human behavior but also to constitute human identity itself'.[10] In *She Would If She Could*, Etherege explores codes of behaviour – decorum, manners – for this very end, to display it theatrically for the very social thing it is: a purely artificial mode of elegance to which all the fashionable individuals acquiesce entirely, a façade of calculated linguistic and behavioural signs by which they project their identities and conceal their inner selves and feelings. Although *She Would* lacks the sceptical tone typical of most comedies of manners – as evident in Etherege's final play, *The Man of Mode* – Etherege displays his characteristic, detached amusement as he examines without judgement and represents with relish the extent to which individuals construct identities and conduct themselves according to social dicta, fashioning for themselves a social mask, a veneer of civility and an external persona (one applied as easily as make-up and costume) intended to hide their natural instincts and emotions that lie just beneath the surface. Their comic struggle stems from their attempt to find a way of expressing those desires and feelings within the boundaries of the current acceptable 'mode' which mandates that one's feelings remain masked and imperceptible to prevent one from yielding power and control to another. And in his depiction of his aristocratic and fashionable cadre of characters from both town and country, no character escapes audience scrutiny, for each one is held up to the light for closer inspection of those codes of behaviour that each adopts to exemplify style, evade social restraints, gain personal ends, and ultimately define self.

Typical of many plays in its genre, *She Would If She Could* anatomises manners and decorum by establishing a characterological dialectic between radical and orthodox values, a set of opposite characters whose behaviour marks stark antitheses denoting the play's countervailing forces defined variously as liberty vs restraint, libertine vs dupe, wit vs would-be wit, new vs old, nature vs artifice, and a host of similar polarities used to demarcate the new social mode from the old conventional code. On one side stand the youthful characters – the pair of gay couples – who represent the new cultural hegemony, the new standard of fashion and decorum of their class, and on the other side the somewhat older country aristocrats who, despite their attempts to emulate the new and spirited Cavalier ethos, remain emotionally and psychologically tethered to the past age's repressive, indecorous, and stifling way of life. The juxtaposition of these two ideological factions works by contrast to underscore the singular importance that all characters place on style and form as the exemplars of social status.

The young quartet of lovers – like all gay couples in comedy of manners – seek liberty from the restraints of convention to express their natural desires, rebel against repressive custom, attempt to control their own fates, view life and courtship as a playful game, and arm themselves with a pragmatic, unsentimental attitude toward love, marriage and constancy. Courtall and Freeman, the young gallants of the town, govern their lives by libertine doctrine. Both conspire to find pleasure at every turn, as Freeman indicates in response to Courtall's inquiry about the day's activities that they 'follow the old trade; eat well, and prepare ourselves with a bottle or two of good Burgundy that our old acquaintance may look lovely in our eyes' (I,i,4–7). Their seduction of women provides them the town's most satisfying diversion, but the chase itself also proves entertaining; their pursuit and discussions of women contain metaphors from warfare or recreational sports (hunting, fishing, horse-racing, falconry), indicating their perception of the love-chase as a battle or game, a contest of wills in which they intend to be victorious. True to the libertine spirit, they prefer numerous affairs simultaneously, and while poised to entertain familiar female acquaintances as they also manoeuvre an introduction to Sir Joslin's nieces, they must out of masculine necessity stop to exchange flirtations with the masked women in the Mulberry Garden – for after all, 'a single intrigue in love', as Courtall wittily informs Freeman, 'is as dull as single plot in a play, and will tire a lover worse, than t'other does an audience' (III,i,113–16). They espouse libertine attitudes toward marriage and fidelity, Courtall asserting 'a wife's a dish, of which if a man once surfeit, he shall have a better stomach to all others ever after' (III,iii,296–8). And while hoping to avoid marriage at all costs because it means a loss of their liberty, and yet to reap the sexual benefits of conjugal life, they hold to the fundamental libertine premise that marriage, though based on mutual love and sexual attraction, can be most palatable if a 'pretty country seat' and a 'handsome parcel of land' (V,i,516–17) are part of the nuptial bargain – the very arrangement they secure at the end of the play.

Though both men display the conventional attributes of the new Cavalier gentleman – libertinism, materialism, hedonism, scepticism – they are not, however, identical. Of the two, Courtall is the wittier and more resourceful, the masterful leader and consummate manipulator of others, directing roles for everyone to play in his various escapades, taking control of every opportunity or situation, and always extricating himself with éclat from any potentially embarrassing entanglement. In the Mulberry Garden (II,i), he devises the plot for Freeman to detain Sir Joslin and Sir Oliver at the tavern until he returns from his meeting with Lady Cockwood so that Joslin will, true to habitual practice, bring the two men home to meet his nieces; at the New Exchange (III,i), he enlists Mrs Gazette as his accomplice in ridding himself of Lady Cockwood and helping him secure a rendezvous with Gatty and Ariana; at the Bear (III,iii), Courtall hits on the idea of disguising Ariana, Gatty and Lady Cockwood as tavern wenches to elude Sir Oliver's detection; and at the Cockwoods' lodgings for the denouement (V,i), he establishes amity and harmony by saving both himself and Lady Cockwood from discovery by Sir Oliver, Ariana and Gatty with his quick thinking, concocting the tales that Sentry provided both him and Freeman entry to the Cockwood home to give them access to Ariana and Gatty, and that Lady Cockwood had Sentry forge the letters in order to frighten the girls into more respectable behaviour.

Courtall, the more experienced and worldly, also serves as Freeman's tutor in all things regarding feminine nature as well as the proper rakish method of chasing and courting women. Like all libertines, he believes he understands the depths of female psychology, offering the perpetually anxious Freeman continual snippets of his worldly advice: after Freeman expresses his anxiety that Ariana and Gatty will rebuff them for having broken their promise not to speak with other women prior to their next encounter, Courtall nonchalantly allays his friend's apprehension with a characteristically self-confident observation that women actually prefer wild libertines who present the challenge of domesticating them: 'whatsoever women say, I am sure they seldom think the worse of a man, for running at all, 'tis a sign of youth and high mettle, and makes them rather *piqué*, who shall tame him' (III,i,109–12). Similar to most of his libertine counterparts, Courtall is multifaceted, capable of adopting various guises to suit the present situation and company: to Freeman he is the perfect rakish mentor, to Sir Oliver and Sir Joslin he is the libertine ethos incarnate and the man whom they try to emulate, to Gatty he is the honest gentleman wit and potentially faithful mate, and to Lady Cockwood he is the dashing courtly lover, respectful of her honour and reputation.

The protean nature of Courtall's identity demonstrates the remarkable dexterity of this libertine, but the myriad roles he plays for each character – ranging from the functionaries like Sentry and Gazette to the major figures in the play, each of whom expects a different identity of him and for whom he willingly performs different roles – also casts in bold relief the extent to which identity and self-image in this society derive not necessarily from an awareness of one's inner self but rather from the external forms of manners and mode, leaving open to question both the true nature of the individual behind his many guises and the influence of manners on the construction or erasure of self-identity. Courtall performs so many roles out of his sense of social protocol and fashion that one is hard pressed to distinguish which, if any, reflects his true nature. Admittedly, some scholars contend that Courtall's various impersonations demonstrate his compliance with his era's desiderata of wit and dissembling and that he possesses a keen understanding of the difference between the many masks he wears as a necessary social façade and his true motives and personality underneath, and to corroborate this assessment of Courtall's (as well as Freeman's) self-awareness, critics cite the only textual evidence of such self-cognisance: 'I hate to dissemble when I need not; 'twould look as affected in us to be reserved now w'are alone, as for a player to maintain the character she acts in the tiring- room' (V,i,351–4).[11] These lines, however, are spoken by Gatty in confidence to Ariana, and thus to attribute a level of cognitive mastery to Courtall by the circuitous route of a confession made by Gatty alone seems both a curious sleight of hand with Etherege's dialogue as well as a quantum leap in character analysis that cannot be bridged with collateral evidence. In fact, nowhere in the play does Courtall offer any dialogue or asides that reveal interiority, and even in his private colloquies with his friend, both he and Freeman refrain from frank discussions and remain, as Kathleen Lynch observed, 'constrained to make clever remarks regarding their love intrigues', perpetually engaged in some type of 'conversational game'[12] with one another, keeping up their pretences, hiding motives, and ultimately obscuring their true identities.

The ambiguity of Courtall's character suggests that through his adherence to manners and style, he has come to rely on outer forms only, neither able to understand his true nature nor capable of separating himself from the many roles he plays. Two examples serve as prime cases in point: Courtall's relationship with Lady Cockwood and his cagey acceptance of Gatty's matrimonial proviso. Courtall leads Lady Cockwood to believe that he will satisfy her sexual desires, though he has no intention of doing so, and his reasons for such tactical – though thoroughly non-libertine – evasions are presented as specious: he complains to Freeman that Lady Cockwood is 'the very spirit of impertinence, so foolishly fond and troublesome, that no man above sixteen is able to endure her' (I,i,265–7), that she 'will give her lover no more rest, than a young squire that has newly set up a coach, does his only pair of horses' (I,i,279–81), and that with the variety of women in town, he will not settle for 'horseflesh' when 'good meat' is plentiful (IV,ii,159–60). However, Freeman's final response to Courtall's excuses – 'This is rather an aversion in thee, than any real fault in the woman' (IV,ii,161–2) – points up Courtall's libertine rhetoric as pure casuistry, a fabricated pretence to mask his true motives which he either does not fully understand himself or prefers not to articulate for fear of disclosing the bogus nature of his libertine ethos. Libertine philosophy promulgated that sexual appetites were natural instincts for both men and women – and there is much Cavalier poetry dedicated to convincing trepid or reluctant women to subscribe to such proffered truths – but Courtall resists the advances of a woman who offers him the variety in sexual adventure that he purports to prefer because she is, in point of fact, the very embodiment of a female libertine who, in accordance with the tenets of libertinism, possesses a libidinous nature equal to that of any man. More specifically, Courtall evades her sexual advances not because she's unattractive (Freeman and Sir Oliver find her otherwise), nor because she's burdensome or sexually experienced, but rather because she has usurped the masculine prerogative as the aggressor, turning Courtall into the feminine role of a sexual object of desire, casting herself as the hunter and him the helpless victim. The imagery he uses to describe Lady Cockwood as a bird of prey – 'Why, this ravenous kite is upon wing already, is fetching a little compass, and will be here within this half hour to swoop me away' (III,i,65–7) – reverberates back to him as well when Gatty accuses him of similar aerial scouting for live quarry: 'I find you daily hover about these gardens, as a kite does about a back-side, watching an opportunity to catch up the poultry' (IV,ii,200–2). Preferring to play the hunter rather than the hunted, Courtall cannot wholly embrace the libertine doctrine he spews so readily because at heart he subscribes to the more conventional views of male–female relationships – particularly regarding female propriety and feminine virtue – though he fails to see the hypocrisy in his preference for sustaining a double standard that libertinism allegedly and tacitly disavows.[13] Those 'golden laws of nature' on which libertinism is partially founded actually undermine male sexual politics, and libertines like Courtall (though certainly not like Horner) eschew sexually aggressive females because they threaten their masculinity by robbing them of the opportunity to play out their cherished role as a rake: the predator who finds his greatest pleasure in asserting his masculine superiority by battling with reluctant and virtuous females and emerging the victor who seduces them into sexual compliance. Courtall, a patent pretender to libertinism who finds female sexual aggressiveness disquieting, does not recognise that his version of its ethos is nothing short of rhetoric and sophistry, a character whom Etherege found amusing as he dons his feigned role of courtly lover with Lady Cockwood to avoid the very type of sexual liaison that his life's philosophy proffers.

Courtall negotiates through society by adopting numerous disguises and strategies to achieve his ends, but his inability to extricate himself from his inveterate role-playing is perhaps best evident in the fifth act when, in response to Gatty's proviso of a month-long probation during which he and Freeman may court her and Ariana and prove their fidelity, he couches his response in characteristically libertine language: 'If the heart of a man be not very deceitful, 'tis very likely it may be so' (V,i,572–3). Coupled with the ambiguity of his character throughout the play, Courtall's non-committal posture here has provoked considerable confusion and critical disagreement as to the likelihood of a happy resolution either after a month's trial or in the marriage itself, should it take place. Given that throughout the scheme of Restoration comedy a libertine's entire existence revolves around seducing women while avoiding matrimony, his last-act conversion to or rejection of marriage understandably garners considerable critical attention, most notably because the marital state is likened (as in many comedies) to a 'state of grace' – that is, an acceptance of traditional social values toward which the libertine has been guided – thereby translating his redemption or recidivism into the singular most important action which crystallises his character overall and signals, respectively, social harmony or continual anarchy at large. Etherege, however, forgoes the conventional happy ending and concludes on a note of irresolution because he was after other game. His interest lies not in positing some Hegelian synthesis (via marriage) between libertine and orthodox views but rather in dramatising the libertine as so wedded to the posturing and rhetorical evasions inherent in the cultural ideal of social codes that he fails to distinguish where performance ends and reality begins. Here Gatty's allusion to the tiring-room proves most relevant, for Courtall, the habitual actor, continues to enact the libertine at a time when his performance should have concluded, but the mode to which he subscribes allows him no way of revealing his feelings and desires without dropping the guise of libertine detachment. Manners and custom have shaped his identity, and his conditional phrasing in response to Gatty's proviso conveys that he – like a method actor – has internalised social codes and transformed them into his self-identity. Whether Courtall will obey the terms of the proviso, wed Gatty, remain faithful to her, and live in marital bliss remains unclear – not unlike Dorimant's situation at the conclusion of *The Man of Mode* – but his expression of his own self-doubt – whether real or affected – suggests the improbability of Courtall's capacity to locate his real identity and true feelings beneath the layers of his feigned behaviour.

Courtall's side-kick, Freeman, begins as a novice rake of sorts, untutored in the proper protocol of gentlemanly behaviour in sexual intrigues and so impetuous and overeager to find new game that Courtall must periodically remind him to cool his heels. In the first scene, Freeman fails to appreciate social decorum, wishing to meet the gentlewoman who has called on his friend, but Courtall, forcing him into a closet from where he may eavesdrop, has to explain that 'for decency sake' he cannot be visibly present during their private conversation, and at the scene's conclusion, as Courtall muses over the recent developments in the 'weighty affairs' of pursuing new mistresses, Freeman stands at the door's threshold and bids him to hurry, 'Come along, come along' (I,i,296), so that they may begin the chase at once. At the Mulberry Garden, Freeman, having left Sir Oliver and Sir Joslin at the tavern and still acutely anxious for an immediate introduction to Joslin's nieces, follows Courtall with the intent of accompanying him to Lady Cockwood's to meet them – 'What do we here idling in the Mulberry Garden? Why do not we make this visit then?' 'Since we know the bush, why do we not start the game?' (II,i,11–12, 15–16). Once again Courtall must instruct him as to proper etiquette – 'Gently, good Frank; first know that the laws of honour prescribed in such nice cases, will not allow me to carry thee along with me' (II,i,17–19). Although he remains habitually rash in his desire for sexual pleasure and conquest – 'Faith, let us dispatch this business; yet I never could find the pleasure of waiting for a dish of meat, when a man was heartily hungry' (V,i,652–4), he tells Ariana in response to the month's trial courtship – his willingness to take direction from his mentor ('I am ready to receive your orders' [III,i,100]) results in his mastering some of the libertine's quick thinking and complaisance.

Most notably, Freeman graduates from apprentice to full-fledged libertine, learning the rake's art of duplicity and confirming what many libertines from later comedies of manners know instinctively but prefer not to voice – there is no honour among rakes, despite their insistence that male bonding and friendship are superior ties to those men forge with women. Freeman deceives Courtall not once, but twice. Aware of his friend's dispassion for Lady Cockwood, Freeman reveals his attraction to her – 'if this lucky business had not fallen out, I intended with your good leave to have outbid you for her lady-ship's favour' (IV,ii,162–4) – but Courtall forbids such a match ('I should never have consented to that' [IV,ii,165]), admitting that despite his lack of interest in Lady Cockwood, his male compet-itiveness would require him to fight for her affection. Freeman's admission is, of course, entirely disingenuous, for the audience learned from Lady Cockwood in the previous scene that Freeman had already made advances toward her at the tavern ('he secretly began to make an address to me at the Bear' [IV,i,191–2]). Boldly countermanding Courtall's wishes, Freeman keeps his clandes-tine meeting with Lady Cockwood in the next and final scene, and when Courtall confronts him about this tête-à-tête, Freeman yet again lies to Courtall, telling him he intended to enlist Lady Cockwood's help in healing the rupture between them and the young ladies. Freeman's dissimulation and duplicity with his closest friend signify his maturation as a libertine, but his betrayal of Courtall prefigures his potential for more serious breaches and violations against Ariana. Although his acceptance of the proviso contains slippery references to futurity that could be read as libertine posturing – 'A month is a tedious time, and will be a dangerous trial of our resolutions; but I hope we shall not repent before marriage, whate'er we do after' (V,i,575–7) – the scepticism he voices accrues added weight in light of his double-dealing with Courtall and his attempted assignation with Lady Cockwood, an assignation that took place just minutes before the proviso scene and one that he will no doubt attempt again. Freeman has learned from the master, but his education was lim-ited to developing his role as a rake rather than cultivating an individual personality and clear understanding of his own nature and desires divorced from the bondage of role playing. Given the nature of his mentor, however, Freeman could learn little else.

In the spectrum of rakes, Courtall and Freeman possess a level of control and geniality that sets them apart from their Etheregean brothers: more refined than the boisterous and rude Sir Frederick and wanting the maliciousness and sexual acquisi-tiveness of Dorimant, they are rakes with a light touch, idle young men looking for sexual adventure rather than vicious predators who seduce naïve or unwilling victims. While their comparatively benign and gentlemanly conduct can be attributed

to the relatively conservative tenor of 1660s comedies in general
as opposed to the following decade's more acrid and brutal plays
that featured rampant illicit sex and violence against women,
Etherege does take especial care to portray Courtall and Freeman
as libertines unfulfilled – unsuccessful in their attempts to secure
a range of mistresses and reduced to chasing the only young virgins apparently available in the town – and this deliberate
characterisation of each gallant as a rake *manqué* does work thematically to foreground his satirical and ironic commentary on
manners and style. By preventing his libertines from fully actual-
ising their roles, Etherege points out the wide discrepancy
between Courtall's and Freeman's perceptions of themselves as
irresistible rakes to whom women come flocking and the reality
that their self-characterisation is an illusion they have wrought
through their language rather than their actions. As Robert Wess
put it, Courtall and Freeman 'talk a much more subversive game
than they actually play.'[14] Specifically, their libertine rebellion
against the status quo is made transparently impotent and
innocuous, limited only to their rhetoric, which they have aptly
filled with aphorisms touting their appetites for sexual variety,
attracting prey to the lure, and denouncing constancy, and it is
their ability to replicate current manners and fashion – to talk the
talk of libertine wit and walk the walk of elegant carriage – that
has convinced them that they are indeed the very embodiment of
the role they opt to play when in fact they fall markedly short.
Living in a quasi-Pirandellian world of illusion, they believe 'it is
so if you think so', and they spend an inordinate amount of time
discussing or defining their identities along lines consistent with
how they wish to perceive themselves and thus have others perceive them. Through his comic would-be libertines, Etherege
shows the power of cultural ideals and social codes in shaping
one's quest for identity, and, equally important, the power of language (especially self-referential speech acts) in transforming
one's image of self into an identity that corresponds to the desired
illusion. Courtall's and Freeman's inability to recognise their failure to embody the role they believe they enact so consummately
is as funny as it is revelatory of the purely performative nature of
their self-fashioned identities. And their incapacity to discard
their libertine roles at the end, forcing them to remain linguistically rebellious in their responses to the proviso, relays the

marked degree to which outward forms have superseded all other means of human communication and interaction.

Ariana and Gatty, the wealthy, precocious and lively heroines of the gay-couple plot, are the play's most enjoyable characters. Recognising their uniqueness in Carolean comedy, Charlene Taylor described them as 'Etherege's most significant innovation',[15] two emancipated young sisters who are the predecessors of such spirited Restoration heroines as Etherege's Harriet and Congreve's Millamant. Ariana and Gatty have accompanied their kinsman Sir Joslin Jolly and the Cockwoods to London where they played 'mad reaks' the previous summer, and they now intend once again to enjoy the freedom that the capital offers. Though country ladies, these independent women possess a keen understanding of precisely how the world operates, holding no illusions about a male libertine's sexual motives or potential for inconstancy. In their first encounter with Courtall and Freeman, they immediately see through the men's playful protestations of love as a deliberately feigned guise reminiscent of the *précieux* mode which cast the male as a courtly lover who spiritually deified rather than physically lusted after the object of his affection – a mode used successfully by many men to seduce unsuspecting and naïve women. And these sprightly ladies, with a linguistic finesse that clearly piques the men's interest in them, deflect these false platonic sentiments with equal mockery throughout this exchange, most notably in their refusal to remove their masks lest their honour and reputations be ruined (II,i,135–8).

In addition to sharing with the men an antiplatonic view of love, these young women, like their male counterparts, understand the ephemeral nature of love and sexual attraction. In a world in which nothing is absolute and loyalties shift according to political-cum-personal exigencies, constancy in one's emotions and passions cannot be guaranteed. Thus, both women, after confessing to each other their feelings for Courtall and Freeman, reflect on love's impermanence: Ariana likening her love to 'some stain' that 'will wear out of itself', but hopefully 'not in such a little time as you talk of, sister', and Gatty retorting immediately that love 'cannot last longer than the stain of a mulberry at most; the next season out that goes, and my heart cannot be long unfruitful, sure' (V,i,300–5). Notwithstanding such sentiments,

Ariana and Gatty deem the love-chase the major town attraction, and after settling in London they immediately don masks and head for the Mulberry Garden to find (if not potential husbands) at least some entertainment; in fact, their initial remarks to Freeman and Courtall indicate their very willingness to engage in invigorating verbal swordplay in order to test the wit and fitness of these men whom they find attractive. In the love-chase, Ariana and Gatty prove linguistically gifted women who understand the combative nature of courtship and appropriate to themselves a mastery and freeness of expression that indicates their ability to control their lives, to dominate the male realm of language, and to place themselves on equal footing with their male counterparts. Because of their incomparable fiery spirits and nimble wit, Ariana and Gatty eclipse Courtall and Freeman in every encounter, and their candour and unpretentiousness with one another enables them, as Peter Holland observed, to 'usurp the rake's normal role as audience's confidant'.[16]

Though both possess free spirits and vivacity, they are, like the libertines, also clearly differentiated. Ariana is the demure and trepid sister, reluctant to acquiesce to Gatty's cajoling that they transgress social protocol by venturing out unchaperoned, as her sister apparently convinced her to do during their previous visit to London. She chides Gatty for her assertiveness, calling her a 'mad wench' for her impetuous and unorthodox antics. Content to remain confined in their London lodgings, Ariana is more inclined to pastoral sentimentality, preferring to take in the country's fresh air and amble in its pleasant groves (I,ii,130–1). She holds more romantic notions than does her sister about the longevity of love and fidelity, and, according to Gatty's playful accusation that she favours those melancholy songs by some 'amorous coxcomb, who swears in all companies he loves his mistress so well, that he would not do her the injury, were she willing to grant him the favour, and it may be is sot enough to believe he would oblige her in keeping his oath too' (V,i,357–61), Ariana clings to the myth of courtly romance, one that could potentially cause her to relinquish her virtue if the suitor promised to guard her honour and remain faithful. Once smitten, Ariana is easily reduced to a degree of plaintiveness and self-absorption that Gatty finds annoying and foolish: 'I'd rather be a nun, than a lover at thy rate; devotion is not able to make me half so serious as love has made thee already' (V,i,364–6). Though more reserved than Gatty, Ariana holds her own once the sparring begins with Courtall and Freeman, keeping pace with her sister's clever rejoinders without missing a cue.

Gatty, referred to repeatedly as 'mad-cap', relishes life more heartily and delights more freely in her rebellion against conventional attitudes. Of the two sisters, Gatty is the more pragmatic, sceptical, and self-aware: she especially eschews the sentimental and conventional notions of love's permanence, voicing on more than one occasion the potential erosion of romantic affection, most notably in her choice of a love song that differs markedly from the cloying madrigal that Ariana prefers and one that mirrors her view regarding love's transitoriness – 'How long I shall love him, I can no more tell,/Than had I a fever, when I should be well' (V,i,344–5); and it is Gatty alone who recognises the social requirement for dissembling in all matters concerning the outward display of love and emotion but nonetheless is fully cognisant of her true feelings and self once she steps into the 'tiring-room' – aware always of the role she must play but never mistaking her mask for her real identity. Unlike Ariana, Gatty finds the country tiresome: 'how glad I am we are in this town again' (I,ii,128–9), she exclaims with an excitement and eagerness to partake in all its diversions and pleasures, and as she reprimands her sister for continually bewailing the loss of the country, she convinces Ariana to be more adventuresome first by likening their situation as single women to monotonous imprisonment – 'dost thou think we came here to be mewed up, and take only the liberty of going from our chamber to the dining-room, and from the dining-room to our chamber again? and like a bird in a cage with two perches only, to hop up and down, up and down?' (I,ii,148–53) – and then by inveighing against the custom that robs women of their freedom by requiring them to venture outdoors with a chaperone who monitors their encounters with men, controls their selection of suitors, and treats them like commodities – 'Wouldst thou never have us go to a play but with our grave relations, never take the air but with our grave relations? to feed their pride, and make the world believe it is in their power to afford some gallant or other a good bargain?' (I,ii,155–9).

Driven by her desire for the same freedoms accorded men, Gatty, willing to violate sacred social protocol and jeopardise both her safety and her reputation by going abroad masked and unchaperoned, will use her wits and cunning to gain a modicum of liberty typically denied to her sex. She is the clever instigator determined to flout authority and convention, qualities which make her fit as the leader of the two, and she, more so than Ariana, embodies the new cavalier woman whose perspicuity, boldness, pragmatism and self-reliance enable her to survive and succeed on her own terms in her challenge against the social order. Quite fittingly, Gatty is the one who initiates the attack against society's double standard that articulates female resentment of male privilege and finally galvanises her partner into action:

> GATTY: How I envy that sex! well! We cannot plague 'em enough when we have it in our power for those privileges which custom has allowed 'em above us.
> ARIANA: The truth is, they can run and ramble here, and there, and everywhere, and we poor fools rather think the better of 'em.
> GATTY: From one playhouse, to the other playhouse, and if they like neither play nor the women, they seldom stay any longer than the combing of their periwigs, or a whisper or two with a friend; and then they cock their caps, and out they strut again.
> ARIANA: But whatsoever we do, prithee now let us resolve to be mighty honest.
> GATTY. There I agree with thee.
> ARIANA: And if we find the gallants like lawless subjects, who the more their princes grant, the more they impudently crave –
> GATTY: We'll become absolute tyrants, and deprive 'em of all the privileges we gave 'em –
> ARIANA: Upon these conditions I am contented to trail a pike under thee – march along girl.
>
> (I,ii,163–75)

These emancipated women, for all their subversive talk, however, know that in their quest for a small slice of personal freedom, they must perforce behave within the boundaries of female propriety and remain 'mighty honest' – that is, virtuous. Thus, in their rebellion against seventeenth-century convention – specifically, their rejection of the double standard – they are actually confined to the realm of language only, from where, at best, they can become 'absolute tyrants' in their battle against male liberties forbidden to women by 'plaguing' men verbally, but they can in fact do little by way of their behaviour to revoke male privilege or extend all those privileges to themselves. Gatty and Ariana are forced to acquiesce to the double standard, which Etherege implies cultivates male–female warfare, and they do so not because they are constitutionally or morally committed to virtue or chastity but because social imperatives make it so. Gatty's song tells it all: 'But oh how I sigh, when I think should he woo me, / I cannot deny what I know would undo me!' (V,i,348–9). Ariana calls her sister 'wanton' for expressing her sexuality so freely, though she herself does not deny similar physical desires. At heart, these are female libertines who would cavort with male-like abandonment – that is, they would if they could – but patriarchal society dictates otherwise. Like Courtall and Freeman, their anarchy against convention is manifested solely through discourse, but for Ariana and Gatty this is a restriction not of their own making.

In conveying the comic and combative nature between these gay couples, Etherege wastes no time to set the requisite, playful tone by calling for visually amusing pictures in their first encounter that translated the love-chase into humorous, physical action. Courtall and Freeman stand just upstage of the proscenium doors at left, where they discuss their convoluted plot to gain an introduction to Sir Joslin's nieces when, at that very moment, the women they seek, Ariana and Gatty, coincidentally enter through one of the doors down left. The ladies take a quick note of the handsome gallants, and then 'pass nimbly over the stage' as a way of feigning indifference while enticing the men to follow. After a brief and fruitless discussion about the questionable beauty of the faces hidden behind the ladies' masks and whether it's worth pursuing these women, the libertines take the bait that the audience knows they cannot refuse: they opt to follow them post haste and rush off after them at stage right. In a few seconds the women enter once again through one of the proscenium doors at left, and their quick reappearance on stage without any sign of Freeman or Courtall provokes audience laughter, for surely these hot-blooded libertines should have outpaced the women. Ariana, glancing behind her toward off-stage left, notes that the men are close at their heels, and Gatty decides to put the gallants' interest and resolve to the test by keeping the chase going. As the sisters scurry one more time across the stage and through the doors at stage right, Courtall and Freeman rush in behind them at stage left, out of breath and stopping for a minute to get a rest while noting that 'whatsoever faults they have, they cannot be broken-winded' (II,i,83–4). Unwilling to forgo the chase and more curious than ever about these elusive women, Freeman suggests that Courtall head them off at the cross-walk while he follows behind them. Repeating their first manoeuvre, much to the audience's amusement, they dash off one more time through the stage-right door in their pursuit of the women, and seconds later Ariana and Gatty enter yet once again through the stage-left doors without any sign of Courtall and Freeman – a repeat of the visual gag moments earlier. Within seconds, however, Courtall startles them when he appears behind them through the lower door at left, and Freeman likewise surprises them when he pops through the upper door at stage right to halt their progress in his direction. After a tiring chase around the Mulberry Garden, the men have finally cornered the women, leaving them no avenue of escape, just as the ladies had wished. While the physical pursuit is over, the love-chase now begins in earnest with Courtall and Freeman trying to catch their breaths as they initiate a conversation which, despite their hopes for an imminent sexual conquest, proves to be a battle of wit from two ladies not so easily seduced. This visual action of the males literally chasing down the coy and resourceful women vivifies the central action of Etherege's comedy, a game of pursuit and evasion that plays out in all their subsequent scenes, with the men typically suffering a degree of discomfiture or embarrassment at the hands of these able and clever women.

In contradistinction to these young couples stand the older characters whose behaviour telegraphs an absence of wit and a wealth of hypocrisy and affectation. Poised to enter the fashionable world of London, these characters adopt roles necessary to enact their own performances as pleasure seekers, attempting to play parts in which they have woefully miscast themselves. For these country denizens, the town is the locus of the new post-Cromwellian world, one that accommodates the naturalistic, lib-

ertine ethos fostered in large part by its priapic monarch and his
courtiers, and it is here only that they can take their prerogatives
as aristocrats and act out the new social roles ostensibly reserved
for their class. London provides them not only anonymity[17] –
unlike the country where local inhabitants learn quickly of one
another's profligate conduct, as Sir Oliver explains to Freeman
(I,i,86–102) – but also a quasi-carnivalesque venue where they can
enjoy the vitality and freedom in a playful world inhabited by
similarly minded people. Their conduct, however, manifests only
the outward trappings of their appetitive instincts, for they lack
the true spirit and vigour that give rise to such behaviour: they
act out of pretence and aspirations to *au courant* social behaviour
but they have no correlative substance. Sir Joslin Jolly and
Sir Oliver Cockwood are bookends, or, as Freeman describes
them: 'They are harp and violin, nature has so tuned 'em, as if she
intended they should always play the fool in consort' (II,i, 3–5).
Quite clearly, these country knights provide a symphony of social
faux pas to warrant laughter at their expense from the younger
characters and the audience as well. Sir Joslin Jolly, as his name
suggests, is a comic fool, a country bumpkin hoping to fit into
fashionable society, but his lack of judgement belies his pretences
to urbanity. He is the instigator of fun and frolicking, inducing his
friend Sir Oliver to join him in the tavern with his penitential suit,
and he is the one who finds the whores for both himself and his
companion. Ever eager to sing, dance, drink and carouse, he is an
innocuous merrymaker who limits his cultural activities in
London to tavern entertainment, and he is fool enough in his poor
judgement to regard Rakehell, Rampant and their throng of
cohorts as suitable company. When drunk, he habitually escorts
male drinking companions to his home as potential suitors to
Ariana and Gatty, and his last attempt to bring his nieces a few
gallants – Madam Rampant (dressed as a man) and her pimp –
shows the depth of his well-intentioned folly. Though a good-
natured fellow, Sir Joslin, a coarse man whose songs and dialogue
reek of gross sexual innuendoes, signifies the rake's base sexual
drive without its veneer of civility.[18]

Sir Oliver Cockwood possesses all of Sir Joslin Jolly's aspirations to rakish behaviour, but his hypocrisy and self-delusion
turn his performance as a would-be town gallant or libertine hero
into a ridiculous and familiar caricature of a married man

attempting to recuperate his youthful and virile identity through adultery while maintaining marital harmony. His predilection for judging only the appearance of things leads him to misapprehend his outward behaviour as a true reflection of his inner self, and thus he remains incapable of seeing not only that his 'gentleman-like recreations' – drunkenness and whoring – show a lack of heroic grace and a misunderstanding of the spirit and tenets of libertinism, but also that his attempt to fashion for himself a public persona of libertine and private persona of faithful husband renders him an outward identity of hypocrite and fool. Moreover, his inability to penetrate surface appearances to perceive the truth prevents his distinguishing between the masks and true natures of those around him: he believes that Courtall is his friend and that Lady Cockwood is virtuous. His delusions about others enable him to inhabit a world that corresponds to his needs and desires, just as his delusions about his libertine behaviour facilitate his self-characterisation as sexually potent when in fact the opposite is true (he has to take cantharides to enhance his sexual performance).

While Sir Oliver's pretence to two completely incompatible roles – loving husband and wild blade – provides truly comic moments for spectators as they watch him fluctuate continually between rakish bravado and emasculating contrition, the marked disparity between these two roles and the alacrity with which he can shift from one to the other communicates once again the performative nature of identity in this society. Needing the world at large – in particular the males – to perceive him as a robust and virile lover, he transforms into the molester of tavern wenches and the braggart who seduces country girls, but wanting his wife (whom he believes is an honest and caring spouse) to regard him as a faithful and loving husband, he lapses into the penitential sinner (complete with costume) displaying paroxysms of remorse over his debauched behaviour. And this cycle, as the action suggests, continues *ad infinitum* with Sir Oliver shuffling back and forth in an unending display of two irreconcilable identities that make it impossible to discern if either of the two roles best approximates his true character and which of the two he perceives as his real identity.

Withholding a clear-cut answer as to Sir Oliver's real nature – other than perhaps the obvious interpretation that Sir Oliver is a patent fool and dupe – Etherege also complicates matters further by deliberately providing contradictory dialogue that precludes an unambiguous grasp of Sir Oliver's character. Sir Oliver reveals to Courtall that he had 'an intrigue with a tinker's wife in the country, and this malicious slut betrayed the very ditch where we used to make our assignations, to my lady' (II,ii,165–8), but Lady Cockwood avers to Sentry that despite her husband's propensity for talking 'of strange matters behind my back', he 'is not able to play the spark abroad thus, I assure you' (I,ii,50–5). Surely both statements cannot be true: either Sir Oliver seduced a married woman who confessed all to Lady Cockwood (who apparently prefers to remain deluded as to her husband's fidelity), or he fabricates the tryst in order to enhance his rakish profile. The spectator is left to wrestle with this discrepancy which – like others in this comedy – suggests that role-playing, while accommodating one's need to project a desired self-image to others, is a performance that can easily fool an intended audience as well as the actor who wishes to internalise his character. Furthermore, although Sir Oliver fails magnificently in his enactment of the libertine, his attempt to emulate the role interrogates the role itself, for it brings to light the sheer histrionics involved, and his ridiculous behaviour juxtaposed to Courtall's more effective performance highlights the latter as clearly the more accomplished performer, one accomplished enough to give acting advice to novice players.

Lady Cockwood also desires to satisfy her natural instincts and appetites while in London by finally consummating her long-standing relationship with Courtall, who has deliberately kept her at bay by manipulating obstructions which enable him to pretend concern for her honour, which she carefully guards, while promising to deliver the 'happiness' she longs for at the first safe opportunity. Like Courtall, Lady Cockwood is a consummate predator, tenacious in her quest for sexual liberty, and a clever actor, skilful in her manoeuvring with Sir Oliver, Gatty and Ariana in order to get what she wants, but in light of Courtall's deliberate evasions of her at all costs, her wasted energies, jealous reactions, and frantic behaviour, all aimed at orchestrating an adulterous assignation with him, render her foolish and pathetic. Lady Cockwood's primary flaw, however, is not her sexual appetite, for this is a natural instinct; rather, it is her desire to satisfy this appetite while retaining a public façade of virtue and a personal belief in her honour.

Yet Lady Cockwood's hypocrisy is not entirely of her own
making, for she is forced, like Wycherley's Lady Fidget and
Congreve's Lady Wishfort, to comply with the codes of male
sexual politics which allow women only one valuable commodity
– their virtue – and thus in her battle against the double standard
that forecloses sexual freedom to females, Lady Cockwood, frus-
trated in an unhappy marriage with a husband who no longer
finds her attractive and cannot satisfy her sexually, must perforce
play the hypocrite by pretending to the honourable behaviour
which social convention demands as she seeks the same sexual
fulfilment and pleasure reserved for men only. In her quest, however, Lady Cockwood has so completely internalised this code of
conduct that she fails to grasp the contradiction between her
vows to honour and her thirst for illicit sex, as her servant, Sentry,
recognises in her mistress's paranoia over the loss of her prized,
unsullied reputation: 'this is a strange infirmity she has, but I
must bear with it; for on my conscience, custom has made it so
natural, she cannot help it' (II,ii,110–12). Self-deluded, she thoroughly believes that her virtue will remain irreproachable so long
as her lover is a gentleman who treats her gallantly and hon-
ourably and who also believes in her scrupulous character to the
same degree that she does. As a result, Lady Cockwood must
forestall sexual consummation until she is absolutely sure that
her virtue and reputation will not be compromised, as she tells
Courtall: 'I shall deny myself the sweetest recreations in the
world, rather than yield to anything that may bring a blemish
upon my spotless honour' (III,i,146–8) – she will forgo adultery if
it means loss of her self-image as a virtuous woman. Clearly,
Lady Cockwood 'would if she could', as the play's title implies,
and the obstructions to her sexual satisfaction stem as much from
Courtall as from herself.

Lady Cockwood, a familiar Restoration portrait of the sex-
starved female, is intended as a source of amusement not sympathy, though Etherege, while not interested in problematising
the double standard to which she (like Ariana and Gatty) is
victim, did afford clues as to the genesis of her frustration and
unhappiness. Of all the characters in this comedy, Lady
Cockwood is the only one not paired with another, and as she
stands in marked isolation riddled with bitterness and loneliness,
it is clear that the source of her vexation is Sir Oliver. His struggle

to gain dominance over his wife at the beginning of their marriage has led to a union fed not by love (as both would have the other believe) but by power politics: 'I have had a design to break her heart ever since the first month that I had her, and 'tis so tough, that I have not yet cracked one string on't' (II,ii,172–5), he tells Courtall, and from that moment it appears that Sir Oliver – the 'tyrant' who accuses his wife of trying to 'usurp my empire' (II,ii,176) – instigated a marital battle for control over Lady Cockwood, who survived by withdrawing, as Edward Burns observes, 'into almost total psychological isolation'.[19] Alienated emotionally from her husband, Lady Cockwood survives her loneliness and satisfies her sexual appetite by latching onto a willing lover toward whom she has no feelings other than lust – 'so much precious time fooled away in fruitless expectation' (IV,i,63–4), she rails when she realises Courtall's true inclinations are toward Gatty. And after briefly bemoaning the lost time before she must retreat to the country, she wastes not another second in her designs to gain some sexual pleasure by turning her sights toward Freeman, a more willing suitor than Courtall. And should that affair not materialise, Lady Cockwood will no doubt take Courtall's advice and find an 'able chaplain' (V,i,636–7) who will satisfy her religiously.

In characterising these country fools and deceivers, Etherege, as he does so brilliantly throughout the play with the gay couples, uses stage directions to create exceedingly comic moments that convey the ridiculous and dual natures of both Lady Cockwood and her equally foolish husband. In particular, the scene at the Bear Garden (III,iii) provided audiences with one of the play's most humorous segments. Amid all the drunken revelry and surrounded by his fellow carousers, Sir Oliver cuts a ludicrous figure in his outrageous penitential suit and sporting the fashionable accessories of a periwig, hat and sword as he knocks back a glass of wine and waits lustfully for Rakehell to deliver a few wenches for his and Joslin's entertainment. Enter Lady Cockwood tentatively, disguised in a gaudy though revealing dress and vizard. Mistaking his wife for one of the prostitutes Rakehell promised, Sir Oliver grabs her before she can make her escape and bounces her around the dance floor as he romps with abandon while she frantically attempts to hold her mask in place. With the dance concluded, Lady Cockwood still has no means of escape, and her

agony and discomfiture intensify as Sir Oliver and Sir Joslin make
her the centre of attention – fondling her freely, rhapsodising on
her alluring figure, and singing her a bawdy tune for everyone's
amusement. When Sir Oliver's sexual advances escalate into a
proposed contest among the men, Lady Cockwood, in desperate
need to halt her husband's plans, feigns a fit which enables her to
cover her tracks and turn the tables on Sir Oliver. Not only has
Etherege created a highly comic and visually animated scene, he
also provided audiences with a delicious gestic moment that
merged the dual identities of both Lady Cockwood and Sir Oliver
into one visual image: Lady Cockwood with her pretence to
honour is decked out like the wench she truly is and is treated
accordingly, while Sir Oliver's eclectic dress conflates the polarities of contrite sinner and rakish scoundrel that he enacts with
unwitting absurdity.

From Lady Cockwood, Sir Oliver and Sir Jolly to Courtall,
Freeman, Ariana and Gatty, Etherege constructs antitheses – new
vs old, youth vs age, libertine vs dupe, freedom vs constraint –
that recur throughout Carolean and later Restoration drama and
form the central polarities by which audiences judge the course of
dramatic action. In *She Would If She Could*, Etherege sets up a dramatically functional dichotomy of characters whose attitudes and
values, by their very contrast, heighten audience understanding
of the extremes of both and enable spectators to read one off the
other: the older, titled faction from the country – those who
symbolise the hypocrites and fools of the past generation who
allowed the execution of its monarch, embraced the repressive
dogma of Cromwell without the slightest resistance, and then
invaded the capital to enjoy the carnivalesque freedom fostered
by the restoration of Charles – alongside the younger faction –
those who embody the brave new world of the Restoration ethos
made possible by their Cavalier ideals and loyalties and who
represent the liberation from the past and failed ideologies of the
previous age. In his binary character construction, Etherege does
not necessarily privilege one group over the other, for the characters in both factions ultimately share more commonalities than
differences. All substitute form for substance, engaging in a
wealth of pretence by adopting roles intended to project an external identity that chimes in with their own personal images,
desires, and motives. For all their efforts to embody roles that

they have chosen to enact, however, it is not insignificant that their successes have been limited to discourse alone: they verbalise their rebellion against conventional morality but never achieve it – Courtall and Freeman fall short of true libertinage, Sir Oliver seduces no one, Ariana and Gatty gain few liberties, and Lady Cockwood remains faithful to her husband. And the open-ended denouement which shows no marked change in any of the characters and offers no definitive answers (do the gay couples marry? do the Cockwoods mend their ways and retire happily to the country?) suggests that each will continue to define himself by words rather than actions, failing to translate idea and language into reality. This marked discrepancy between the characters' descriptions of their self-identities and their actual behaviour provides an interpretative perspective through which spectators view them clearly as little more than actors striving to perform their parts, to act themselves out according to the customs and manners dictated by a society in which stylistic modes are the ultimate gauge of worth. That they fail to recognise that their performances fall short of their ideal or that they have misplaced their highest value on their performances over all else unites them as comic figures equally deluded in their belief that they are indeed the characters they attempt to enact.

Though heralded by many later critics as the first new type of comedy in the Carolean period, *She Would If She Could*'s inauspicious beginning has plagued its stage history, for during the seventeenth century it received only ten productions, a handful more in the eighteenth century when it enjoyed periodic revivals for actors' benefit performances, and was then shelved completely during the nineteenth century. The twentieth century did not respond very favourably to it either, for only one notable production, Jonathan Miller's at the Greenwich Theatre in London in April 1979, marks the sum total of its professional revivals. Miller, taking his cue from the National Theatre's 1960s revivals of Restoration comedies (particularly Congreve and Farquhar) that downplayed the artificiality of the characters' demeanours and stressed a more modern and realistic approach, rid his revival of similar conventions, but in so doing he removed the crucial core of this comedy that presents those artificial manners as a source of tension among characters who try to conform to its rules while concomitantly attempting to express their natural desires within the confines of the requisite, fashionable language and behaviour of the day. The gay couples' conflict between their profound sexual attraction toward one another and their need to restrain that sexuality within the boundaries of current modish conduct, as well as Lady Cockwood's unbridled passion that she must contain under the guise of virtue, generate a palpable tension within the characters that creates a good deal of the play's humour, and the absence of these modish imperatives to which characters try to adhere as they grapple with their sexual and emotional urges rendered Miller's revival of this comedy little more than 'a repetitive recital' with an 'air of sedate dullness' that yielded negligible laughter.[20] While Miller's de-emphasis on the artificiality of manners would work for Wycherley's satires, it will not succeed with Etherege's comedies, for artificial manners and mode are the centrepieces around which the action revolves. Miller's misstep should serve as a warning to future directors who try to find modern equivalents in their productions of Etherege's manners comedies: beneath the surface of the characters' artificial and stylistic demeanour resides a living humanity struggling to express itself through the required façade of linguistic and behavioural codes which, ironically, is intended to mask passions and desires. Etherege interrogates this conflict between internal emotions and external forms, revealing characters caught in an ironic 'catch-22' of their own making and from which they can imagine no viable alternative that allows them freedom from a set of artificial conventions to which social custom requires them to remain comically welded.

5
The Man of Mode:
Comedy and the Masquerade

Eight years after the less-than-stellar reception of *She Would If She Could*, Etherege's last play, *The Man of Mode; or, Sir Fopling Flutter*, revived his reputation among contemporaries as the finest dramatist of manners comedy. First performed by the Duke's Company on 11 March 1676, this play appealed particularly to the court, who reportedly attended numerous performances, and it was immediately hailed by audiences at large as not only Etherege's best comedy but also the best to date on the Carolean stage. Until the end of the century it continued to enjoy a number of revivals, including a production in Brussels on 3 October 1679 specially staged for the Duke of York, and a revival performed at Whitehall in 1685 for the newly enthroned James II.[1] The enormous contemporary success of this comedy has been attributed in part to its purported verisimilitude, in particular its alleged naturalistic portrayal of lifelike characters whose manners, motives, and behaviour reflected the temperament of the significant number of court-based spectators and their acolytes who relished seeing their lifestyle enacted on the London stage. The play's realism proved so noteworthy that its topical lifelikeness sparked particular mention from commentators, such as

Langbaine, who lauded Etherege's 'art and judgment' and reported the play as 'acknowledg'd by all, to be as true Comedy, and the
Characters as well drawn to Life, as any Play that has been Acted
since the Restauration of the *English* stage'.[2] In fact, so pervasive
was this opinion of the play as a mirror of Carolean life and
personages that it generated speculation among contemporaries
as to whom Etherege used as models for his characters, and
general consensus had it that Etherege based Dorimant on the
infamous rake Lord Rochester, Sir Fopling on the well-known fop
Beau Hewit, and Medley on himself.[3]

The assessment by Etherege's contemporaries of *The Man of
Mode* as a naturalistic representation of London life in the 1670s
has significantly affected critical evaluations of the play, for it has
led to an ongoing debate – one that began in the early eighteenth
century and continues today – as to the comedy's dramatic
impact and thematic import. Some 35 years after the première of
the comedy, Richard Steele penned an indictment of it in *The
Spectator* (No. 65, 15 May 1711), denouncing it as 'a perfect
Contradiction to good Manners, good Sense, and common
Honesty' and censuring Dorimant as 'a Knave in his designs',
particularly for his 'falsehood to Mrs Loveit, and the barbarity of
triumphing over her anguish'. Responding a decade later to
Steele's more middle-class reading of the play – a reading that
reflects a bias against Carolean comedy in favour of the early
eighteenth century's changing critical attitudes about exemplary
heroes, stage decorum and character propriety – John Dennis,
also reading the play as a simulacrum of Carolean life, defended
it against claims of immorality, asserting that Etherege wrote a
didactic satire that worked by negative example, drawing a portrait of a realistic 'young Courtier, haughty, vain, and prone to
anger, amorous, false, and inconstant', and thus by 'shewing us
what is done upon the Comick Stage, to shew us what ought
never to be done upon the stage of the World'.[4] These two polar
views of *The Man of Mode* as either an amoral and naturalistic
comedy or a corrective satire continue to dominate critical evaluations of the play, leaving many to question, as does Norman
Holland, 'what, if anything, Etherege wants us to take seriously'.[5]

Clearly the crux of this debate over the play's merits hinges, of
course, on Dorimant, for in Restoration comedy the curve of dramatic action is most typically plotted by the central male charac-

ter's behaviour, which serves as the barometer for measuring a play along cultural, ideological, political or thematic lines; or, as David Wilkinson put it in more phallogocentric terms when assessing the significance of all lead males in Restoration drama, 'it is *his* conversation that is the epitome of elegance, evasiveness and insolent imperturbability, and it is *his* actions that must be taken to suggest the more commendable values in these plays – however ironically they may be presented'.[6] In the case of Dorimant, however, commendable values seem elusive, and his extreme rakish behaviour – in particular his predatory nature, irascible temperament, and callous treatment of women – has continued to spark considerable disagreement not only as to what moral values the comedy reflects relative to contemporary society but also as to whether Etherege intended his character to serve as a hero representative of his age, a contemptible libertine, or a satiric portrait of the contemporary gentleman.

The difficulties in pinpointing both Etherege's dramatic intent and Dorimant's exact nature stem in large part from *The Man of Mode*'s dark, non-judgemental tone as well as its ambiguous resolution. Unlike Etherege's earlier comedies which display an 'all-in-fun' atmosphere featuring such innocuous, gentlemanly rakes as the playful and roistering Sir Frederick (*The Comical Revenge*, 1664) or the non-sexually aggressive Courtall and Freeman in *She Would If She Could* (1668) – all of whom steer clear of sexual consummation despite their libertine talk and apparently make a fifth-act resolution for social propriety and monogamous marriages to women they love – *The Man of Mode* exhibits a harsher and more sobering view of libertinism with Dorimant depicting a malicious and appetitive individual whose sexual corruption and reprehensible behaviour receives neither explicit nor implicit disapproval and who is nonetheless rewarded at the end of the play with the heroine's love, only to repay her just seconds after vowing his love to her by conniving to secure a secret rendezvous with Bellinda, a young virgin he had recently bedded. Whether Dorimant will follow Harriet to Hampshire and live in wedded bliss, remain a bachelor in London and continue his seductions, or marry and enjoy illicit relationships proves uncertain – a sixth-act resolution that cannot be plotted definitively given Dorimant's machinations and the denouement's ambiguity. What is patently clear, however, is that Dorimant represents a new type of libertine, one that made his appearance in the 1670s with the rise of sex comedies, which include such problematical plays as Wycherley's *The Country Wife* (1675) and *The Plain Dealer* (1676) and Shadwell's *The Virtuoso* (1676).[7] These comedies, which surfaced concurrently with the advent of other dramatic genres that involved such horrific actions as rape and are symptomatic of the jaded tone in the plays of this decade, took a good deal of licence with moral propriety, featured male rakes (e.g., Horner) with great cunning, viciousness, and cynicism, and, moreover, did not moralise on the aberrant social and sexual behaviour of the male characters, thereby rendering the rakes' status as heroes ambiguous and questionable and obscuring consentaneous and cogent assessments as to how their actions could suggest any positive, overarching dramatic point.

It is this play's very lack of a moral centre or ideal – most usually signified by the male hero – that has generated such contradictory analyses, for this moral ambivalence creates an interpretive lacuna that cannot be bridged with the traditional heuristic device of reading one group of characters against another in order to glean a 'right way' versus 'wrong way' interpretation vis-à-vis corrective comedy or satire. Typically, both social satire and didactic comedy do afford a moral norm by which the actions of those foolish or deviant characters can be judged, as in the case of Etherege's earlier works in which clearly polarised characters represent either emulative or censorious behaviour. In the case of *The Man of Mode*, critics have posited such readings by dividing the characters into binary opposites such as the Truewits (those ideal characters such as Dorimant, Harriet, Young Bellair, Emilia) versus the Witwouds (those ludicrous individuals such as Fopling, Old Bellair, Lady Woodvill), but these critics have failed to convince completely because they cannot reconcile the fact that those would-be wits, though foolish enough to warrant our laughter, are not vicious and morally bankrupt individuals deserving our contempt and censure, and they cannot ignore the reality that those characters who ostensibly deserve our admiration fail to spark such wonder or respect, despite their keen wit, social finesse, and artful manoeuvring: Young Bellair and Emilia are much too anaemic characterologically to inspire our interest, and both Dorimant and Harriet display (though to differing degrees) sufficient maliciousness to abort our wholesale approbation.[8] The line between 'right' and 'wrong' in this comedy proves so severely blurred as to render untenable any simple binary analysis viewed through the lens of corrective comedy or traditionally plotted social satire. However, recent critical theory, such as deconstruction, has demonstrated that elisions can be factored in to fill heuristic gaps, and thus, in the case of satire, the play need not necessarily depict characters representative of a central norm or ideal by which other characters' actions are measured and assessed, most especially in those instances where the object of satire underpins the totality of action and embraces the entire cast of characters in order to suggest that the 'ideal' is conspicuously absent. In sum, the blatant absence of the 'ideal' works effectively to foreground it, making it ever-present as a disturbing erasure. Such is the case with *The Man of Mode*. Etherege did not limit his satire to the blatantly foppish and fatuous, but rather he aimed his satiric shots at the full spectrum of characters whose want of both social and moral decorum emblematised a society that had substituted the traditional ideals believed to underlie human existence with vacuous forms and pretences. Indeed, though Etherege was himself driven by the imperatives of libertinism and materialism, he did not fail to see behind the nascent philosophies' appealing and alluring surface an iconoclasm void of substance.

Etherege, by his deliberate omission of character 'substance' or some viable 'ideal' in *The Man of Mode*, telegraphs his intent to underscore not only its absence but also its antithesis: specifically, to dramatise the artificiality and vacuity behind the new stylish mode of behaviour that characterised the late seventeenth century's leisure class. This new code of conduct began with Charles II's restoration as the fashionable society attempted to carve out for itself a new cultural identity that jettisoned the dull trappings of Puritanism by embracing manners that set them apart as the socially elite and re-established the social hierarchy. Fashioning a new cultural and ideological identity modelled on the king's self-indulgent court and wrought by language, manners, and dress, aristocrats aimed at establishing cultural signs that separated them from the working class and especially from the rising middle class, whose financial enterprises threatened to vitiate and perhaps eclipse the power, wealth and prestige of the gentry. By the 1670s, this new 'mode' had, in effect, burgeoned into a façade

of pretences with little substance to buttress it, and in this comedy Etherege turned the typical Carolean themes of nature versus
artifice or real versus affectation on their heads by erasing the real
and natural in the equation, providing no normative or ideal
characters and concentrating instead on vivifying the extent to
which society was obsessed with the outward show of forms and
manners, which were ostensible indices of the inner substance of
the individual. In effect, the mask – that central symbol of
Carolean drama – is foregrounded in this play as a veneer, an
artificial construct crafted with sartorial details, physical posturing, and witty dialogue, and Etherege intimates that despite the
attractive or seductive lure of the mask, there is actually nothing
behind it.

Masquerading consumes the lives of the central characters, and
although much of Restoration drama revolves around the theme
of appearance versus reality with its proliferation of characters
who don figurative masks and assume roles to conceal their true
motives or identities and thus further their own ends, in *The Man
of Mode* the maskings, impersonations and playacting form the
gist of every scene. Not only do most of the characters' conversations focus principally on the apt or artless execution of manners
and modes by others within their circle of acquaintance, but characters intentionally stage scenes for each other or for public spectacles. Dorimant, for example, who orchestrates many scenes for
others to play (sometimes unwittingly), creates an amusing spectacle at the theatre by purchasing box seats for one of his prostitutes, directs Bellinda in her scene with Mrs Loveit so as to initiate his break with the latter, stages Loveit's encounter with Sir
Fopling in order to finalise his break with her, and he also enacts
the role of Mr Courtage to deceive Lady Woodvill; likewise,
Harriet and Young Bellair impersonate young lovers to fool Old
Bellair and Lady Woodvill, Young Bellair and Emilia mask their
true feelings from Old Bellair, Harriet imitates Dorimant's mannerisms to expose his affectations, and so on. From the first curtain with Dorimant's morning ritual of outfitting himself for his
day's activities to Sir Fopling's outrageous appearance in masquerade dress, characters remain principally concerned about
public appearances – theirs and others – and they devote a good
deal of their energies to examining their past performances,

critiquing the performances of others, or planning their next performance.

The behaviour of the characters in Etherege's comic world, which placed a premium on the social importance of not only being seen literally but also being seen – that is, perceived – as a person of certain quality and characteristics, mirrored the sophisticated world of London where, simply put, everyone sought to be on stage. Like Etherege's characters, London's elite congregated at fashionable public places such as coffeehouses, taverns, parks, and the patent theatres to watch others and, more importantly, to be watched by others. To them, life was an elaborate and playful spectacle aimed at the pursuit of personal pleasure, a daily, public masquerade in which everyone – from the court to the literary world – seemed to participate, and often with scandalous results: court ladies routinely disguised themselves as orange sellers and attempted to ply their wares on London streets; the Earl of Oxford, after unsuccessfully trying to seduce a well-known actress, secretly concocted a sham marriage to her in order to consummate his lust; the playwright George Farquhar unwittingly married a fake heiress and became quick fodder for gossip throughout London; and even Charles II, accompanied often by his queen, would don a disguise and visit the homes of unsuspecting Londoners, many of whom failed to recognise them.[9] Such masquerades were habitual in the daily life of London's *beau monde*, and while the civically organised masquerades as a sanctioned form of public amusement and celebration did not take hold until the eighteenth century, it appears that the seventeenth century's socialites anticipated this cultural phenomenon by a number of decades, perhaps with encouragement as well from the lavish masked entertainments held by Charles II at Whitehall – especially influential for those who wished to emulate the king's inner circle. In an age where surface seemed to rule over substance and subterfuge replaced plain-dealing, the masquerade provides the most apposite symbol of the era, especially its spectatorial qualities.[10] Explaining the connexion between personal gratification and the masquerade, Terry Castle notes 'one took one's pleasure, above all, in seeing and being seen. With universal privileges granted to voyeurism and self-display, the masquerade was from the start ideally suited to the satisfaction of scopophilic and exhibitionist urges.'[11] Castle's description can apply readily to Etherege's comedy.

So insistent is *The Man of Mode* to foreground masquerading, performance and gamesmanship as the core of its action that directors of recent productions have, through their use of set designs, stage blocking and characters' business, translated these themes into palpable visual details.[12] Declan Donnellan, in his 1986 'Cheek by Jowl' production, used a stage that symbolised the game motif: a circular dance floor that simulated a dart-board with its round wooden platform composed of alternating segments of light and dark wood with a bull's eye at centre. When on stage, characters moved with mechanical regularity, periodically circling each other gracefully or moving around the circle's perimeter as if taking part in a stately dance, and this highly stylised bit of choreography, which made the characters seem to move 'with sinister precision from one intrigue to another', recalled for *The Spectator* (5 April 1986) a group of 'mechanical creatures caught up in an endless cycle of mindless repetition'. In counterpoint to the actors' continual, ballet-like circular movements were their choreographed frozen stances, and the juxtaposition of these two contrary and striking visual pictures evoked images of characters more mechanical and void of feeling than lifelike and sentient: 'all its incessant circular moves and chases, plus the trick of freezing several groups in postures of desire or amazement while another group jerks into speech and motion insistently suggests the operation of a wind-up toy' (*The Times*, 26 March 1986). While the dart-board stage afforded a clever scenic metaphor for the satiric barbs thrown by the characters at one another, the stylised movements that Donnellan incorporated provided an apposite, visual analogue to the seventeenth century's formal displays of manners and etiquette that had become so entrenched and habitual as to suggest not only the robotic essence and emotional detachment of those performing them but also the hollowness at the centre – or at the bull's eye, if you will – of a game of manners and mode that all the players regarded as their *raison d'être*.

Just as this production stressed 'the nature of an artificial and exquisite society, largely drained of feeling and possessed by the need for elegance of language and manner',[13] so, too, did it highlight the scopophilic and voyeuristic nature of the masquerade to which Terry Castle alludes. The actors, when not performing, sat offstage outside the circle, from where they interjected their verbal and non-verbal critiques of their peers' actions: groaning at the slightest mention of the country, applauding the conclusion of a scene or one another's sparkling wit and striking poses, and shooting disdainful grimaces at the paying audience if it attempted likewise to express any reactions. The theatrical artifice and voyeurism inherent in all the graceful manners and seductive masks were again underscored a few years later in Garry Hynes's 1988 production by the Royal Shakespeare Company. Opting, as did Donnellan, to forgo period scenery and replications of seventeenth-century locales, Hynes used a relatively bare stage with a ramp of black doors and screens which had holes punched through them, a symbolic set which suggested to one critic 'a stark black box with burning peep-holes, craters randomly gouged out of the gloom to signify an infernal dungeon of emotions', while for other reviewers, the black panels and the splintered holes through which the light filtered stressed 'the artificiality of the world we are spying on' and suggested 'the falsity of display'.[14] On this colourless and bare set stripped of any elegant scenic details, the characters stood clearly in *bas relief*, and their demeanour, gestures and business were calculated to foreground the performative nature of their lives: 'Everyone is acting and then standing back to assess the effect of a gesture, an expression, a phrase. It is a world without privacy.'[15]

In both Donnellan's and Hynes's productions, one moment the actors are Etherege's characters performing their myriad roles and disguises and the next they are characters-cum-spectators scrutinising and evaluating the performances of others. The line between the character as 'performer' and 'spectator' is clearly demarcated, and each participant involved is acutely aware of the synergistic relationship between both roles: the controller of the 'gaze' from others during his performance at centre stage, and the voyeur-spectator whose presence and responses are necessary for the performer's existence. Like actors on a stage, Etherege's characters thrive on the scopophilic power of their performance – each character deeming the others as an adoring audience eager to collude in the game – for, indeed, there is little purpose in all the rehearsals devoted to perfecting the proper gestures and poses, cultivating the proper language and wit, and selecting the proper sartorial accoutrements without anyone to watch the performance. And, of course, the power of the gaze goes to the best performer, the one who can upstage the others with *éclat* – much like both men of mode, Dorimant and Sir Fopling, try to achieve whenever they make an entrance.

In their productions of *The Man of Mode*, Donnellan and Hynes scratched beneath the play's surface of elegant manners to show a society besotted by artifice and appearances. These revivals eschewed the common, stereotypical interpretations of Restoration comedy as lightweight fare with sparking wit, playful frivolity, and sophisticated elegance to reveal something more sinister and unsettling, and for those spectators and critics who preferred to have their Carolean comedies served up as museum pieces that replicated this age of reputed grace and refinement among a select social sect, both productions seemed flawed. Reviewing Donnellan's revival for the *Daily Telegraph* (26 March 1986), Eric Shorter longed for the absent polish and style so as 'to relish the language as the characters relish it, to share their joy in their elegance, that faith in the frothy which made the pursuit of gallantry an art in itself', while the critic for the *Sunday Telegraph* (30 March 1986) faulted the actors for failing 'to point their lines in such a way that they emerge as witty', asking rhetorically 'Is this Restoration *comedy*?' Donnellan and Hynes excised the 'charm' ostensibly at the heart of this play and in its place offered a disturbing glimpse of 'the pain and cruelty' as well as 'the sterility that underlies desperate pleasure-seeking'[16] by revealing the venality of these characters, exposing them, noted the *Spectator* (5 April 1986) 'as cruel, obsessive and limited'.

Of the two revivals, Hynes's afforded audiences the more sobering interpretation, showing them 'that when you strip away the artifice of vanity fair you are left with a world of resonant solitude and sexual cruelty' (*Guardian*, 15 July 1988). Hynes chose also to accentuate the play's rampant male chauvinism, and in so doing she made for 'an uncomfortable but compelling evening' (*Time Out*, 20 July 1988) for those spectators more accustomed to regarding misogyny as an innocuous, victimless game. While exposing 'the raw nerves underneath the theatrical artifice' and 'the constant tension between artifice and angst', Hynes deftly revealed a society 'in which foreplay is bloodsport and seduction the death of a reputation'.[17] In this world of 'decayed passion, masculine cruelty, and narcissistic solitude' – as one critic

(*Guardian*, 15 July 1988) characterised the revival overall – male carnality is neither romantic nor sensual: it is self-centred, sadistic, and savage.

The source of this savage and brutal tone derives, of course, from Dorimant, Etherege's central character and his supreme masquerader. In fact, so varied and disparate are the roles he plays in order to achieve his libertine imperatives that critics face an impossible task when trying to plumb the depths of his artifice to find the central core underneath. Compounding this problem in deciphering Dorimant's true self from the myriad roles he plays deliberately to mask his true motives is the absence of any dialogue from him (asides, soliloquies) that affords a clear glimpse of any characteristics that approach interiority.[18] Etherege's non-judgemental detachment toward this character complicates matters further, but his less univocal and more prismatic delineation of Dorimant further occludes a concise and clear interpretation. Not only does each scene afford a different perspective on Dorimant's character, each perspective fails to add up to a discrete, whole personality; and the constantly shifting angles from which we view Dorimant, coupled with the contradictions between how characters describe or regard him and how the audience actually sees him behave, generate a fragmented sketch rather than a complete, composite portrait. Confronted by the ineluctable and impossible task of trying to discern the actor from the role, audiences are typically – and not surprisingly – left with conflicting reactions and opinions about his 'real' character. Perhaps Edward Burns was right when he summed that 'One must describe Dorimant, one cannot analyse him.'[19]

With the very first scene, the audience witnesses Dorimant in all his rakish glory – vain, arrogant, abrasive, affected and yet at turns witty and charming – as he enters wistfully as if from his bed to ready himself for the day's adventures. Alone on stage, he addresses the audience directly, expressing his indifference to the letter that he has composed to Mrs Loveit, a jealous mistress with whom he has had a long affair but plans to cast-off now that her charms no longer hold any allure. His insouciance is palpable as he waves the letter with a flick of his wrist – 'What a dull insipid thing is a billet doux written in cold blood, after the heat of the business is over?' (I,i,3–5) – and as he strolls leisurely about his dressing room, unmoved by Loveit's affection for him, the portrait of a self-controlled and self-absorbed libertine comes quickly into focus. With the entrance of Foggy Nan, a bawd in the guise of a fruit-seller, and her news that a young gentlewoman with 'a hugeous fortune' who saw him yesterday at the Exchange and 'is so taken with you' has arrived with her mother in London, Dorimant scents yet another seduction. And when Medley, Dorimant's disciple, confidant, and a lover of gossip, arrives, identifies the young lady as Harriet Woodvill, confirms that she is witty, charming, and wealthy, and follows with a lyrical description of her physical beauty, Dorimant emits a no doubt familiar proclamation: 'Flesh and blood cannot hear this, and not long to know her' (I,i,161–2). Alone with Medley, Dorimant reveals his devious plot to rid himself of Mrs Loveit, a plot he knows Medley will relish: after sending Loveit the letter blaming (albeit falsely) his two-day absence from her on business, Bellinda, the latest young woman whom Dorimant has secretly been trying to seduce, will visit Loveit to disclose her knowledge of his infidelity with an anonymous woman, and shortly after Dorimant will arrive on cue, endure Loveit's fury, confess his roguery, swear her ill humour makes her intolerable, and thus force Loveit to initiate the break. Medley is duly impressed.

With the arrival of Tom the shoemaker and Handy, Dorimant's valet, the action gains momentum as the main business of the scene begins, that is, dressing Dorimant: fitting his new shoes, assisting him with his clothes and peruke, and scenting him – the typical morning ritual performed with much care and finesse and accompanied by the usual sharing of the day's gossip among companions, including Young Bellair, an honest and good-natured young man and the last of Dorimant's friends to arrive. The discussion of fashion leads to ridicule of Sir Fopling Flutter, an Englishman 'lately arrived piping hot from Paris' (I,i,397) where, in his attempt to emulate the modish people of Paris, he acquired the affectations of a frenchified fop, and the mere mention of this outrageous pretender sparks in Dorimant another idea as to how to use a character to his advantage: Fopling will serve as a catalyst in his split from Loveit. While Young Bellair is out of the room briefly, Dorimant's conversation with Medley reveals his true feelings toward his absent companion: 'He's handsome, well-bred, and by much the most tolerable of all the

young men that do not abound in wit' (I,i,461–3), and he discloses further his more nefarious interest in his friend – that is, his
acquaintance with Bellair positions him well to bed the virtuous
Emilia, his friend's intended wife: 'I have known many women
make a difficulty of losing a maidenhead, who have afterwards
made none of making a cuckold' (I,i,486–8). Bellair returns with
troubling news that his father, who does not know of his relationship with Emilia, has just arrived in London, is residing in the
very house where Emilia lives, and has prearranged his son's
marriage to an unidentified woman, a match to which Bellair
must agree or suffer disinheritance. As Bellair runs off to inform
Emilia, Dorimant receives a letter from one of his prostitutes,
Molly, who writes quite illiterately of her 'mallicolly' and penury.
Dorimant decides to send poor Molly money so that she can pur-
chase a box at the theatre 'and perk up i' the face of quality'
(I,i,558), and he and Medley both enjoy a superior laugh at this
poor wench and the very spectacle of her seated in the playhouse's most expensive seats. Pleased by the various plots he has
managed to devise this morning, Dorimant, with Medley by his
side, leaves to dine at a fashionable eatery, singing cheerfully as
he exits.

In this lengthy, single-scene first act, Etherege accomplished
much toward shading in an outline of Dorimant's character. Of
course, the exposition did work in other dramatic ways: disclosing the play's various plot lines and introducing all the main
characters either directly or referentially, most especially the
eponymous Fopling who is described in much detail here and
elsewhere so as to create considerable audience anticipation for
his late arrival on the scene in the third act. But the entire first act
belongs to Dorimant – the action takes place in his dressing room
and a host of characters congregates there to interact with this
notorious rake in order, as Dorimant no doubt suspects, to bask
in his brilliance. Dorimant's state of undress accentuates further
his reigning supremacy and control over not only his environment but also his satellites, and recent productions have embel-
lished Etherege's stage directions to drive home this crucial point
– from Terry Hands's RSC 1971 revival which showed Dorimant
'languishing naked in an elegant bath as he plots the seduction of
an heiress while gargling champagne and having his back
scrubbed'[20] to Hynes's which revealed him lounging around his

room in his underpants. The physicality and immodesty of the character is immediately grasped by audiences, and for the seventeenth-century spectator in particular, this first scene must have conjured up thoughts of yet another infamous rake, Charles II, during his morning ablutions with his attendants ministering to him and awaiting his royal commands. More especially, of course, audiences particularly recognise at the outset that Dorimant's clever banter with his acolytes, for all its flash and polish, is calculated here (and elsewhere) to put focus on his verbal finesse and artistry, to render himself cynosural in a performance he both directs and performs in. His clever witticisms are, as Robert Markley notes about this opening scene, 'self-dramatizing', intended 'to call attention not to what he is describing but to his verbal artifice, to whatever role he is playing at the time'.[21] For Dorimant, life is an unending performance, a series of stratagems deployed to further his own ends, and his need to upstage all others, to retain his status as London's regnant libertine sporting the finest fashion, quoting the popular poets, inventing the sharpest quips, and seducing the most women remains paramount, a reputation that when threatened, as happens later with Loveit, exposes his villainous strain.

Through its depiction of this young gentleman's morning *levée* with the usual routine of dressing and gossiping, this initial act affords audiences more than just a heavy dose of atmosphere and a realistic enactment of a libertine readying himself for his day's activities of pleasure-seeking, for peppered throughout this leisurely dialogue are hints to Dorimant's darker nature. He regards people as easily discarded pawns whom he can manipulate for his own egocentric ends: Loveit, the woman to whom he had earlier professed undying love, can be cast off for her friend, Bellinda, and she in turn can facilitate his plot against Loveit, while Fopling, a fool at whom he jeers, can likewise aid him in that direction. Most disturbing, to be sure, is Dorimant's hypocrisy toward his honest and amiable best friend, Young Bellair. Not only does Dorimant complacently tell Medley that he regards Bellair as a man of little wit and that he consorts with him because Bellair's respectable reputation about town will serve his own ends, he nonchalantly proclaims his ignominious plot to cuckold Bellair and corrupt the innocent Emilia. Certainly male sexual competitiveness and aggression permeate Restoration comedy and are typically deployed by dramatists to provoke the audience's laughter, but in Dorimant these pathologies are symptoms of a malicious and vindictive personality that wields its force most especially over women. Explaining his plan to extricate himself from Loveit's passionate grasp, Dorimant tells Medley: 'next to the coming to a good understanding with a new mistress, I love a quarrel with an old one, but the devil's in't, there has been such a calm in my affairs of late, I have not had the pleasure of making a woman so much as break her fan, to be sullen, or forswear herself these three days' (I,i,216–21). That his powerful ego – one that presumes women lack the power to resist him – dictates first that women should fall into paroxysms of anger and despair when he jilts them, which of course he invariably does, and second that he both relish in and boast of witnessing such feverish displays denotes a sadistic rather than emotional connexion on his part. Dorimant, unlike most literary libertines who derive pleasure from sexual intimacy, finds joy mainly in possessing and then tormenting his conquests, and by conflating sex and power into a form of 'bloodsport' alluded to earlier, Dorimant asserts his domination and superiority over women.

Within this context of male sexual warfare, the opening segment's action reveals even richer iconography. Amidst the continual chatter about Dorimant's control of his mistresses – either past, present or future – as he carefully dons his clothes, straightens his cuffs, fluffs his cravat, and positions his wig, the image is brilliantly cast of a young and vain rake who regards the careful orchestration of his appearance in ways consonant with his manipulation of women. The analogy struck here is both forceful and deliberate, one Harold Weber astutely notes as 'the arming of an epic hero', the meticulous cap-à-pie suiting of a combatant who 'readies himself for a sexual combat that resembles an actual state of war'.[22] This splendid theatrical image – wrought by the harmony between the characters' dialogue concerning the women in Dorimant's life and the scripted stage business for the actor – vivifies the key element of Dorimant's character: his singular and unchecked passion for power and control over the world around him and the people – most especially women – who inhabit it. From his selection and arrangement of the sartorial appurtenances of battle, his barking commands to his inferiors

(Foggy Nan, Tom, Handy), his devising dramatic spectacles for the unwitting women (Loveit, Molly) to enact for his own amusement, to his contriving to seduce Bellair's fiancée, Dorimant is motivated by a Hobbesian lust for power – a power manifested here in the first scene and one that intensifies with brutality in subsequent acts, most especially in his exchanges with his chief opponent in his battle to maintain his supremacy, Mrs Loveit.

Audiences get a clearer glimpse of Dorimant's darker side early in the next act when he arrives at Loveit's home to act out the scene he has devised with Bellinda. Loveit's subscription to courtly passion blinds her to the type of extreme malice a libertine such as Dorimant can demonstrate when his freedom and reputation are at risk. She does, however, find out quickly when he enters, finds her pacing and ranting over his reported infidelity, and begins his stinging insults immediately: 'What, dancing the galloping nag without a fiddle?' (II,ii,144). Dorimant's cool and oblique admission of his unfaithfulness pushes Loveit's rage to its zenith – she tears her fan to pieces and collapses weeping. Dorimant's only retort is mockery: 'So thunder breaks the cloud in twain, And makes a passage for the rain' (II,ii,181–2). To Loveit's angry reminder of his earlier oaths and vows of constancy, he offers clipped responses intended to enrage her further – that his indifference springs from a lack of love and the capriciousness of youth – and each retort grows more bitter and abusive while his delivery becomes increasingly condescending. His false accusations that she has turned her attentions toward Fopling bring Loveit to distraction, at which point Dorimant, having planted the seed for his later scheme with Fopling and won this match against his opponent, callously dismisses her pleas to reconcile and leaves her in the fit of agitation that he has created deliberately and with great satisfaction – after three days of no histrionic displays from a female, he finally provoked one to break her fan. But Dorimant's motive for such abrasive treatment remains unclear, and while some critics suggest that his callous behaviour is for Bellinda's benefit, she, at any rate, perceives that he has gone too far: 'H'as given me the proof which I desired of his love, but tis a proof of his ill nature too' (II,ii,308–9). Without any precise dramatic motive to interpret Dorimant's brutal attack on Loveit, audiences must perforce view it as demonstrative of Dorimant's aggressive and sadistic strains.

In his next encounter with Loveit – at the Mall for the prearranged meeting with Fopling – Dorimant suffers unexpected public embarrassment at her hands that instigates in him a level of vengeance disproportionate to his discomfiture. Unfortunately, Dorimant's need for spectators to witness his masterful performances and to publicise his conquests over women prompts him to invite Medley, the one observer on whom Dorimant can count to broadcast his triumph over Loveit, but when Loveit feigns interest in Fopling in order to turn the tables on Dorimant and make him jealous, Medley's presence quickly becomes a liability to Dorimant's cherished reputation. Medley's barbed observations ('She entertains him as if she liked him', 'She takes no notice of you', 'Would you had brought some more of your friends, Dorimant, to have been witnesses of Sir Fopling's disgrace and your triumph' [III,iii,260, 294, 350–3]) hit their mark, and Dorimant, now vulnerable and vowing to get revenge by forcing Loveit to 'pluck off this mask and show the passion that lies panting under' (III,iii,361–3), asks Medley for a few days' reprieve in relaying this incident to anyone until he has sufficient time to offer Medley evidence that his reputation has not been compromised. At risk here is Dorimant's public image, and vengeance is the only course of action he can fathom when that image has been threatened. Appearances are everything, and he will orchestrate events in order to ensure that the public mask he wears – unlike Loveit's which he intends to rip off – remains intact.

Driven by his public humiliation and his failure to assert his superiority over Loveit, Dorimant accosts her one final time in a scene that patently discloses his acrimonious and vengeful temperament. Once Dorimant extracts from Loveit an admission that her behaviour with Fopling was intended to wound him, he tries to convince her that it is his love for her that will bring him ridicule if she does not publicly rebuff Fopling:

> DORIMANT: Should I be willing to forget it, I shall be daily minded of it, 'twill be a commonplace for all the town to laugh at me, and Medley, when he is rhetorically drunk, will ever be declaiming on it in my ears.
> MRS LOVEIT: 'Twill be believed a jealous spite! Come, forget it.

> DORIMANT: Let me consult my reputation, you are too careless
> of it. (*Pauses*) You shall meet Sir Fopling in the Mall again
> tonight.
> MRS LOVEIT: What mean you?
> DORIMANT: I have thought on it, and you *must*. 'Tis necessary
> to justify my love to the world; you can handle a coxcomb
> as he deserves, when you are not out of humour, madam!
> MRS LOVEIT: Public satisfaction for the *wrong* I have done *you*!
> This is some new device to make me more ridiculous!
> DORIMANT: Hear me!
> MRS LOVEIT: I will not!
> DORIMANT: You *will* be persuaded.
> MRS LOVEIT: Never.
> DORIMANT: Are you so obstinate?
> MRS LOVEIT: Are you so base?
> DORIMANT: You will not satisfy my love?
> MRS LOVEIT: I would die to satisfy that, but I will not, to save
> you from a thousand racks, do a shameless thing to
> please your vanity.
>
> (italics added; V,i, 245–72)

During this exchange, Dorimant is anything but the aloof and
unruffled libertine that Loveit contended with earlier in Act II: his
desperation to mend his reputation has released his fulminant
vitriol, and his casuistical entreaties for her assistance would be
droll and brilliant were they not so transparent and vicious.
Dorimant, who has scant regard for Loveit's reputation or her
public embarrassment, demands vehemently that she aid him in
his plot to recuperate *his* image, forgetting, of course, that he
instigated his own humiliation by orchestrating the rendezvous
between Loveit and Fopling for his machiavellian delight in
humiliating her in front of witnesses. Loveit sees through his
hollow protestations of love, and despite the full force of his
wrath, she refuses to placate Dorimant's ego. Loveit does help to
to reinstate Dorimant's reputation, but only inadvertently: in the
next and final scene when, still stinging from Harriet's biting
rebuke ('Mr Dorimant has been your God Almighty long enough,
'tis time to think of another' [V,ii,434–6]) and no longer able to
endure Fopling's folly, she contemptuously dismisses him and
then rebuffs the entire crowd before her quick exit, and although

Dorimant did not directly precipitate this ocular proof he had promised for his companion Medley, Loveit's outburst proves fortuitous: Medley proclaims Dorimant's unequivocal mastery over women: 'Dorimant! I pronounce thy reputation clear – and henceforward when I would know of woman, I will consult no other oracle' (V,ii,487–9).

Despite his acrimony toward Loveit and his delight throughout the play in torturing her, Dorimant has been acquitted by many scholars for his abrasive, insensitive treatment of this woman to whom he has professed love. Loveit's non-modish behaviour – her unchecked fury, demonstrative passion, jealous possessiveness – all mark her as a prime and fitting target for taunts from the modish crowd who regard such emotional displays as anathema. Although familiar with the voguish forms of dissembling, as she shows in her encounter with Fopling in the Mall where she brandishes her fan with panache and plays to perfection the fashionable socialite – so much so, in fact, that she rekindles Dorimant's interest and sparks his jealousy – Loveit cannot sustain the feigned indifference or artificial demeanour that are requisites in this society. Not unlike Lady Cockwood, she holds tenaciously to the outmoded *précieux* myths of courtly love, and while she may lack Lady Cockwood's paranoia over her reputation, her desire for absolute control over and deification by her lover makes her not only a natural candidate for the town's ridicule but also an easy victim for Dorimant's sexual acquisitiveness and power. As a woman who submits foolishly to the blandishments of a rake and then faults him for his inconstancy and rejection, Loveit was, by seventeenth-century standards, a dupe. However, today's audiences – more sensitive to misogyny and male sexual politics – seem less inclined to view Loveit as risible. Filtering their remarks through a twentieth-century perspective, critics at Hynes's revival found Loveit, in her refusal to mollify Dorimant's vanity (V,i), 'striking a blow for female dignity', and likened the torment between Dorimant and Loveit in their final encounter as having 'a racking cruelty that puts you in mind of Strindberg'.[23]

Although Dorimant reserves his calculated abuse against women for Loveit, Bellinda, through her own naïveté, suffers nonetheless at his hands. Aware of Dorimant's reputation and having witnessed at first-hand his treachery with Loveit, she regardlessly trusts in his oaths of love and capitulates to his advances. Like her friend Loveit, whom she has betrayed and who learns too late that Dorimant garners 'more pleasure in the ruin of a woman's reputation than in the endearments of her love' (V,i,207–9), Bellinda acknowledges his duplicity only after he has made his conquest:'Other men are wicked, but then they have some sense of shame! he is never well but when he triumphs, nay! glories to a woman's face in his villainies' (V,i,298–301). Clearly, Bellinda does not endure the same mistreatment as does Loveit – and Dorimant does guard her reputation despite the cajoling from Fopling and others – but once she discovers Dorimant in Loveit's chamber after their liaison, she realises her folly and vows never to repeat it: 'Let me but escape this time, I'll never venture more' (V,i,331–2).

While Bellinda is often considered a minor character who does little more than provide the classic and stereotypical dramatic caveat against female, premarital sex, her character actually provides crucial commentary, both direct and tacit, on Dorimant's character – commentary that is not lost on the audience. Etherege deliberately supplied this minor character with more asides, as Judith Fisher astutely noted, than any other character (as much as double the number given to Dorimant or Loveit), and this glimpse into her interiority 'establishes her as a character we can rely on to show real rather than performed passion'.[24] Equally important, Bellinda's openness affords her a unique relationship with the audience, especially in a play where characters seldom reveal their interior thoughts and feelings. Thus, while her verbal and non-verbal responses to Dorimant's behaviour do not quite elevate her to the status of chorus, they do carry significant weight in spectators' assessment of Etherege's rake hero. Indeed, audiences can readily extrapolate from the charm and sexual allure that they witness Dorimant bestowing on Bellinda in order to bed her, those types of strategies he used on Loveit during the initial stages of their affair and long before boredom overtook him. Most significantly, in Bellinda's seduction scene, audiences get one of the most distasteful glimpses at this libertine who, for all his talk about love and passion, equates sexual intimacy with a game in which winning against his opponents is his singular goal. After Dorimant and Bellinda make their exit from the bedroom to the drawing room, their post-coital conversation is played in counterpoint to Handy standing upstage 'tying up linen' (IV,ii), an image that denotes a routine, household chore. This forceful and offensive slice-of-life picture belies the myth of the rake as a sensual lover consumed by rapture and relishing the mutual ecstasy of his mate. Rather, the vulgar stage composition merely reduces Bellinda to nothing more than one of many young virgins whom Dorimant has seduced, and it diminishes Dorimant to a sexual predator whose appetites cannot be satiated. As Harold Weber commented, this scene conveys Dorimant's perception of the bedroom as 'a battlefield', a place of 'grim struggle to assert one's superiority over one's partner'.[25] The emotional void at the heart of this scene was captured succinctly for audiences at Hynes's revival: as Bellinda scurried to find her clothes and dress, Dorimant, detached and depressed, remained seated on the bed and 'slumped like a Hogarthian rake',[26] showing male concupiscence at its basest.

Both Loveit and Bellinda – in succumbing so readily to Dorimant's disingenuous oaths of love, lacking the emotional fortitude to resist his advances, and failing to distinguish the actor from his many disguises – present little challenge to Dorimant's acquisitive nature and immense ego. In Harriet, however, Dorimant encounters not only less easy prey, but also a formidable opponent who can penetrate his libertine façade and kindle in him something more profound than animal lust and sexual conquest. For Dorimant, Harriet is markedly different from the other women (the Loveits, Bellindas, and Mollys) with whom he consorts. Her roguish and rapier wit, keen intellect, self-possession, lack of affectation, inviolable honour, and irrepressible fieriness enable her to play his game so expertly that she elicits in this libertine, who had mocked love and marriage as a contrivance calculated to deny men their liberty, an attraction and passion that distinguishes her as the suitable match for him.

At the first sight of Harriet Dorimant is smitten. Arriving at the Mall where he plans to execute his plot against Loveit (III,iii), Dorimant accidently stumbles upon Harriet and Bellair walking and, remaining at a distance and rhapsodising on her beauty, he proclaims 'I'll follow the lottery, and put in for a prize with my friend Bellair' (III,iii,42–3). For the first time, the audience sees Dorimant drop his libertine guise to reveal a heroic lover whose immediate reaction to a female sparks the very unrakish-like

thought of marriage (i.e., the 'prize'). Having learned earlier that
Harriet took notice of him at the Exchange and thus believing he
has the upper hand here, he approaches her to engage in a conversation that he presumes will captivate her. But he no sooner
begins his heretofore foolproof pose of gallant – bowing gracefully to her and gently chiding her for her sullenness ('A thousand
smiles were shining in that face but now' [III,iii,70–2]) – than he
realises he has encountered a woman far less pliant and gullible
than those to whom he is accustomed and one excellently suited
to maintain a brilliant parry in his game of verbal swordplay.
Beneath the civil and courteous surface of their highly metaphor-
ic banter is a layer of sexual innuendo that masks their true
feelings toward one another, revealing to audiences the sexual
tension underneath. Sublimating their emotions in a cerebral
fencing match, Dorimant and Harriet prove equal partners, with
Harriet controlling the conversation's direction and demonstrating her facile intellect by rapidly shifting metaphors, and
Dorimant countering each move quickly with a clever rejoinder.
But when Dorimant pushes innuendo too far and manoeuvres his
quips to a more personal insinuation about gaining her 'favour',
Harriet halts the conversation and tells Bellair 'Let us walk,'tis
time to leave him, men grow dull when they begin to be particular' (III,iii,101–2). With another woman, Dorimant's sly retort
would have earned him a coy look and a reprimanding giggle,
both of which would have intimated the lady's mutual interest,
but Harriet's exception to his forwardness surprises and stings
him. To retaliate, he tries to regain the upper hand by exposing
her professed loathing of flattery as a ruse, doing so by describing
the behaviour he just witnessed from her as she passed through
the Mall and gave a deliberate performance for the fops who eyed
her: 'the thousand several forms you put your face into; then, to
make yourself agreeable, how wantonly you played with your
head, flung back your locks, and looked smilingly over your
shoulder at 'em' (110–14). Harriet's instinctive response: ridicule
him in return. But Harriet takes her retort one step further; she
not only describes his affected demeanour among the ladies – 'a
sly softness in your looks and a gentle slowness in your bows, as
you pass 'em' (III,iii,116–18) – she punctuates her description
with a parodic imitation of his behaviour, acting out the affected
traits she has just limned. Harriet's pantomime is the final word

in this minor skirmish, for the exchange ends abruptly with the arrival of Lady Woodvill, but she emerges as the clear winner of this round: she not only seized control of the badinage, she got in the final jab with an amusing pantomime that most certainly deflated Dorimant's vanity.

Harriet's mockery of Dorimant's affected *honnête homme* pose identifies her as the only character sufficiently astute to read his inveterate masquerading. Not even Dorimant's close friend, Bellair – to whom she earlier said of Dorimant, 'He is agreeable and pleasant I must own, but he does so much affect being so, he displeases me' (III,iii,28–9) – can discern Dorimant's artifice; as he tells her, he believes that all Dorimant 'does and says, is so easy, and so natural' (III,iii,30–1) and, surprised at her observation, adds the telling comment 'I never heard him accused of affectation before' (III,iii,35–6). Etherege appropriates to Harriet the role of chorus here, for if audiences had not by this point gleaned that Dorimant – despite his throng of idolaters who sing his praises and flock to his side (and even to his dressing room) – is a habitual poseur, then Harriet's perfect enactment of his every calculated manoeuvre (that is, her very ability to mimic him exactly) signals that his behaviour is studied, rehearsed and executed like that of an actor whose careful preparation results in a such a natural and lifelike performance that his artifice remains indistinguishable to the spectator. Harriet is a woman who will brook no pretensions and requires from her mate a level of self-awareness that Dorimant has to achieve, and her mimicry here is her first step in helping Dorimant reach that awareness.

During their next encounter, at Lady Townley's, Dorimant – disguised at Harriet's request as Mr Courtage, 'that foppish admirer of quality' (III,iii,377) – continues the same tactic of feigned gallantry with Harriet because his flawed ego, which deludes him into thinking that he can 'fathom all the depths of womankind' (as he told Medley in the previous act, III,iii,389), continues to encourage his belief that his artful posturing as the heroic lover, a pose that facilitated his many previous conquests, is the single most effective method of winning a woman's heart. Harriet, however, instructs him differently. She immediately mocks his pretence, answering his exaggerated bow with a 'demure curtsy' and explaining that 'Affectation is catching I find; from your grave bow I got it' (IV,i,120–1). His attempts at playful

charm evoke her cool reception, and as he struggles to elicit a
warm response from her, he realises the depth of his feelings for
her 'I love her, and dare not let her know it' (IV,i,164–5).
Although libertine imperatives dictate against revealing one's
true emotions so that one's opponent cannot gain the
upper hand, Dorimant cannot resist broaching the subject of
love in order to elicit from Harriet some admission of her
feelings:

> DORIMANT: Think of making a party, madam, love will
> engage.
> HARRIET: You make me start! I did not think to have heard of
> love from you.
> DORIMANT: I never knew what 'twas to have a settled ague
> yet, but now and then have had irregular fits.
> HARRIET: Take heed, sickness after long health is commonly
> more violent and dangerous.
> DORIMANT: (*aside*) I have took the infection from her, and feel
> the disease now spreading in me. (*To her*) Is the name of
> love so frightful that you dare not stand it?
> HARRIET: 'Twill do little execution out of your mouth on me
> I am sure.
> DORIMANT: It has been fatal –
> HARRIET: To some easy women, but we are not all born to one
> destiny. I was informed you use to laugh at love, and not
> make it.
> DORIMANT: The time has been, but now I must speak –
> HARRIET: If it be on that idle subject, I will put on my serious
> look, turn my head carelessly from you, drop my lip, let
> my eyelids fall, and hang half o'er my eyes – thus while
> you buzz a speech of an hour long in my ear, and I
> answer never a word! Why do you not begin?
> DORIMANT: That the company may take notice of how pas-
> sionately I make advances of love, and how disdainfully
> you receive 'em.
> HARRIET: When your love's grown strong enough to make
> you bear being laughed at, I'll give you leave to trouble
> me with it. Till when pray forbear, sir.
>
> (IV,i,167–97)

Harriet once again emerges the victor in their exchange. While she not only maintains her feigned indifference to his role as the romantic suitor, she also establishes the ground rules for their relationship. Although she acknowledged her feelings for Dorimant during their first encounter ('I feel as great a change within; but he shall never know it' [III,iii,73–4]), she continues to dissemble out of necessity – that is, she must guard her honour by remaining inviolate and not become one of his victims – and will continue to do so until she is certain that she has won Dorimant on her own terms. She informs him that his passionate oaths, so effective on other 'easy women', have no impact on her, and as proof of this, she forestalls his confession of love by mocking the role he expects her to perform as the demure recipient of his blandishments. If Dorimant intends to prove his love to her, words alone will not suffice: the proof that Harriet requires from him is his willingness to shed his pretensions and vanity by professing his love for her publicly, risking the type of laughter and ridicule that he has so readily inflicted on other men, like Bellair, who put their love above their own egos.

In the final scene, Dorimant gives Harriet the proof she wants. In a lengthy exchange that runs some 185 lines, Harriet, refusing to let Dorimant win her easily, continues her manipulation of him to the point of emotional torture for them both. At each plea by Dorimant that she let him open his heart to her, she stops his entreaties with scepticism – 'Do not speak it, if you would have me believe it; your tongue is so famed for falsehood 'twill do the truth an injury (*Turns away her head*)', and 'In men who have been long hardened in sin, we have reason to mistrust the first signs of repentance' (V,ii,135–7;150–2). Only after Dorimant openly admits his love does Harriet show her heart: 'I would, and never will marry another man' (V,ii,374–5) except Dorimant. Notwithstanding this confession, however, Harriet does not transfer control to Dorimant and transform into the typical comic heroine spewing cloying sentiments of love, for such a metamorphosis is not in her nature. This strong-willed woman with a sharp tongue (as she demonstrated to Loveit) possesses a coldness and toughness that will enable her to meet Dorimant head on as an equal not a subordinate. As for sentimentality, she leaves that to Dorimant: to his final confession of love, 'The first time I saw you, you left me with the pangs of love upon me, and this day my soul has given up her liberty' (Vi,ii,476–8), she responds not in kind but in quips – 'This is more dismal than the country! Emilia! pity me, who am going to that sad place. Methinks I hear the hateful noise of the rooks already – kaw, kaw kaw' (V,ii,479–81).

These final lines that Etherege assigns Dorimant and Harriet can easily be lost on the audience as the remainder of the scene – which includes only 9 lines and a celebratory dance – follows apace. Yet this last exchange between this gay couple, the most famous gay couple in Carolean comedy, figures prominently in clarifying the true nature of these characters and presaging their future together should they opt to marry. At the end of the play, Harriet maintains her ascendancy over Dorimant, as demonstrated by her continued mastery at verbal manoeuvring and dissembling, and this sustained, artful use of language, even after Dorimant has confessed his love and agreed to journey with her to Hampshire for a trial courtship, telegraphs Harriet's intention to remain a free spirit, to reject the traditional role of subservient wife, and to deploy wit as an erotic substitute for the lure and excitement of London if she intends to enjoy and survive connubial bliss in the country, a place which she, like Dorimant, equates with boredom and dull domesticity. For Harriet, love does not transform her – she required no transformation to make her complete – nor does she demand a metamorphosis from Dorimant. To his oath that he will renounce friends, drinking, and other women, she responds 'Hold – though I wish you devout, I would not have you turn fanatic' (V,ii,159–60). Harriet expects his fidelity, but she also means to continue instructing Dorimant that love cannot be sustained by oaths and vows, for these can be easily broken and typically engender feelings of entrapment; rather, love is sustained by honesty, and it is to be given freely if it is to be given at all. This beguiling woman, whose playful banter and roguish strain attracted Dorimant at the outset, understands the dangers in a world of transient emotions and fleeting happiness, and her resilience and wit will help to nourish her relationship with Dorimant and, more importantly, help to ensure her own survival should they eventually marry. Dorimant, on the other hand, remains unable to reconcile the concepts of love and marriage with personal, individual freedom – which Harriet clearly offers him – to achieve a new level of self-awareness. The roman-

tic effusiveness of his final lines – as well as those spoken to
Harriet throughout their 'courtship' in this final scene – suggests
that he has pinioned himself to the role of romantic lover, unable
to discard this mask because he cannot imagine any alternative.
As a libertine accustomed to masquerading according to clearly
demarcated character types, Dorimant equates love and passion
as traits of the heroic lover, and he will probably play this part
with her *ad infinitum*, despite Harriet's instruction otherwise.

Equal to Dorimant's inability to discard his mask of romantic
lover with Harriet is his inability to discard his guise as a libertine. While professing his love to Harriet, he informs Loveit in
confidence that he still loves her but he must marry Harriet 'to
repair the ruins of my estate that needs it' (V,ii,327–8; see also
Dorimant's comment to Bellair, IV,iii,211–13). He tells her also
that had she not been so jealous and demanded his fidelity, she
could have been his mistress in London while Harriet remained
his wealthy wife in the country: 'To satisfy you I must give up my
interest wholly to my love, had you been a reasonable woman, I
might have secured 'em both, and been happy' (V,ii,315–17).
Moments later, he turns to Bellinda – the woman for whom he
had earlier left off his wooing of Harriet in order to satisfy his lust
('The hour is almost come I appointed Bellinda, and I am not so
foppishly in love here to forget; I am flesh and blood yet'
[IV,i,382–4]) – and tries to arrange their next assignation. Some
critics opine that Dorimant does not actually intend to pursue
either woman but merely wishes to keep his libertine reputation
intact, but such interpretations strain credibility given the character Etherege shows us, and they actually substantiate the view
that Dorimant has not shed his rakish impulses since he remains
compelled to protect this reputation even on the brink of matrimony. Admittedly, this reading does help to put a positive spin on
the negative aspects of Dorimant's character: that is, it exonerates
him for his cruelty and duplicity by fashioning him as a converted rake redeemed by love. However, Etherege supplies no concrete evidence of such a complete conversion. In fact, Dorimant's
oaths to Harriet ring hollow in light of his many specious
justifications for his broken vows to Loveit and Bellinda: in his
first confrontation with Loveit, Dorimant excuses his lies by
explaining that 'Love gilds us over, and makes us show fine
things to one another for a time, but soon the gold wears off, and

then again the native brass appears' (II,ii,221–3), and in the final
scene, amidst his profuse, romantic declarations to Harriet,
Dorimant rationalises to Bellinda the male tendency to break
promises of love, 'Th' extravagant words they speak in love; 'tis
as unreasonable to expect we should perform all we promise
then, as do all we threaten when we are angry' (V,ii,335–7).
Dorimant's professions of love to Harriet – professions that he
apparently offers to others so freely and yet retracts so regularly
– may well be short lived, and Harriet's healthy scepticism over
his capacity to reform must inevitably be shared by the audience.

   In ending his play on a caesura – a pause that leaves the audience reflecting back over the entire action of the comedy to wrestle with questions about the gay couple's future, the nature of true
love, and the ephemerality of passion – Etherege deliberately
shows Dorimant not as the libertine converted, but rather as the
libertine confirmed, and although Dorimant may well be
reformed by Harriet's love long after the fifth act concludes and
somewhere on a remote country estate in Hampshire, the picture
that Etherege leaves with the audience is that of an individual
whose habitual masquerading has ultimately enveloped his
entire identity, or, perhaps more precisely, his lack of identity.
From the *honnête homme*, the romantic suitor, the elegant beau, the
libertine wit, to the rakish seducer, Dorimant dons roles and acts
them out according to the audience for whom he performs, cal-
culating always to be attractive and irresistible to the viewer.
Each mask that he wears is presented to others in lieu of his own
face, and in this world where identities can be easily assumed and
just as easily discarded and where appearances are quite deceiving, Dorimant has crafted from his myriad disguises the deceptive illusion of a univocal personality that fools both his audience
and himself. Lost in the fashionable games of artifice and masquerading, Dorimant's mask has become fixed to his face.

In reading *The Man of Mode*, one typically focuses on Dorimant's
seductions and machinations, but in performance, the spectator
cannot avoid the centrality of Sir Fopling, who is, after all, the title
character. Like Molière with his brilliant expository dialogue that
builds audience anticipation for the late arrival of Tartuffe,
Etherege takes especial care to prepare audiences for Fopling's
grand entrance in Act III, scene ii. In the first act, Etherege devotes

34 highly descriptive lines (I,i,396–429) to this creature of 'great acquired follies, the very 'pattern of modern foppery' with his 'pretty lisp' and 'imitation of the people of quality of France', and these lines of dialogue, coupled with Medley's and Young Bellair's burlesque of this affected fop, whose 'head stands for the most part on one side' and whose facial expressions are 'more languishing than a lady's when she lolls at stretch in her coach', all conspire expertly to pique spectators' eagerness to witness for themselves the outrageous and ridiculous antics of this eminent coxcomb. When he makes his first appearance in the third act at Lady Townley's, he does not disappoint. Dressed in a flamboyant and colourful outfit that upstages all the others wearing their more tasteful and fashionable English mode and accompanied by a young pageboy attired in identical garb, Fopling makes a stunning entrance as he stands stock still and, with a limp-handed dismissal of his underling, instructs his miniature to 'wait without'. As the characters facetiously compliment him on his keen sense of style and itemise the details of his dress – from his suit and wig to his shoes and gloves – Fopling enhances their delight as he steps mincingly about the stage and poses for his onlookers to get a better glimpse of him. The drollness of this first entrance is second only to his appearance in Act IV, scene i where, having just left a gala event at Court, he arrives uninvited at Lady Townley's party with his entire entourage decked out for a masquerade. In his 1971 revival, Terry Hands capitalised superbly on this stage direction for this scene by having Fopling enter disguised as the person with whom he probably most identified: Fopling did not enter on foot – he was carried in by his minions in a chariot designed like a sunburst on which he stood regally outfitted like the Sun King, Louis XIV. As always, Fopling controls the 'gaze'.

For all his outlandish conduct, however, Fopling is not a source of vexation; he's pure entertainment for everyone in this modish group. His absence of malice and ire make him innocuous, and his genuine childlike joy for life renders him endearing. Stunningly capturing these latter qualities was John Wood, whose performance in the scene at Dorimant's lodgings conveyed Fopling's guileless nature. Having arrived at Dorimant's after he caused such a big sensation at Lady Townley's, Fopling is in peak form, as described vividly by the designer for Hands's revival, Timothy O'Brien:

Someone says, 'Look, Sir Fopling's dancing' and he's up on a cloud at the end of a wonderfully successful party where he has felt himself the real comet in the sky, and he's celebrating this so nakedly in his Brandenberg with its soft colours and weaving about the stage like some marvellously happy moth. Then he explains that he has written a song, which is teased out of him. It's read over and he's persuaded to sing it. He stands on the bed, starts to sing, and suddenly realises it's a much better song than he remembered. Almost with tears of pride he sings. Then he sits down and his friends say: 'Of its kind it couldn't be bettered and it's particularly remarkable for being in the French manner.' 'That's what I aimed at', he says, and bursts into tears, and then makes a marvellous gesture: he cries 'Slap, down goes the glass and we're at it.' That's not artificial, it's someone so enthusiastic, so capable of enjoying himself, that the artificiality has vanished.[27]

This habitually good-natured fool, with his ebullient personality and extemporaneous dances and poses, provides more than innocent and inconsequential laughter. Although some critics maintain that Fopling adds little to the main plot – Robert Hume, for example, regards him as 'a figure of fun, not the object of serious attack' but concludes he's 'irrelevant to the action'[28] – his presence does contribute significantly to the play's overall tone. On the one hand, each of his entrances somehow impinges on Dorimant's pursuit of pleasure: he thwarts the conclusion of Dorimant's initial exchange with Harriet at the Mall by sauntering in with his seven minions, yelling Dorimant's name, and frightening off Lady Woodvill, who drags Harriet with her; in full masquerade regalia, he interrupts Dorimant's next flirtation with Harriet at Lady Townley's at the crucial point of Dorimant's attempt to coax from her an admission of love; he barges into Dorimant's room after the seduction of Bellinda; and he upstages the courtship of Harriet and Dorimant in the final scene. And with each of Fopling's unannounced intrusions, audiences laugh heartily at this fool's unwitting frustration of Dorimant. On the other hand, Fopling's interferences afford a requisite dose of comic relief that offsets the darker mood cast by Dorimant's behaviour. His fanciful and self-indulgent conduct at Dorimant's lodgings helps to expunge some of the unsavoury aftertaste from

Dorimant's sexual escape with Bellinda, and, more importantly, as John Barnard points out, Fopling's entrance at the end of the play facilitates a traditional comic resolution: he redirects the audience's attention 'away from the dubieties of Dorimant's actions'[29] with Loveit and Bellinda by refocusing their visceral reactions to the pure comic energy that he exudes as he prances delicately about the stage, dancing ineptly and uninhibitedly to the concluding celebratory song.

From a thematic standpoint, however, Fopling plays a far more crucial role in illuminating the central ideas of masquerading and artifice. His pretence to wit and fashion, his transparent vanity, his singular concern for outer appearances, his delightfully obtrusive presence, and his failure to keep within the boundaries of decorum all work to make him the play's colourful and cyno-sural centrepiece from which the satiric thrust of the comedy radiates and by which audiences gauge the artificial conduct of the other characters, in particular Dorimant, the one character to whom Fopling gravitates and regards most like himself – that is, a man of mode.

While at first glance Dorimant and Fopling appear to be oppo-sites – one the true wit and the other the false wit – Etherege actu-ally intimates that they share more commonalities than differ-ences. Their fastidiousness over their dress and appearance links them physically at the play's outset, as established by Bellair's compliment to Dorimant in the first act about his attire – 'No man in town has a better fancy in his clothes than you have' (I,i,392–3) – which precipitates their discussion about Fopling's pretence to fashion. The visual similarities between both – a similarity that includes not only attire but also mannerisms – is underscored by Fopling's initial greeting of his old acquaintance Dorimant, who has also travelled to Paris and apparently absorbed some of its 'culture': 'Dorimant, let me embrace thee, without lying I have not met with any of my acquaintance, who retain so much of Paris as thou dost, the very air thou hadst when the marquise mistook thee i' th' Tuileries, and cried "Hey, chevalier" and then begged thy pardon' (III,ii,170–5). In addition to these compli-ments about Dorimant's French mannerisms, Fopling's reputed requisites for a complete gentleman, requisites that Fopling believes he possesses – that he 'dress well, dance well, fence well, have a genius for love letters, an agreeable voice for a chamber, be

very amorous, something discreet, but not over-constant' (I,i,425–7)
– have been, with the exclusion of just a few points, attributes that
Dorimant displayed in the very first scene. Other similarities, which
include their use of French words, their composition of songs, their
infinite vanity, their graceful bows and languishing glances,[30] yoke
Dorimant and Fopling together not as doubles – for Dorimant is
clearly not as excessive and extravagant as Fopling in his dress or
behaviour – but as opposite sides of the same coin.

Both Fopling and Dorimant are men of mode, and while their
approach to sustaining and displaying that mode differs markedly, each is an artificer representative of an age and *zeitgeist* that
privileged surface over substance. Fopling is a harmless, risible
caricature of society's obsession with fashion and mode: he is all
surfaces, oblivious to the laughter he provokes and capable of
regarding only external signs as the true reflection of one's inner
self. Dorimant, whose elegance of manner does not detract from
his turpitude and viciousness, presents the darker side of the
modish upper class: he is the Hobbesian libertine who uses
artifice for his own personal gain, indifferent and oblivious to the
damage he causes, and, like Fopling, discerning his mask as a
veracious image of his real nature. By juxtaposing Fopling's trav-
esty of this mannered society with Dorimant's drive to remain the
reigning libertine in this artificial world, Etherege provides an
apposite binary construction that allows audiences to read each
against the other, revealing the vacuity behind each's artifice. By
extension, of course, Etherege draws the audiences' attention outward to the entire cast of characters whose lack of meaning and
purpose eludes them because they, like Fopling and Dorimant,
believe in the illusion of a substantive self-identity that each has
crafted for his own performance in an elaborate and hollow masquerade. It would seem, then, that Donnellan's revival hit the
mark: these characters will continue their elegant and graceful
movements around the circle's perimeter, repeatedly manoeuvring physically, linguistically and emotionally around each other,
stopping occasionally to strike a pose for special effect and
admiration from the onlookers. And they will not cease their
incessant circling – which gives them the illusion that they are
actually doing something and getting somewhere – until they
wind down and collapse after having spent all their energy playing a game at which everyone loses.

6
Wycherley and the Carolean Theatre

William Wycherley (1641–1715), the eldest of six children of Daniel and Bethia (*née* Shrimpton) Wycherley, was born in the town of Clive, north of Shrewsbury, just one year prior to the English Civil War.[1] Daniel Wycherley, a gentleman by birth with a genealogy reaching back to the reign of Henry IV and a landowner of considerable property, had served as High Steward (land steward) to the Marquis of Winchester, and when the latter was imprisoned by the Puritans during the war, Daniel continued to manage his estates, acquiring property for the marquis as well as himself and in turn building a considerable sum of money for his family. With his father's means and wealth, young William received an excellent education, beginning with a classical curriculum that included Greek and Latin. At age 15, William completed his pre-university education, as was the custom among young gentlemen, by sojourning at his father's expense in France where he spent four years in Angoulême – a southwest, provincial town, home to the school of *préciosité* – studying culture, manners, and language with Jesuit tutors and members of an elite circle of nobility and ultimately converting to Roman Catholicism. Prior to the restoration of Charles II, William returned to England and in October 1659 enrolled as a student in the Inner Temple, one of the Inns of Court in London, but by July 1660, he had left London for Oxford, where he studied and took up residence with the eminent Thomas Barlow, provost at Queen's College, librarian at the Bodleian, and a staunch Anglican, who was probably instrumental in Wycherley's reconversion to Protestantism. Wycherley did not matriculate at Oxford, however, and by November 1660 he was once more on the move, returning to London and enrolling again in the Inner Temple to continue his law studies, which, in all likelihood, he did not complete.

Wycherley's activities during the first decade of the Restoration are sketchy, but his residence in London, a city now lifted from its austere Puritan trappings and newly rejuvenated by Charles's return, no doubt afforded him myriad diversions from his law books. His residence in the Inner Temple gave him convenient access to the fashionable society and its favourite venues to patronise (viz., the coffeehouses, taverns, theatres) and preferred places to promenade (e.g., St James's Park, Covent Garden, the galleries of Whitehall Palace), and the well-to-do young student, who had spent a good deal of time consorting with the cultivated society in France, must have gravitated toward these popular London haunts, which catered to the sophisticated and urbane. In fact, Wycherley set each of his comedies either completely or partially in locales situated in this general area known as 'the Town', which suggests not only his familiarity with this region and its inhabitants but also his personal sense of affinity with those who populated and played in London's elite cultural centre. In 1662, Wycherley's name appears on the army roster for a summer tour of duty in Ireland, a brief diversion for a gentleman wishing for adventure and the opportunity to demonstrate his mettle, but by December he was back in London and presiding as 'controller for the Christmas' at the Inner Temple. No other evidence of Wycherley's activities surfaces until 1664, when in January he took a post as attaché to Sir Richard Fanshawe, Britain's new ambassador to Spain. Wycherley's apprenticeship in diplomatic service lasted approximately one year, and by February 1665 he had returned from Spain to join the British navy in the Second Dutch War (1664–7), engaging in the June 1665 attack with the victorious Duke of York (Charles's brother, James, and successor to the throne in 1685) against Opdam, a bloody battle which Wycherley describes in an undated poem penned years later.

After his service in battle, Wycherley returned to London, but the city had changed drastically from the gay and glamorous playground he had left it: devastated by the Great Plague of 1665, much of the city was closed down, including the two patent theatres, which did not reopen until late autumn 1666, following the Great Fire that levelled almost the entire old City of London. With activities curtailed in London, Wycherley may well have spent his time pursuing his law studies, writing poetry (as did most gentlemen of this period), and consorting with gentlemen wits, such as John Wilmot, Earl of Rochester, and Charles Sackville, Earl of Dorset, two men with whom he most likely made acquaintance during the Dutch War. For the next four years Wycherley's activities are unknown, though in 1669 his first published work appeared, the poem *Hero and Leander in Burlesque*, a burlesque (a genre made popular by Samuel Butler's satirical portrait of the Puritans in *Hudibras*) parodying the two celebrated lovers in Greek legend.

In the next decade following the Restoration – specifically 1671–6 – Wycherley would pen the four plays that comprise his total output as a playwright.[2] In March 1671 at the King's Company's Theatre Royal in Bridges Street, Wycherley's first comedy, *Love in a Wood; or, St. James's Park*, enjoyed an exceptionally successful première. This initial play shows the author's familiarity with both the Spanish comedies of Calderón – a familiarity he most surely gained during his earlier stay in Madrid while attaché to Fanshawe – and the popular 1660s multiplot comedies which typically contained three lines of action: high, middle, and low. For the Fletcherian high plot of *Love in a Wood*, Calderón's untranslated intrigue play *Mañanas de abril y mayo* (1632) which features the tribulations of two heroic lovers, Ana and Juan, provided Wycherley with the primary source for the love–honour trials of his noble characters, Christina and Valentine.[3] Having duelled with and wounded an adversary who has impugned Christina's honour, Valentine is exiled to France, leaving Christina to mourn his absence by cloistering herself in her home and vowing 'to see the face of no man' until Valentine returns. To this serious high plot Wycherley grafted the more native components of wit comedy in the middle plot: the drinking and wenching recreations of Ranger, Valentine, and Dapperwit. Ranger, a 'free-ranging' libertine in love with the chaste and witty young Lydia, perpetually chases other women, in particular Christina, whom he wrongly believes is enamoured of him; Dapperwit, a vain fop and would-be wit in love with the sound of his own voice and insipid similitudes, feigns friendship with Sir Simon Addleplot in order to trick him into furthering his pursuit of Gripe's daughter, Martha, to gain her inheritance; Vincent, a plain-speaking libertine dedicated to claret and carousing, aids his friend Valentine when he returns to London and vows revenge on Ranger, whom he believes has stolen Christina from him. The Middletonian comedy in the low plot features the cullying escapades of an assortment of upper-class fools, petty crooks and wily cozeners: Lady Flippant is a lustful widow near financial ruin whose protestation against remarrying masks her avid search for a potential, wealthy husband; Alderman Gripe, Lady Flippant's brother and a wealthy, hypocritical, self-righteous city Puritan who rails against lechery but attempts to rape a young wench, Lucy, is made the victim of a blackmail scheme for his sexual advances on her; and Sir Simon Addleplot, a coxcomb, simpleton and rival to Dapperwit, disguises himself as a clerk to Alderman Gripe in order to gain access to Martha, seduce her, and then marry her for her money. At the end of the play, Valentine learns of Christina's fidelity, Ranger realises the depth of his true love for Lydia, Dapperwit marries Martha who really just wanted a husband for her unborn child, Gripe plans to wed Lucy to disinherit Martha for marrying a fool, and Lady Flippant unites with Sir Addleplot, both of whom neither loves the other nor possesses the fortune each presumes the other has.

Wycherley's first play demonstrates more than a rehash of previously successful comic forms made popular in the previous decade by Dryden, Etherege and Sedley, for *Love in a Wood* contains embryonic material for the biting social satire that he would develop more fully and sardonically in his last two plays. With a malicious tone that Wycherley would shade even darker in his final comedies, *Love in a Wood* attacks the pretences, hypocrisy and aggressiveness of coarse, selfish and unprincipled characters who cheat others for their own materialistic or carnal gain while cloaking their real motives behind a façade of respectability, friendship, and honour. In his profile of morally bankrupt individuals, Wycherley anatomises marital motives, and excluding the romantic idealism of Valentine and Christina – an idealism that surfaces in each of his comedies – his first play explores the purely mercenary or sexual impetus that forges many conjugal unions, a theme that *The Country Wife* examines even more profoundly. Many of *Love in a Wood*'s characters will resurface again in Wycherley's last two comedies, but their reincarnations will be far more brutal and disturbing as the playwright's comic critique of his society's moral vacuity grows increasingly disdainful and derisive.

Not only did *Love in a Wood* prove an instant success for both the King's Company and the fledgling playwright, it also afforded Wycherley a meteoric rise from a country gentleman of relative obscurity to an esteemed playwright earning recognition throughout London as a man of wit, and it also brought the acquaintance of Barbara Palmer, Duchess of Cleveland, one of the king's mistresses, through whom he gained personal access to the royal court. Wycherley's brief affair with the duchess introduced him to London's most elite and desirable social circle, the Court Wits, and within a short time Charles II grew to cherish Wycherley's friendship and often 'chose him for a Companion of his leisure Hours, as Augustus did Horace'.[4] In fact, Charles was so fond of Wycherley that when the playwright fell seriously ill of a fever a few years later, the king visited him at his private lodgings in Bow Street and gave him £500 for a recuperative holiday in Montpellier.

Emboldened by the success of his first comedy, encouraged by friends and fellow wits to continue his playwrighting, and perhaps eager to solidify further his reputation as a gentleman writer of appreciable literary talents, Wycherley began to craft his next play, *The Gentleman Dancing-Master*, in the winter months following his debut as a dramatist. As with his first comedy, Wycherley's second play derived in part from Calderón, specifically his *El maestro de danzar*, which features a young heroine (Leonor in Calderón's play, Hippolita in Wycherley's) who tricks her father (named Don Diego in both comedies) into allowing her suitor into his home by disguising the gallant as a dancing instructor. Less complex in structure than *Love in a Wood* with 21 scenes, 11 major characters, 10 different locales, and 3 plot lines, *The Gentleman Dancing-Master* has 6 scenes, 5 main characters, 2 locales (with all but one scene taking place in Don Diego's home), and only one well-defined main plot: Hippolita and Gerrard outwitting both Hippolita's father and her aunt. By Carolean standards, the plot is exceedingly simple. Sir James Formal, an English merchant who reveres Spanish customs and codes of honour and thus has adopted Spanish mannerisms and dress (even changing his name to Don Diego), arranges the marriage of his daughter, Hippolita, to her cousin, and to ensure her virtue and his honour until the ceremony, he imprisons her at home with her aunt, Mrs Caution, as her guard. Hippolita, an intelligent and resourceful 14-year old who possesses the maturity to understand the hazards of contemporary life but is young enough to remain uncorrupted by them, is determined not to wed her cousin, Nathaniel Parris, a Francophile fop who apes French manners, dress and language and prefers the name Monsieur de Paris. With Monsieur's unwitting assistance, Hippolita encounters the handsome town gallant Gerrard, who, per Monsieur's instructions, breaks into her home to meet her, and he is immediately attracted to Hippolita's beauty, spirit and charm, as she is likewise captivated by him. When her father returns home unannounced, he finds Gerrard and threatens to kill him, but Hippolita cleverly passes him off as a dancing master whom Monsieur has hired to instruct her. The bulk of the action revolves around Gerrard's attempts to escape and elope with Hippolita, a plan that is continually thwarted by various obstacles, including Hipppolita's own uncertainty over Gerrard's love for her rather than her fortune and the repeated intrusions of Don Diego and Mrs Caution on their private conversations. When Don Diego realises that Gerrard is not a dancing master, fighting ensues, and to quell the mêlée, Monsieur pushes Gerrard, Hippolita and the parson (whom Monsieur had brought to officiate his marriage to Hippolita) into another room. Moments later, Gerrard and Hippolita emerge and announce they have been married, and all ends happily as Don Diego promises them his entire estate.

The comparative simplicity of *The Gentleman Dancing-Master*, its repetition of similar farcical incidents throughout the action, and its absence of strikingly novel characters or scenes may account for its tepid reception by audiences at Dorset Garden, where the Duke's Company played it for only five days after its première on 6 February 1672. Although Wycherley's second play is a farce with very slight and uncomplicated intrigue, he did pack into it a critique of some of those social follies that echo through his plays: the ridiculous posturing of Don Diego and Monsieur de Paris bespeaks Wycherley's contempt for the prevailing pretences of the 'masquerading age', as Caution calls it – the 1670s when outward appearances and forms were deliberately donned and manipulated as a mask either to affect a new persona or to project an image that could fool others as to one's true nature, which was typically quite contrary to the affected external façade (see Chapter 5); and Hippolita's determination to reject the conventional and base motives for marriage and to find a loving and compatible partner with whom she can be guaranteed marital happiness reflects Wycherley's advocacy of ideal or romantic love and his abhorrence for his age's common practice of prearranged marriages, a subject he revisits with more seething contempt in his comic portrayal of Pinchwife and Margery in *The Country Wife*. Like all Wycherley's comedies, *The Gentleman Dancing-Master* explores the vanity, carnality, and hypocrisy hidden behind a false veneer of honour and respectability, a society in which the difference between appearance and reality is deliberately made indiscernible.

Within one month after the première of *The Gentleman Dancing-Master*, the Third Dutch War (1672–4) broke out, and with it came a significant change in Wycherley's life that put his playwrighting efforts on hold for over two years. In June 1672, shortly after the war's inception, Wycherley received the appointment of captain-lieutenant under his friend the Duke of Buckingham, for whom he secured and trained troops in Yorkshire. At the end of the war, he was appointed captain of the regiment in February 1674, but he resigned the post after one week's service and returned to London, taking up residence in Covent Garden's Bow Street and placing himself once again at the centre of London's theatrical and social activity.

In the following year, on 12 January 1675, the King's Company produced Wycherley's third comedy at the newly built Theatre Royal in Drury Lane. Still smarting from the poor reception of *The Gentleman Dancing-Master*, Wycherley referred to himself in his new play's prologue as 'The late so baffled scribbler', but any trepidation he may have felt due to his second comedy was quickly allayed by the immediate and spontaneous enthusiasm which greeted *The Country Wife*. Briefly, the comedy depicts the rakish Horner who feigns impotence in order to seduce married women whom he knows are willing though wary of their reputations, and Margery, a young and artless country wife who makes her first visit to London with her tyrannical, elderly husband and falls captive to Horner's sexual allure. For this comedy, Wycherley borrowed some plot devices from three sources: from Terence's *The Eunuch* he took Horner's sexual ruse; from Molière's *L'École des maris* (1661), Wycherley cribbed the foolish husband's comical complicity in his wife's adultery by serving as the unwitting courier of letters to her lover; and Molière's *L'École des femmes* (1662) provided the prototype of the overly jealous guardian whose neurosis over cuckoldom encourages him to marry a country naïf. Notwithstanding Wycherley's minor adaptations from these sources, his comedy remains completely original, and one far more lurid and savage than those sexually tepid comedies by his contemporary French counterpart. In *The Country Wife*, the farcical atmosphere evident in Wycherley's first two plays remains intact, but he yokes to it a darker, more cynical tone, and where the playwright had earlier displayed his detached amusement and mild distaste for society's hypocrites, pretenders, and tyrants and remained optimistic by crafting happy resolutions to his plays, he now reveals a palpable disdain for the excesses, falsity and self-interest of his society. In this play, farcical comedy segues into biting and acrid satire, and pessimism precludes harmonious closure or character transformations: the play's rampant adultery and subterfuge will continue *ad infinitum* long after the final curtain. Wycherley reserves his strongest indictment for marital unions based on sexual motives, financial benefit, or parental coercion, dramatising the hostility and rancour that inevitably fester in loveless marriages. Although the romantic ideal that Wycherley posits in his earlier plays finds expression through one happily united couple, *The Country Wife*'s denouement suggests that such marital concord based on mutual affection and respect is at best an anomaly in a world populated mostly by deceitful, appetitive and selfish individuals.

The following year witnessed Wycherley's fourth and last comedy, *The Plain Dealer*. Audiences at the play's première on 11 December 1676 were initially perplexed as to Wycherley's intent, but when prominent literary figures and friends of

Wycherley immediately hailed it as an excellent and instructive satire, the play gained sudden approval from theatregoers and became part of the King's Company's repertoire. The uncomplicated plot of this play contains two threads of action: Manly, a sea captain intolerant of society's hypocrisy and immorality, has just returned to London to reclaim his fiancée, Olivia, and the fortune he entrusted to her care, only to find that she has taken his money and married his friend; in the second plot line, Freeman, Manly's lieutenant, attempts to trick a litigious widow devoted only to her money into marrying him so that he can acquire her wealth. After getting his revenge on Olivia, Manly is united with Fidelia, a young lady who, driven by her love for Manly, had disguised herself as a cabin boy and followed him to sea, while Freeman blackmails the widow for her attempt to commit perjury, forcing her to clear his debts and pay him a hefty annuity. In crafting this play, Wycherley culled from more sources than for any of his other comedies – six sources to be exact – but most obvious are his borrowing from Shakespeare's *Twelfth Night* with Manly's (Orsino's) use of the disguised Fidelia (Viola) to court Olivia on his behalf and Olivia's sexual attraction to Fidelia, and his liberal use of Molière's *The Misanthrope* (1666) with Manly's (Alceste's) bitter vilification and renunciation of all society as well as Olivia's (Celimène's) preference for the pleasures of that society.[5]

In this final play, as with his earlier appropriation of dramatic sources, Wycherley shapes his borrowed materials into a wholly new finished product that is unquestionably unique and unmistakably his own creation. In *The Plain Dealer*, Wycherley takes his invective one step further by widening and darkening his attack on English society. Where his previous plays, most especially *The Country Wife*, had brilliantly merged social commentary with farce to create a frothy though serious satire on a small section of society corrupted by specific social conventions, *The Plain Dealer* offers a much broader canvas that paints all individuals in society as willing and eager accomplices in a hypocritical, corrupt and evil world. Wycherley's earlier risible indictments of a few fools who capitulate to social follies and forms have been extended into a harsher attack on the world at large populated by unattractive and malicious individuals, and although he offers a glimmer of hope via the romantic ideal of Fidelia, Manly's fifth-act posture that all of society, despite his new friendship with Freeman and love for Fidelia, remains 'odious' to him presages not only the hero's refusal to accept his lot as a member of society but also society's unlikelihood of forging a more harmonious, civil, and unselfish existence.

After the enormous successes of *The Country Wife* and *The Plain Dealer*, Wycherley's fortunes declined precipitously. In the summer of 1678, he became seriously ill of a fever which kept him bedridden for months. With Charles II's financial assistance, Wycherley travelled to France in the winter of 1678 to regain his health, and although the following spring he returned to London with restored physical vigour, the fever, perhaps encephalitis, had apparently left him mentally impaired, for acquaintances commented on his diminished mental agility and loss of memory, a debilitating condition from which he never recovered fully. At the age of 47, Wycherley's literary career was virtually over. While he did write poetry in his later years, his inability to connect thoughts and develop ideas for an extended period rendered his poems banal, rambling, and tautological. He never again tried his hand at playwrighting.

Just as Wycherley's health took a dramatic downward spiral, so, too, did his financial situation decline, leaving him in a continual state of penury from which he could likewise never escape. Shortly after his return from Montpellier, Wycherley received an invitation from Charles II to tutor his illegitimate son, the seven-year-old Duke of Richmond, for an exceedingly generous yearly salary of £1500 plus a handsome annuity (in perpetuity) when his tutelage ceased. Before taking up his new post, Wycherley travelled to Tunbridge Wells where he met the young and beautiful Lady Laetitia-Isabella, Countess of Drogheda, courted her and married her, all without consulting the king. When Charles learned of the marriage, he was not amused: perhaps deeming Wycherley's marital commitments as impediments to his full-time obligations as tutor, or regarding Wycherley's marriage to a woman of nobility as a breach of protocol for which he should have at the very least sought royal consent, the king, offended by Wycherley's seemingly cavalier disregard either for his generous offer or for his royal prerogative, immediately withdrew the position and severed all ties with Wycherley. Regrettably, Wycherley had no idea at this time that the financial benefits from Charles's offer would have saved him from the ignoble fate that awaited him in three years when heavy debts – his own as well as those from the estate of his wife, who died in 1681 – would land him in a debtors' prison. In 1682, Wycherley, in dire financial straits, attempted to regain the king's favour by writing an epistle to him claiming his outrage at the attacks levelled against Charles because of his refusal to capitulate to Parliament's Exclusion Bill that would have prevented his Catholic brother, James, from succeeding him to the throne. Wycherley received no response from Charles, and although he did borrow money from a few wealthy friends, he was unable to raise the near £1590 owed to creditors and was sent first to Newgate Prison and later transferred to The Fleet prison, where he remained for four years.

Following Charles's death on 6 February 1685, James II ascended the throne, and later that autumn Wycherley made an indirect appeal to his old acquaintance and James's newly appointed Lord Chamberlain, John Sheffield (Earl of Mulgrave), for some form of assistance. On 14 December 1685, *The Plain Dealer* received a special performance at Whitehall, which prompted James to complain of Wycherley's long absence from court and to inquire about his welfare. Upon learning of Wycherley's imprisonment, the king ordered his debts to be paid, and when Wycherley was released from The Fleet the following spring, James II granted him a £200 pension. Wycherley, as a gesture of gratitude for James's generosity, reconverted once again to Catholicism. Unfortunately, when the Glorious Revolution of 1688 forced James II from England to clear the throne for his Protestant successors – his daughter Mary and her husband William of Orange – his generous annuity to Wycherley ended.

Wycherley's release from debtors' prison did not free him from continual financial worry, for having misrepresented his total debts to James as only £500, no doubt out of embarrassment, he was again plagued by his old creditors, and he also had to resume his battle with litigators against his deceased wife's estate. Lacking James's pension or any other means of support, Wycherley had to rely on his father for financial assistance, which he received for nine years until 1697 when Daniel Wycherley died. Although William was Daniel's eldest son, his father, keen to bequeath the family estate to heirs who could provide progeny to carry on the Wycherley name and probably equally reluctant to leave his estate to a son he regarded as a profligate, willed his

property to one of William's nephews (son of his deceased brother, John), leaving William £1000 to pay off his creditors and only
a fixed income from the family estate in Shropshire, a modest
annual sum of approximately £200 that enabled him to live com-
fortably but was not sufficient to keep him permanently out of
debt. When William appealed to his nephew to sell or mortgage
some of the properties to help him financially, his nephew
refused, and once again Wycherley had a brief stay in prison in
1715 when he was sued by a former servant for £30 in unpaid
wages. Rescuing the 74-year-old Wycherley from debtors' prison,
his cousin, Captain Thomas Shrimpton, was a thoroughly
unscrupulous man who probably convinced Wycherley to get his
revenge on his callous nephew by marrying a young woman who
would, according to the terms of Daniel Wycherley's will, be enti-
tled to a hefty annual jointure on the Wycherley estate, a jointure
that would also enable William to pay off the debts that deeply
concerned him. Shrimpton introduced the ailing and infirm
Wycherley to Elizabeth Jackson, and on 20 December 1715 they
were quickly married. Eleven days later, on New Year's Eve,
William Wycherley died, and shortly after her husband's death,
Elizabeth married her lover, Shrimpton – a series of calculated
events that read like a mercenary-marriage subplot right out of
Restoration comedy, and one which would have greatly amused
Wycherley.

Although Wycherley spent his later years subsequent to his
release from The Fleet in the 1680s embroiled in law suits over the
estates of both his wife and his immediate family and struggling
to ward off debt, he always managed to stay in good spirits, keeping himself pleasantly entertained by occasionally writing poetry
and visiting with familiar companions at Will's Coffeehouse,
where he was accepted as a leading figure among the distinguished wits, reigning poets, and aspiring writers who congregated to discuss literature and the arts. His old circle of friends had
diminished considerably – Buckingham, Dorset, Dryden, Sedley,
Etherege and many others had predeceased him – but at Will's,
Wycherley made new literary acquaintances, William Congreve,
John Vanbrugh, Thomas Southerne and Nicolas Rowe among
them, and he no doubt spent many convivial evenings with them
discussing the new collection of poems that he had been crafting.
Following a protracted delay, Wycherley's *Miscellany Poems*

finally appeared to a tepid reception in 1704, the same year he met the 16-year-old Alexander Pope, whose reverence for Wycherley was matched by the playwright's esteem for the young poet's talents, an esteem that Wycherley demonstrated by introducing his young admirer to London's most influential writers and critics, which proved instrumental in securing the publication of Pope's early poetry. Over the years, their friendship deepened, and in 1706 Wycherley asked Pope to correct and finesse the newest volumes of poems and epistles that he wished to have published. Pope agreed, and he spent years working with Wycherley to reshape the playwright's dull and repetitious writings into acceptable verse, never, of course, showing his exasperation or offending his elderly companion to whom he felt indebted. Four years later, after Pope's repeated but tactful criticisms of the many tautologies and solecisms in his poetry, Wycherley, without taking offence, asked Pope to return his manuscript pages and ended their collaboration, though not their friendship. Thirteen years after his death, Wycherley's last volume of poems finally appeared in print, first through Lewis Theobald, who acquired Wycherley's papers from Shrimpton and had them published under the title *Posthumous Works*, and in the following year, 1729, through Alexander Pope, who oversaw the production of his edited volume, *The Posthumous Works of William Wycherley*.

Clearly, Wycherley's poetry has been long forgotten, and justifiably so, but his plays have endured as examples of the finest comedies of the early Restoration. Wycherley, along with Etherege and Congreve, forms the canonical triumvirate of Restoration comedy, and he carved out his place between Etherege (c1636–92), the complacent sceptic who crafted the first significant comedy of manners, and Congreve (1670–1729), the restrained pragmatist who brought comedy of manners to its apogee, by serving as a satirist of the very society Etherege and Congreve depicted in their coruscant portrayals of the *beau monde*'s sophistication, polish, breeding and glamour – that is, striking a compromise between manners comedy and social satire by focusing on the fashionable world with its pretences and modes of behaviour while probing well beneath the layers of its artifice to reveal the unpleasant and inglorious human nature that actually lies beneath the deceptively attractive façade of social conventions and decorum. While Etherege sought to dramatise the surface details of carefree, elegant and witty individuals obsessed with conforming to the current mode and manners, in turn eliciting audiences' admiration for many of his characters' artful mastering of a world besotted by masquerading, Wycherley wished to expose the extremes of human follies and vices hidden behind the mask of false motives or feigned appearances – exaggerated misanthropy, greed, aggression, lechery, vanity, affectation, hypocrisy – through a wide range of characters who evoke not sympathy or approval but sardonic laughter. In his own day, Wycherley was lauded as a supreme moralist and satirist, and his mastery of satire over that by any rival playwright stemmed from his adroit avoidance of didacticism. Wycherley does not preach – he establishes characters who illustrate specific vices or extremes and allows them, by their own attitudes, eccentricities, stupidity, or blindness, to fall victim to absurd or outrageous situations of their own making: they are the architects of their own ridiculous dilemmas. And it is the absurdity of the situations into which the characters inevitably and unwittingly place themselves that evokes the heartiest amusement and laughter.

Relying on humour through character and farcical situations rather than witty exchanges, Wycherley deploys language quite differently from Etherege. Having no interest in exploring the sexual attraction and antagonism of the gay couple or demonstrating the linguistic finesse of the libertine world, Wycherley uses little of the witty badinage typical of manners comedy, and although he could craft a clever turn of phrase to be savoured or quoted by spectators, he lacked the poetic skill to write sustained and sparkling repartee. Rather, his dialogue bristles with snippets of aphorisms, similes, double entendres, and sexual innuendo, and he uses bold, blunt and vigorous language that reveals (rather than conceals, as with Etherege) the inner nature of each character and precisely suits the character's temperament: Pinchwife's vituperative allusions to disease and pain, Lady Fidget's crafty perversion of words such as honour, and Manly's violent images of animals and sex are cases in point.[6] For Etherege, speech and wit are the 'mode' or 'manner' which characters adopt to signify their sophistication and superiority, but Wycherley reserves wit for exposing the falsity behind the veneer of manners and social convention, unmasking characters to reveal the differences between outer appearances and true identities, and ultimately showing the characters' profound and unsavoury deviation from the ideal presumed to be embodied in the superficial niceties of social discourse and decorum.

Wycherley's comic world – alternately shocking, ironic, theatrical, aggressive, and farcical – depicts an unpleasant place populated by selfish, cruel and appetitive individuals who seldom undergo any significant metamorphosis or experience life-altering epiphanies. Using one-dimensional characters emblematic of specific attitudes, emotions or motives, Wycherley positions each to be read against the other in order to reveal the thematic focus of his social criticism. And within his astringent, satiric social commentary, rarely does any character escape Wycherley's comic attack, even his ostensible heroes: from the libertine, businessman and parent to the lawyer, politician and sea captain, most characters engage in some form of duplicity, anti-social behaviour, or immoral activity that deliberately exploits or harms others and contributes to the overall ugliness of the world and its moral decay. Unlike a number of his contemporary comic dramatists, Wycherley was not morally neutral to the affectations, dishonesty and corruption of the *beau monde*, but he did, however, write with sufficient detachment as to fill his plays with ambiguities that continue to plague critics who attempt to find definitive character interpretations or singular thematic messages. Although he affords no clear-cut, ideational stance from which to judge his comic characters, satirical invectives, or moral indictments – leaving each spectator to fill in the gaps on his own, based on his own ethical viewpoint – Wycherley did provide the most satirical and harshest view of Carolean society, and it was his perspective and dramaturgy, not Etherege's, that formed the legacy to later seventeenth-century drama in the emotionalism and nihilism portrayed by playwrights such Thomas Otway, Nathaniel Lee, and Thomas Southerne.

As the foremost Carolean satirist among a group of comic playwrights otherwise committed to mirthful dramatisations of the superficies inherent in the cultural ethos that enveloped the seventeenth-century leisure class, Wycherley has been isolated as an atypical figure in this cadre of writers. His acrid and derisive satires have led some critics to appropriate to him traits belonging to such characters as the callous libertine Horner or the surly misanthrope Manly, whose abusive attacks on society have been interpreted as the playwright's true sentiments. Fuelling this argument is Wycherley's willing acceptance of the soubriquet 'manly Wycherley' from such contemporaries as Dryden, Rochester, Congreve and Pope, as well as his own use of the appellation 'the Plain Dealer' in the preface to his *Miscellany Poems*. However, by all accounts from those who knew him well, Wycherley bore no close resemblance to any of his outspoken and idiosyncratic characters, nor did he harbour a Puritan loathing for society's mores. Like all the young gentlemen of the day, Wycherley subscribed to the tenets of libertinism, scepticism, and rationalism, as his poems clearly attest, and although biographers have no anecdotal evidence of his debauched and reckless behaviour – as they do for Etherege, Rochester and Sedley – Wycherley's close companionship with such notorious rakes suggests that he embodied the same spirit and embraced the same *carpe diem* philosophy as they did.

Compared to the extrovert Etherege, Wycherley was reserved, a handsome and statuesque gentleman who never spoke ill of friends and thought it distasteful and disloyal to do so. Long-time companions held Wycherley in high esteem, particularly for his civility, good nature, affability, and loyalty. George Granville (Lord Landsdowne), characterised him as 'The best good man, with the worst-natur'd muse' who 'has all the softness of the tenderest disposition; gentle and inoffensive to every man in his particular character',[7] and many others who limned his traits echoed Granville's assessment. Wycherley, always cordial to all those he met, enjoyed lively conversations but 'would never be wiser than his company', and this gentleman, who possessed 'a Wit sprightly, entertaining, and inoffensive', was 'a valuable companion, and a sincere friend'[8] to many: on more than one occasion, he demonstrated his sincere spirit of generosity and loyalty, mentoring Pope in his early career, supporting Buckingham after his imprisonment in the Tower without concern for royal backlash, and soliciting financial support for impoverished friends. Wycherley's congenial nature never flagged, not even in those years of dire financial difficulty, and during his long stay in The Fleet prison, he never cavilled over his predicament, though he did offer a characteristic quip when he noted in a letter written while imprisoned that his greatest disappointment was having to lose so many new acquaintances to the gallows.

Wycherley was a man of substantial wit and tolerance who derived enormous amusement from the world as he saw it. In his dramatic critiques of society, he unveils the comic absurdity of attempting to live as a social being in a world where conventions mandated deceitful behaviour: private desires versus public form and social conformity. And individuals who attempted to pretend to the civility of society while satisfying their personal needs without discovery – and often without concern for the consequences or the harm done to others – afforded Wycherley a mixture of laughter and disdain, as well as a wealth of comic material ripe for his unique brand of satire.

7
The Country Wife:
Love, Marriage and Sovereignty

No Carolean comedy has garnered such a range of critical opinion, some of which borders on moral indignation, for its prurient content as Wycherley's acknowledged masterpiece, *The Country Wife*. Premièring at Drury Lane in January 1675, just one year prior to Etherege's *The Man of Mode* and during the height of Carolean drama's heavy proliferation of 'sex comedies' in the 1670s, Wycherley's mordant play, which features not only a salacious libertine hero, aptly named Horner, who has deliberately spread the false rumour that he has suffered irreversible impotence after a botched operation for the pox so that he can seduce the willing wives of gullible and unwitting husbands, but also a host of equally libidinous and compliant women whose raw appetites for physical passion far exceed the boundaries of acceptable female propriety, has been labelled everything from 'the most bestial play in all literature',[1] an Ibsenite portrait of contemporary society, an exposé of male homosocial bonding, an attack on Hobbesian self-interest, a romping and innocuous comedy, an indictment against the age's moral turpitude, a dramatised exegesis of masculinity, to anything else that falls in between the polarities of harmless farce and biting satire.[2]

While these twentieth-century interpretations are based in modern critical theory very much removed from seventeenth-century aesthetics and phenomenology, they nonetheless do suggest the gamut of possible responses from Carolean spectators, for late seventeenth-century theatregoers, like those today, were not so homogeneous – notwithstanding the court-based contingent – as to react singularly and uniformly as a collective group. As Rothstein and Kavenick have suggested in their polysemic readings of Carolean drama, those comedies of the 1670s with their open-ended resolutions and ambiguous main characters – especially the unrepentant rake heroes who continue to threaten society's moral code well after the fifth act – appear to offer no overriding thematic significance (other than perhaps nihilism), and this significant break from expected orthodoxy and traditional comic dramaturgy inevitably fostered 'different provisional images to different members of the same audience'.[3] Thus, some spectators enjoyed living vicariously and painlessly through Horner's sexual athleticism and gauged their masculinity vis-à-vis his successful seductions, others – specifically some of the female 'citizens' who now began to frequent the playhouses – certainly identified in part with the unhappy and mercenary marriage of Lady Fidget and recalled their own fantasies or realities of adulterous liaisons, while even a few young women living under the tyranny of a loveless and abusive husband cheered silently for Margery's emotional rebellion and awakening. Depending on where they sat figuratively, each spectator entered into his own 'compromise formation', as Rothstein and Kavenik call it, responding to Wycherley's group of dysfunctional individuals, who seek to use one another for personal gain or carnal pleasure, with varying degrees of engagement and detachment, and no doubt with occasional empathy.

Although no precise account of Carolean audiences' reaction to *The Country Wife* can be reconstructed with any degree of exactness, theatregoers in the main responded to it with shock and approval, for extant (albeit scarce) theatre records indicate that the comedy enjoyed a regular place on the Restoration stage and retained its popularity well into the mid-eighteenth century. Even after suffering a hiatus of some 150 years during the comparatively staid decades of the late eighteenth and entire nineteenth centuries, Wycherley's hard-hitting, ribald satire re-entered the repertory where it has remained the most produced and studied play in the Restoration canon. Its enduring popularity can be attributed to its frothy and wildly comic situations in which fatuous characters – that is, most of the men – become the architects of their own well-deserved undoing, as well as its proliferation of droll and often lewd double entendres – such as those in the infamous 'china' scene – which underscore the patent stupidity of laughable and pathetic dupes. However, while idiotic buffoons, risqué allusions, and sexual escapades verging on the indecent provide sufficient lures for patrons, these ingredients alone do not completely account for *The Country Wife*'s pervasive attraction to theatregoers. Wycherley's comedy provides a unique admixture of graphic sexual farce that evokes the audiences' laughter (sometimes in spite of themselves) and sardonic frankness that concomitantly startles the viewers and elicits their engagement. The play's humour is savage and unremitting, and while its candid and shocking glimpse at marriage and the dicey subject of adultery makes some spectators uncomfortable, the heightened farcical elements leaven the performance experience and keep theatregoers – some, perhaps, with their mouths wide open – focused on the fast-paced action and vulgar innuendoes. Simply put, the play makes audiences laugh at sex – not romantic sex but gratuitous sex (e.g., procured quickly with a lover as one's clueless spouse is on the other side of a locked door) – and loveless, mechanical copulation is, as portrayed by a master like Wycherley, embarrassingly titillating, brutally honest, and inherently disquieting. The play's action both entices and disturbs spectators, and whether one views it as a misogynist tract against female sexual liberation, a harmless fable, or an obscenely dirty joke, *The Country Wife* generates strong reactions from theatregoers: it leaves no one ambivalent, for few can remain indifferent to a play that deals so boldly and derisively with sexual impropriety and the repudiation of conventional morality.

As representative of the darker comedies of the 1670s – cynical comedies, as John Harrington Smith labelled them[4] – *The Country Wife* dramatises the era's most sceptical attitudes toward love, marriage and sex. Unlike the Carolean comedies of the 1660s – such as the earlier plays of both Etherege and Wycherley – which featured the obligatory 'gay couple' whose mutual antagonism-cum-attraction provided the requisite dose of benign sexual energy that resolved itself happily in romantic love and consensual marriage between the subversive libertine and inviolable heroine, comedies of the 1670s featured a preponderance of lecherous men and married women who opted for dispassionate and illicit sex and denigrated marriage altogether. This radical shift in attitude toward the sanctity of marriage presented in the plays of this period mirrored the prevailing anxieties among society at large, a change in perspective that took well over a decade to evolve and whose roots lie in the socio-political conditions during the Interregnum as well as the subsequent realities of a promised 'restoration' that never fully materialised.

During the seventeenth century, conventional attitudes about marriage were being debated seriously as a result of the Civil Marriage Act of 1653 which, by removing the jurisdiction of marriage from the ecclesiastical courts to the state, had redefined marriage not as a sacramental bond per se but more a civil contract between partners. This secularisation of marriage contributed inevitably to a challenge against the entrenched analogy between monarch–subject and husband–wife that had granted and validated complete familial sovereignty to the male and had relegated women to the mandatory role of a loyal subservient, one whose treasonous acts against her spouse, like those by any against the government, could be punishable by death. Although Charles overturned the Interregnum laws, the residual effects of this legislation were palpable: a radically new concept of women as less the obedient subjects of their husbands and more as free agents in their own right burgeoned, and with it an onslaught of published debates in the form of broadsides arguing the pros and cons of absolute patriarchal power and privilege. Of course, seventeenth-century women never enjoyed the exact rights and laws accorded men – in fact, the horrific practice of burning women at the stake for criminal offences against their husbands (specifically for murder, and even in those cases of self-defence) continued during the Restoration – but the controversy over male sovereignty within marriage, as well as the value of marriage itself, lasted for decades and manifested itself in a flurry of pamphlets, culminating many years after the polemic began with Mary Astell's *Some Reflections upon Marriage* (1696), in which the author argues cogently and tactfully against the divine right of kings and husbands.[5]

Contributing equally to the erosion of conventional views of marital relationships was, of course, the monarch himself, for Charles II's reign was characterised by a high level of infamous duplicity in both political and personal matters – not the least of which were his multiple, notorious affairs and 14 illegitimate children – that diminished the value and credibility of sacred oaths and vows made to loyal subjects to nothing more than meaningless and empty promises (see Chapter 1). Most significantly, Charles's maladminstration and negligence engendered the erosion of all hope that had been held by everyone in May 1660 for the promised changes that would reconstitute those political, social and ideological beliefs that had forged Britain's pre-Interregnum national identity, and this loss of confidence and sanguinity in the return of the earlier ideals and myths generated a level of cynicism that was conveyed obliquely in much of the literature of the 1670s, including dramas. Indeed, just as the comedies of the 1660s mediated the high level of public optimism in Charles's ability to orchestrate imminently a level of stability, unity and trust out of the chaos that preceded him, so too did the comedies of the next decade reinscribe the pervasive disillusionment generated by the unlikelihood of such a complete national recovery. Using the marital state as a metaphor of the envisaged national harmony that Charles would effect, those early Carolean comedies depicted transgressive libertines whose anarchy against all conventional values and morals initially threatened the social order, but whose ultimate fifth-act acceptance of marriage symbolised the reinstatement of peace, concord and stability. By the 1670s, marital relationships in the comedies were dominated by characters, like embittered subjects to a seemingly disloyal and detached king, whose scepticism and disenchantment over matrimony bespoke the general malaise and dissatisfaction with the current state of Britain's restoration, and their want of fidelity, trust, and affection toward their mates, as well as their illicit sexual liaisons, signalled a covert rebellion against a bond that neither party found tenable. As Susan Staves notes, Charles had not only failed to bring about the restoration of the old myths and ideas embodied in Caroline England, he also failed to provide new and viable myths that would galvanise his subjects and unify his country.[6] Not surprisingly, the marital plots' formulaic denouement used by comic playwrights in the 1660s seemed invalid over a decade later in part because Charles offered no ersatz myth that augured a happy resolution, and the ambiguous and open-ended conclusions that proliferated in the 1670s 'cynical' comedies reflected the continual uncertainty and insecurity over Britain's future, intimating that chaos still reigned and that any possibility of a harmonious closure was perhaps within reach but not yet fully realised.[7] Wycherley's comedy concludes on such an unresolved note.

Thus, when Wycherley penned *The Country Wife*, marriage as both a sacred institution and a metaphor for the body politic had undergone considerable perceptual changes, and many Carolean playwrights reified these altered attitudes in their plays, anatomising the state of matrimony and sussing out those pathologies – both cultural and individual – that led to isolation, bitterness and betrayal in a sacred union – whether personal or political – that was meant to provide emotional well-being, personal security and lifelong succour. Understandably, these acerbic portraits of marriage can be misinterpreted easily as blanket denouncements of matrimony by the playwrights and the public at large in preference for the more naturalistic state of sexual freedom which the marital state precludes for both sexes. However, neither Wycherley nor other playwrights advocated the abolition of marriage, for at the very least patriarchal and patrilineal cultures depend on legitimate wedlock for their own self-perpetuation and survival, and there is no practical alternative that can guarantee the permanent cultural inscription of this sacred status quo or, perhaps equally important, accommodate romantic love and sexual attraction.[8] Wycherley, like many of his fellow dramatists writing in all the popular genres, focused his attack not on conjugal life in general but rather on the socially accepted practices and attitudes regarding matrimony that destroyed the spirit, fostered enmity, and negated personal happiness. Emboldened by the current changes in attitudes about the condition of marriage within his patriarchal culture and the unsettled status of the state, as well as the prevailing licence with stage decorum, Wycherley crafted a bawdy, spirited and acrid satire that exposed his era's most egregious violations against the most sacrosanct of human bonds.

Each of the three plots in *The Country Wife* explores different stages of marital relationships to reveal the discord that develops when matrimony is based on factors other than mutual respect and reciprocal, selfless love: the relatively established marriage between Sir Jaspar and Lady Fidget exposes the acrimony and distrust that must eventually evolve in a relationship built solely on mercenary motives; the newlyweds Pinchwife and Margery vivify the jealousy, brutality and betrayal that erupt quite early on when men procure wives for their own sexual pleasure alone; and the betrothed Sparkish and Alithea signify a caveat against marriage based on external appearances and social convention only. That Wycherley intentionally has all three couples reside in different geographic areas – the Fidgets from the city where London's commercial district lies, the Pinchwifes from the country which typically represents bucolic serenity and guilelessness, and Sparkish and Alithea from the town where elegance and sophistication reign – suggests that these disastrous marriages cut across all boundary lines when individuals marry for personal concupiscence, self-aggrandisement and monetary gain.

The latter point – financial motives – is the most crucial, for it provides one of the significant common denominators that links all three couples and the one which Wycherley found especially distasteful and ruinous. Sir Jaspar and Lady Fidget, though it is not stated directly through the dialogue but only implied, are bound in matrimony by their mutal lust for wealth; Sir Jaspar cares only about business profits and his wife likewise worships money, for though disgusted by Horner's alleged sexual mishap (that is, until she learns the truth), Lady Fidget agrees to play ombre with him only after her husband guarantees her she'll win a tidy sum ('Then I am contented to make him pay for his scurrility; money makes up in a measure all other wants in men' [II,i,567–9]). Pinchwife secured Margery not with her approval but by her parents' consent, and his preference for a naïve wife springs from his desire to eschew paying for mistresses who continue to abandon him; summing his pathetic dilemma, he admits to Horner 'A pox on't! The jades would jilt me; I could never keep a whore to myself' (I,i,510–11). Horner's astute observation, 'So, then you only married to keep a whore to yourself' (I,i,512–13), conveys the nature of Pinchwife's relationship with his wife: a loveless marriage in which Margery is a sexual object whose services are accessible on demand and free of charge – it's a simple matter of economics and sex. Sparkish wants to marry Alithea solely for the £5000 dowry that her brother, Pinchwife, intends to pay him; when he breaks off their betrothal, he admits to her 'I never had any passion for you till now, for now I hate you. 'Tis true I might have married you for your portion, as other men of parts of the town do sometimes' (V,iii,75–8). Although Wycherley detested marriages based on any motive other than genuine affection – as demonstrated in his previous comedy, *The Gentleman Dancing-Master* (1672), which featured the plight of a heroine who outwits her tyrannical father and the unacceptable suitor he intends her to marry – he inveighed particularly against those nuptials that put economic desires above all other considerations, a constant refrain in many of his *Miscellany Poems*, such as 'To a Rich, Mercenary, Matrimonial Mistress', and 'The Poor Lover to His Rich Mistress, about to Marry His Coxcombly Rival'. Financially motivated marriages were, unfortunately, commonplace during the Restoration as upper-class families sought to repair or recuperate their estates seized or depleted during the Interregnum by the expedient method of forcing children to marry wealthy partners. Comic playwrights such as Wycherley took aim against this approach to matrimonial matches which, as P. F. Vernon notes, became 'a family business matter on which more depended than the domestic happiness of two individuals'.[9] No longer a sacred oath binding two people in love, marriage was purely an economic contract, one that could be entered into at will for reasons of survival and material gain or one that could be foisted on incompatible and reluctant individuals; in either case, the end result was nonetheless the same: unhappily married couples whose natural reactions to their detached and dispassionate mates fostered a high degree of contempt and repulsion that led either to misery and suffocation or to treason through adultery – the very options Wycherley's female characters face at the hands of their tyrannical or indifferent male sovereigns.

Atypical of most Restoration plays which featured sexual rebellion on the part of married women and demanded, for propriety's sake, that the adulteresses endure some form of humiliating abuse or punishment in order to eradicate their threat to prevailing sexual politics and reinforce patriarchy's desideratum of female virtue, *The Country Wife* deliberately breaks with such dramatic protocol by presenting a title character who, despite her sexual transgression, remains sympathetic until the final curtain. Similarly, the 'virtuous gang' – Lady Fidget and her cohorts, who speak boldly of their spouses' sexual incompetence and seek physical pleasure outside their marriages – receive no comeuppance at the end of the play and will no doubt continue their use of Horner until they grow bored with his services. Certainly, Wycherley was neither championing women's rights nor advocating adultery, but he did, however, examine male–female relationships in marriage through a lens that viewed husbands as the oppressors – exerting their sovereign and legal rights over their subjects by dictating all aspects of their lives, restricting their personal freedom, negating their human spirit, and, when necessary, even confining them under lock and key – and the wives as rebels who resist the tyranny that attempts to reduce them to meaningless chattels and insensible objects. That the women's rebellion manifests itself in adultery is not, in and of itself, anomalous, for such plots dominate Carolean and later Restoration comedy, and these story lines do, after all, make for good comic material in a patriarchal society where men relegate women to the role of sexual objects only, then contradictorily fault and denigrate them for their sexual power, and finally suffer considerable and unrelieved anxiety (and ironically blame women for that anxiety) over female freedom within the very sexual realm to which they have deliberately confined them. In *The Country Wife* all the abject fools are men – the comic victims of a sexual ethos that they constructed for their own masculine prerogatives, but preserving that arbitrary ethos requires constant vigil to ensure the containment of a very fragile power structure that is always on the verge of collapse at the hands of those whom it oppresses. Hence, surveillance by castrated chaperones or forced house-arrest seem like reasonable solutions to the tyrannical, but when that chaperone proves no eunuch and incarceration can be cleverly circumvented, audience laughter is aimed at the idiots who devised their own undoing by tenaciously holding onto a flawed system of their own making, and the audience's pure delight, though perhaps not its wholesale approval, is given over to the anarchists who exact their revenge by hitting their oppressors where it most hurts.

Of the three marital relationships depicted by Wycherley, that between Sir Jaspar and Lady Fidget paints the most disturbing portrait of the emotional rancour that provides the breeding ground for betrayal and revenge. Unlike Pinchwife and Margery, who make no pretences to sublime happiness and compatibility and who present a disturbing picture of tyranny from a physical perspective, Sir Jaspar's and Lady Fidget's comparatively long-standing union depicts beneath the surface of an ostensibly respectable and civilised marriage the alienation and contempt that constitute the emotional damage brought on by neglect and subordination.

Lady Fidget's loveless marriage to Sir Jaspar stems in part from her husband's exclusive interest in money over all else. As representative of the new entrepreneur whose middle-class wealth was beginning to eclipse that of the leisure class, Sir Jaspar has sublimated all his passion in his business dealings, leaving him with little time or interest in a wife whom he regards as an impediment to his obsession for acquiring money. His primary concern for his wife is to provide her the illusion of male companionship by finding her a safe chaperone to accompany her at the playhouse and other harmless diversions and thus free his time to pursue his singular pleasure in business ventures ('I go to my pleasure, business' [II,i,674–5]), and he makes his priorities between companionship with his wife and men of business clear when he tells Horner to keep the secret that he missed his promised appointment with Lady Fidget because he was at Whitehall, 'advancing a certain project to His Majesty' (III,ii,641–20). Although Sir Jaspar's civility precludes imprisoning and brutalising his wife, he cares nothing about her personal happiness and wishes only to find a foolproof and expedient way of preventing her from dishonouring him without any effort or emotional investment on his part. To a man for whom 'Business must be preferred always before love and ceremony' (I,i,133–5) and who displays only indifference toward his mate, rebellion from a neglected and unhappy wife is inevitable.

That Wycherley has no sympathy for Sir Jaspar, this avatar of the new, bourgeois businessman motivated solely by greed and consumed with his own self-importance, is evident in the famous 'china scene' where Wycherley makes him an unwitting accomplice and witness to his own cuckoldry. Entering Horner's lodgings through the downstage left proscenium door, Sir Jaspar finds his wife and Horner standing on the forestage, locked in an embrace. Startled at first, he believes Lady Fidget's absurd explanation that she sought out Horner's assistance in purchasing some china. Pleased to see his wife helping herself to some of Horner's china – a highly valuable commodity – he not only allows her to exit through the downstage right proscenium door (locking it behind her) ostensibly to search for Horner's stash, he stands idly by as Horner pursues Lady Fidget by way of the upstage right door, moving to the locked door and shouting out a warning riddled with sexual innuendo that clearly escapes him: 'He is coming into you the back way' (IV,iii,144–5). When Lady Squeamish enters at left and insists that Sir Jaspar break down the door, he refuses, for he interprets the noises and moans from behind it as nothing more than his wife's struggle to wrestle from Horner a free piece of china. With hair and clothes dishevelled, Horner and Lady Fidget finally exit from the locked room, the latter carrying the sought-after piece of china. Delighted that Lady Fidget got what she had been struggling for, Sir Jaspar stands smiling and smug, completely oblivious to the series of double entrendres at his expense as both Horner and Lady Fidget discuss their sexual liaison with ironic references to Horner's depleted collection of china. Squeamish catches on to the ruse, pressing Horner for her fair share as well, leaving Sir Jaspar in the middle of the group, grinning like a comic butt whose thorough self-centredness and stupidity warranted Lady Fidget's flagrant and unabashed abuse of him.

Lady Fidget's treasonous act against her uninterested husband seldom garners extended critical analysis, for scholars must perforce acknowledge her adultery as the ineluctable consequence of Sir Jaspar's maltreatment. Thus, having been acquitted of sole culpability for her sexual escapades, Lady Fidget is typically censured for other transgressions that some regard as Wycherley's primary intended targets for satire and commentary: female hypocrisy and pretence to honour. Without question, Lady Fidget and her companions are, as Horner defines them, 'pretenders to honour, as critics to wit, only by censuring others' (II,i,495–6). Her repeated references to her precious honour are attempts to mask her true lascivious inclinations, and her hypocrisy shines through her façade each time she mentions the word, which she does with such regularity as to divest it of its literal meaning and render her ridiculous. Her husband, no doubt tiring of hearing the word from her, tells her she has 'so much honour in thy mouth', to which Horner quips in an aside, 'That she has none elsewhere' (II,i, 464–6). When Lady Fidget later learns the truth of Horner's ruse, she intimates that her interpretation of honour actually has little connexion to her virtue: 'could you be so generous, so truly a man of honour, as for the sakes of us women of honour, to cause yourself to be reported no man?' (II,i,624–6). Her continual skewing of words such as honour in order to create new connotations – for example, she tells Horner with sexual innuendo, 'I have so strong a faith in your honour, dear, dear, noble sir, that I'd forfeit mine for yours at any time' (II,i,641–3) – allows her to preserve the image for others as well as herself that she is indeed a woman of moral righteousness. Such repeated corruptions of language serve her own solipsistic needs: Lady Fidget, by her very manipulation of words and their meaning, redefines and justifies her adulterous affairs, thereby reducing them to minor indiscretions that have not compromised her virtue. Ultimately, Lady Fidget validates Horner's hypothesis that such 'women of quality' who profess their eternal allegiance to honour 'are only chary of their reputations, not their persons, and 'tis scandal they would avoid, not men' (I,i,192–4).

Reputation and scandal, as Horner suggests, are at the core of Lady Fidget's paranoia over the protection of her honourable guise. But while Wycherley may have been satirising such female hypocrisy and pretence in general, his satire actually focuses in more closely on his society's double standard which mandated that women – excluding the whores from whom men expected sexual abandon and licence – deny their own *jouissance* or pleasure, exhibit sexual disinterest, and remain virtuous lest they themselves be likened to whores and suffer the dire consequences of expressing their true sexual nature. Through Lady Fidget's (and the other women's) covert defiance of these unwritten doctrines, Wycherley exposes as ludicrous the double-standard male myth that 'respectable' women constitutionally lack the same natural sexual impulses enjoyed by men and reveals the disastrous results wrought by a sexual-political system that requires complete submission to the suppression or erasure of such basic human needs and pleasures. Yet Wycherley probes the double standard even deeper by demonstrating that female duplicity and hypocrisy are not a result of biological essentialism, as some might opine, but rather the predictable byproducts of a culture that seeks to define and control female identity. As Jon Lance Bacon observes, 'Restoration comedy presents womanly falsehood and concealment as a social response to domestic patriarchalism rather than as a natural inclination'.[10] In a society that denounced female sexual expression and equality and whose sexual currency placed the highest premium on female virtue as a means of containing that sexuality, women were forced into the hypocritical position of either holding onto the only currency they were allowed to possess by repressing their sexuality – which Wycherley shows as a wholly unnatural expectation because women then deny their natural instincts and thus betray themselves – or maintaining the self-protective pretence of virtue when natural desires win over sexual repression – which Wycherley dramatises as a necessary posture that ensures female survival in a world where the loss of such currency is tantamount to personal bankruptcy.[11] Seventeenth-century women had one respectable, professional option – marriage – and the inevitable consequential loss of a mate or a potential mate that their dishonour could occasion led many females to guard their reputations, if not their virtue, with a fierceness and hypocrisy equal to Lady Fidget's:

> LADY FIDGET: Our reputation! Lord, why should you not think that we women make use of our reputation as you men of yours, only to deceive the world with less suspicion? Our virtue is like the statesman's religion, the Quaker's word, the gamester's oath and the great man's honour – but to cheat those that trust us.
>
> (V,iv,113–9)

Women, Lady Fidget avers here in the 'banquet scene', do not differ morally and ethically from the men who set the example by their dishonesty, duplicity, and plotting. And if female honour, like all forms of virtue attributed to men in political, religious and social arenas, is actually a sham – 'the jewel of most value and use, which shines yet to the world unsuspected, though it be counterfeit', says Lady Fidget smirkingly (V,iv,194–6) – then at least the illusion that women comply with this myth which forms the foundation of patriarchal structures must be preserved at all costs even in the face of contrary evidence, as Sir Jaspar and Pinchwife encounter in the final scene but opt to ignore. Ironically, in this world of moral contradiction and hypocrisy, the very guardians of women's reputations were the men with whom they had affairs, but male sexual competitiveness among many men in this libertine society must perforce disregard codes of secrecy (such as the one to which Lady Fidget and her gang agree) and manifest itself in boasting about the number and the identity (sometimes fabricated) of those women who entrust them with their reputations. Thus, Lady Fidget's repeated fore- stalling of sexual consummation with the eager Horner until he promises to protect her honour is as humorous as it is revealing as to the anxiety women experienced over the ruin of their repu- tations (warranted or not) and indicative of where sexual power actually resides.

Lady Fidget's cavalier dismissal of the social mandate for female virtue reeks of resentment and contempt, but its tone pales by comparison with the sardonic and venomous discussion that ensues during the bulk of the 'banquet scene' as the 'virtuous' trio, having agreed to discard their masks of ceremonious hypocrisy and speak uninhibitedly as if drunk, talk openly of their deep-seated loathing for men who, by wielding their oppressive sovereign power, enslave women in a miserable, isol- ated and unfulfilled existence that fosters their hypocrisy and foments their rebellion.[12] Beginning their private colloquy with Horner as now one of the gang, Lady Fidget starts by forging their female comradery with a feminist version of a tavern song, which is typically reserved for men to extol the pleasures of their sexual freedom and bemoan the shackles of marriage:

1
Why should our damned tyrants oblige us to live
On the pittance of pleasure which they only give?
    We must not rejoice
    With wine and with noise.
In vain we must wake in a dull bed alone,
Whilst to our warm rival, the bottle, they're gone.
    They lay aside charms
    And take up these arms.*   (*The glasses)

2

'Tis wine only gives 'em their courage and wit;
Because we live sober, to men we submit.
    If for beauties you'd pass,
    Take a lick of this glass;
'Twill mend your complexions and, when they are gone,
The best red we have is the red of the grape,
    Then, sisters, lay't on,
    And damn a good shape.

                                    (V,iv,31–46)

Husbands are incompetent, unexciting lovers and 'damned tyrants' to whom women must either 'submit' their bodies for, at the very most, only 'a pittance of pleasure' sexually or endure a 'dull bed' while men retreat to their preferred company of male friends and wine. This frank song exposes married life – women's only viable place in society – as an intolerable sham which they, on the one hand, rebel against through their illicit venery and, on the other hand, collude with by their silence at large: the truths that Lady Fidget, Mrs Dainty and Mrs Squeamish admit secretly in this scene could never be revealed openly without retaliation from the men who control every aspect of their lives. As the segment progresses, so too do the candid admissions about sexual fulfilment, marriage, and infidelity. Lady Fidget divulges her habitual sexual eagerness with attractive strangers whose seductions go undetected by a drunken husband, 'No, I never part with a gallant till I've tried him. Dear brimmer, that mak'st our husbands shortsighted', and her wanton code of conduct is seconded immediately by Mrs Squeamish, who openly admits to a variety of sexual partners that undermines patriarchal class structure, 'And for want of a gallant, the butler is lovely in our eyes' (V,iv,52-7) – any man is better than her husband, even a servant. The women express their resentment toward the male custom and privilege of openly taking 'common and cheap' mistresses and lament these men ignoring those 'women of quality' like themselves who are forced either to use their wiles to satisfy their sexual needs or to 'lie untumbled and unasked for' (V,iv,76) – that is, mistresses have taken too many potential lovers out of circulation (obviously tossing back only the bad catches like Pinchwife). Lady Fidget, speaking for her comrades, sums up their preference for sexual partners very different from their spouses: 'we think wildness in a man' is a 'desirable quality' (V,iv,109).

In this banquet scene that brings the play's action near closure, Wycherley presents comic inversion on a number of levels. The women's honest sentiments about the opposite sex parallel the opening scene in which Horner, Harcourt, and Dorilant reveal their feelings about the true nature of women and the supremacy of male bonding and drinking over the diversions offered by mistresses. Most importantly, the banquet scene shows women as quite different from the stereotypical male identity that has been imposed on them, one that Sir Jaspar sums as 'sweet, soft, gentle, tame, noble' creatures 'made for man's companion' (II,i,535–6). The 'virtuous gang' usurp male roles, and their imitation of their oppressors is liberating: singing sexist songs that denigrate their spouses, treating the male as the sexual object (slapping Horner familiarly on the back and proudly claiming him as 'my false rogue' [V,iv,176]), talking openly about their adulterous adventures and female sexual desire, and deploying language and sentiments typically allowed only to men – all of which adds up to the women's candid expression of their unanimous disdain for patriarchal rule and a complete disregard of a double standard that is not of their own making and which seeks to rob them of the only personal liberty allowed to them. If women are sexual objects only, then their rebellion will fittingly take place on the field of battle where their opponents have restricted them. At the segment's conclusion, the women learn that Horner has serviced all three, but Wycherley cleverly eschews the conventional depiction of women battling each other over the same man (as is typically portrayed in comedies harking back to Aristophanes) and opts for a community of women – of which there is no male counterpart in this play – who agree to be 'sister sharers' (V,iv,191–2]) of a man who is of no value to them ('we get no presents, no jewels of him' [V,iv,193–4]) other than that of a sex toy that cannot compromise their reputations.

To many critics, the banquet segment – a parody of bacchanalia – is the play's most disturbing and grotesque scene. Commenting on its 'depravity', Ronald Berman suggests that 'On this rock sinks all that is left of Renaissance ideals of conduct between and among the sexes'.[13] Wycherley would probably respond that those ideals of conduct in the Renaissance were as fallacious then as they were in the latter decades of the seventeenth century, and he might point out as well that the Renaissance woman, unlike her Carolean counterpart and notwithstanding patriarchal canon, had not been robbed of a useful and productive familial role that positioned her as more than an object whose only purpose had been reduced to enhancing her sexual desirability. Of course, women imitating men disrupts and problematises the sacred absolutes of patriarchy's gender definitions, and when a play presents a male pretending to be a eunuch – which then allies him more with the women – and females swilling spirits and behaving like men, anxiety and nostalgia over the loss of ideals, however false such ideals were, speak volumes.

While the Fidgets' failed marriage vivifies the disturbing emotional detritus that patriarchy creates, the Pinchwifes' relationship demonstrates vividly and shockingly the degree of physical and verbal abuse that derives from this system which tacitly grants men indiscriminate and incontestable power over their female subjects. Unlike Sir Jaspar, Pinchwife makes no pretence to civility – he is a sinister, baleful man whose innate hatred of women erupts verbally or physically at every turn. This is no attractive, urbane libertine typical of Carolean comedy who disguises his misogyny under a veneer of cultivation, wit and manners which somehow enables him to deflect attention away from the depth of his emotional pathology: Pinchwife is misogyny incarnate – unmasked, stripped of its deceptive exterior, and exposed to the core of its loathing, malevolence and brutality. His complete subscription to the chauvinistic tenets that women are inherently inferior, malleable, and servile – 'out of Nature's hands they came plain, open, silly and fit for slaves' (IV,ii,63–4) – leads this superannuated rake of 49 to the delusion that he can secure a safe marriage by selecting an innocent child less than half his age (she's probably no more than 18), keep her in ignorance by sequestering her in the country, offer her no love or affection, degrade her continually, terrorise her at will and then expect in recompense his wife's fidelity to her part of their marriage oaths. His fanatical jealousy is his comic flaw, but it is a perverse jealousy, one that springs not from his love for Margery but rather from his possessiveness of her as his sexual property – his 'freehold' and 'baggage', as he puts it. Given his earlier rakish years spent pursuing empty sexual relationships (none of which were apparently fulfilling or long-lasting), Pinchwife has cultivated a distorted view of women that colours his perception of their worth and ultimately leads him to arrange a marriage for the singular reason of satisfying his lust with a naïve child whom he owns and who is thus duty bound to comply. Sex to Pinchwife is the defining role for all females, and not unlike the other males in this play though certainly more candid and vulgar in his expressions,[14] he dichotomises women according to their sexual value only, summing that, for the most part, all of them (including his virtuous sister, whom he calls a 'jill-flirt' and berates as a 'notorious town-woman' [II,i,47–8]), are wanton whores, a 'legion of bawds' (III,ii,615).

Wycherley created Pinchwife in a pre-Freudian era and, therefore, did not feel compelled to explain the motives for his character's destructive and disturbing psychological pathology, but recent critics have attempted to analyse his belligerent, sexist nature. Norman Holland, for example, explains that Pinchwife 'fears and distrusts women; these fears create a hostility that tends to make him an inadequate lover: unconsciously, he satisfies his aggressive instincts by frustrating and disappointing women he makes love to. Disappointing women, in turn, creates further situations that increase his fears. Thus he falls into the typical self-defeating spiral of neurosis.'[15] Holland, however, fails to explore precisely why Pinchwife fears and distrusts women in the first place, which would necessarily explain the aetiology of misogyny altogether. Helen Burke, proffering a more cogent diagnosis, notes that Pinchwife's rage toward women stems from his resistance to the fact that 'women are potentially destructive to the grand design of masculine power'[16] – that is, they have the inherent power to demolish the foundation on which patriarchy is precariously perched. Thus, to stave off such destruction of a system that ensures male privilege and supremacy, misogynists like Pinchwife will contain women within the prescribed boundaries of their rule by demeaning and terrorising their mates, none of whom have been afforded by their sovereign oppressors any legal right to cavil or a restraining order to protect them.

Wycherley, of course, turns Pinchwife's misogyny into comic material by making this repugnant and unsympathetic character the architect of his own well-deserved fate. Through a series of ingenious plot twists devised by the playwright, Pinchwife's every devious effort to keep his possessive hold over his property and thus evade cuckolding backfires and brings him closer to the inevitable. His initial tactic of frightening Margery with the evils of the town and the wicked behaviour of the town's women 'who only hate their husbands and love every man else, love plays, visits, fine coaches, fine clothes, fiddles, balls, treats, and so lead a wicked town life' (II,i,91–4) serves only to pique his wife's desire for freedom: 'Nay, if to enjoy all these things be a town-life, London is not so bad a place, dear' (II,i,95–6). Trying another tactic to deter her from the town's pleasure, he tells her frankly that 'one of the lewdest fellows in town' who saw her at the theatre 'told me he was in love with you' (II,i,129–31), but this admission only heightens Margery's curiosity to the extreme. To conceal his wife from the gallants, he hits on the idea of dressing Margery as a young gentleman when he escorts her around the town, but when Horner encounters her and sees through the disguise, he kisses her and then bids his male companions to do likewise. Enraged by Horner's molestation of his wife and her innocent admission of delight in their encounter, Pinchwife forces Margery to write Horner a rebuking letter, but she substitutes it with her own love letter which Pinchwife unwittingly delivers personally to Horner. Having taught Margery how to write letters to people in the town, Pinchwife finds her penning yet another epistle to Horner, which she cleverly ascribes to Alithea; Pinchwife, willing to give his sister over to Horner to keep him away from his wife, delivers the disguised Margery right into Horner's lair. Pinchwife's increasingly frenetic and failed attempts to maintain his tight grip on Margery amuse audiences because they underscore his thorough impotence in every respect, and render him ridiculous for attempting, like Sir Jaspar, to control female sexuality as a means of preserving his power over his legal property.

Although audiences may laugh at Pinchwife's own undoing, he is by no means an inherently humorous character. Almost every sentence this morose and hateful man speaks is littered with coarse, debasing language that reflects his loathing toward everyone around him. He has no capacity for love: 'damned love – well – I must strangle that little monster while I can deal with him' (IV,ii,65–6), he rails with clenched teeth and fists at

Margery's affection for Horner, knowing full well that he cannot offer, nor has ever offered, his wife a single reason to feel any other emotion toward him but repulsion, for he admits with alarm that 'the sight of [Horner] will increase her aversion for me' (IV,ii,58–9). Most unsettling is his vicious treatment of Margery: his constant and unprovoked insults (such as at his first entrance when he brings his wife to tears and offers no apology), his repeated shoves to force her into a locked chamber, and his threats to kill her pet all presage his very real potential for unchecked violence against her, a potential that erupts into bursts of homicidal energy on four occasions. During his letter dictation to Margery, Pinchwife threatens her twice with the penknife: first he frightens her with the promise to 'write "whore" with this penknife in your face' (IV,ii,110–11) if she does not obey his orders – a shocking and violent image of his desire to brand and disfigure her – and he finally terrorises her into complete compliance with a gruesome threat when he picks up the penknife, puts it to her face, and vows to 'stab out those eyes that cause my mischief' (IV,ii,129–30) if she does not write exactly what he bids her. When he finds Margery writing Horner another missive, he reads it aloud, bemoans the power of women, instructs her to complete the letter – 'But make an end of your letter and then I'll make an end of you thus, and all my plagues together' (IV,iv,44–6) – and draws his sword on her. Sparkish's unexpected entrance and humorous reaction to the sight of Pinchwife chasing his wife with his sword ('What, drawn upon your wife? You should never do that but at night in the dark, when you can't hurt her' [IV,iv,51–3]) deflates the audiences' fear for Margery's safety, but the image of his fierce brutality and murderous nature cannot be expunged. Margery's surprise appearance at Horner's lodgings provokes Pinchwife's last threat to kill his wife, who represents to him all of womankind: 'I will never hear woman again, but make 'em all silent, thus' (V,iv,337–8), he howls as he tries to draw his sword first on Margery and then on Horner. The thwarting of his attempts to use menacing phallic weapons provides an apposite visual image of the source of male aggression toward women: male impotence and sexual insecurity.[17] As a sovereign power who believes that men serve as women's 'politic lords and rulers' (IV,iv,43–4), Pinchwife is an impotent and ineffectual tyrant who must perforce rule Margery by fear and oppression.

Margery is no typical Carolean heroine, spirited and self-sufficient, like Etherege's Harriet, who would battle her oppressor blow for blow; she is an innocent and ingenuous child of nature whose youthful enthusiasm for both life and liberty have been harnessed by an elderly man who wants her only as his sexual property. Unfortunately, she is so untutored and simple that she does not fully understand the magnitude of her imprisonment, both physically and emotionally, until Horner kindles in her the realisation that, by powers not of her control, she has been carved out for an odious and insufferable life: 'I hope you will speedily find some way to free me from this unfortunate match, which was never, I assure you, of my choice, but I'm afraid 'tis already too far gone' (IV,iv,27–30), she writes to Horner in desperation to escape her husband and to find solace in love. Although some critics contend that Margery loves Pinchwife and is satisfied with her life prior to her encounter with Horner,[18] the play actually provides no such evidence. In fact, dialogue from their first scene together indicates that Margery feels at best only the customary obligation and wifely affection that women in such situations, who are told to be content with their lot, find themselves duty bound to exhibit. Her innately kind disposition and eagerness to please enable her to treat Pinchwife tenderly despite his abrasiveness toward her, but when Pinchwife questions her about her affection for him over anyone else, her simple and guileless admission that she indeed likes the actors more, for 'the playermen are finer folks' (II,i,85–6), suggests an underlying (though not fully realised as of yet) disenchantment with a churlish and unattractive mate who pales by comparison to the finely dressed actors with their gentlemanly manners and conduct. And when Pinchwife presses her yet again and more specifically about her love for no one but him, her evasive response, 'You are mine own dear bud, and I know you; I hate a stranger' (II,i,88–9), conjures an image not of a young woman who loves her new husband but rather of a simple-minded, young country girl who, having just moments earlier expressed her desire to leave London and return to their home in the country, has known only an insulated, domestic life in which she was shipped directly from her parents' home to that of her husband, a child who finds comfort in the familiar, however stifling that familiar environment may be to the outside observer. Margery's first awareness of any emotion approaching love – or what she interprets as love – is for Horner, and once she experiences this emotional and sexual awakening, she finally verbalises her true feelings for the tyrant who repulses her:

> Well, 'tis e'en so, I have got the London disease they call love; I am sick of my husband and for my gallant. I have heard this distemper called a fever, but methinks 'tis liker an ague, for when I think of my husband, I tremble and am in a cold sweat and have inclinations to vomit but when I think of my gallant, dear Mr Horner, my hot fit comes and I am all in a fever.
>
> (IV,iv,1–8)

Margery, the play's eponymous character, symbolises a prelapsarian state of innocence that Wycherley deploys to contrast and to satirise the real world embodied in the hypocrisies and subterfuge of the town. Her language, actions and reactions provide a repeated source of delight and amusement, for they reveal a genuine simplicity and honesty that make her humorous, endearing and sympathetic as she manoeuvres through a foreign land where each new experience wholly captivates her and potentially corrupts her. The simplicity of her syntax and her use of expressions such as 'nangered', 'fropish', and 'grum' mark her out as a frank, country naif lacking the linguistic finesse of the *beau monde* which has perfected the manipulation of discourse for the purposes of deceit: her first missive to Horner is, as he notes, 'the first love-letter that ever was without flames, darts, fates, destinies, lying and dissembling in't' (IV,iii,408–10). With her wide-eyed innocence, she misinterprets the 'pox' as some form of general malady endemic to London's environment, she reads the tavern signs in the Exchange with an awe and literalness that misses their obvious sexual signification, she's stupefied that people residing in the same city would write letters to one another when an informal meeting is so easily managed, and she remains perpetually confused as to why she cannot discard a husband whom she has grown to 'loathe, nauseate and detest' (IV,iv,25–6) and make Horner her new spouse, especially when she has daily observed many London women leaving their mates and residing with other men. Like any trusting child unschooled and unexposed to the ways of the world, she accepts everything and everyone at face value, and her artlessness prevents her from fathoming duplicity in others, leading her to believe that Horner would never try to 'ruin' her if he loves her just as she would never do him harm. Margery lives solely by her elemental instincts and emotions – those feelings and drives that all humans possess prior to their socialisation and acculturation – and she seeks, childlike, to satisfy those basic desires and natural instincts, which of course include her uncensored sexuality, without thought of the dire consequences to which she is completely oblivious.

Just as Margery's refreshing plain-dealing, unsophisticated demeanour and unabashed spontaneity foreground the absurdities and hollowness of a mannered society fuelled by rampant artifice so, too, does her inability to grasp the social code of an ostensibly civilised world emphasise the duplicitous motives and emotional vacuity of most of those with whom she interacts. But the extent to which she herself assimilates the guile and pretence of those around her or instead remains in a state of innocence until the final curtain poses a crucial interpretive decision for both an actor and a director, for as the comedy's title character, Margery's characterological transformation or stasis significantly affects the way in which audiences read Wycherley's satire of this cultured and affected society. If, as some critics contend, Margery learns the art of deception early on as evidenced in her first letter to Horner when she realises how to 'shift' (IV,ii,171) like any other London woman who wishes to deceive her husband, her conversion from a naïve and sincere child to a duplicitous and clever townswoman implies that society's evils will corrupt the purest of individuals and that one's survival and acceptance in the adult world mandates the fall from prelapsarian ignorance to cynical enlightenment and double-dealing. Such an interpretation of Margery would obviously require that all her dialogue and actions subsequent to her initial epistle to Horner smack of hypocrisy and cunning premeditation,[19] and it would presume as well that she will be able to 'shift' for herself when she returns to Hampshire and will find ways to subvert her domestic confinement as well as her emotional and sexual dissatisfaction with Pinchwife. Conversely, if Margery maintains her innocence and puerility throughout the play, then her remove to Hampshire suggests a form of banishment from the real world which cannot accommodate honesty, simplicity, and ingenuousness. Clearly, this interpretation garners all audience sympathy for Margery, for though she remains free of inhibitions and any sense of guilt over her sexual tryst with Horner, her singular epiphany that she cannot replace Pinchwife with Horner and 'must be a country wife' forever (V,iv,463) heightens the tragedy of her plight. Having experienced love and sexual fulfilment, she must return to the confines of the country where her newly realised desire for mutual affection and passion will be forever foreclosed, and, most disturbing, the ignorance with which she arrived in London that had previously protected her from understanding the depths of her oppressive and loveless life will no longer provide her the illusion of pastoral contentment. The prelapsarian child has acquired knowledge: she's been handed over by her parents to a loathsome tyrant (in whose presence, unfortunately, she had admitted to loving another man) who will now guard her even more closely in their remote country prison where she will have no escape from his lustful advances, abusive treatment, and emotional bankruptcy.

In his satiric disquisition of love, marriage and sovereignty, Wycherley anatomises the negative consequences that spring from patriarchy's sovereign–subject marital analogue to which his society adhered. Whether the husband is, like Sir Jaspar, detached and indifferent to his spouse or, like Pinchwife, overly watchful and possessive, both extremes reveal a relationship in which men value their spouses as second-class citizens with whom sexual bonds are the only form of intimacy they seek and whose tyrannical hold over their wives to whom they offer neither love nor respect but from whom they expect affection and loyalty encourages rebellion against their male prerogative and dominance by a symbolic form of castration through adultery. Absent in the Fidget and Pinchwife marriages are the deference, trust, friendship, love and compatibility that Wycherley viewed as mandatory for a successful and healthy marriage, and he dramatises the importance of these qualities through the relationship between Alithea and Harcourt. Admittedly, Alithea and Harcourt, as characters in this ribald satire, seem somewhat out of place with their comparatively elevated language and sentiments which ally them more with the love–honour 'high' plots in heroic plays rather than with the sexual escapades of a fast-paced, raucous comedy.[20] Easily eclipsed by the bawdy dialogue and behaviour of Wycherley's other figures, Alithea and Harcourt can be readily overlooked as thematically relevant to the play if one misreads the comedy as only a lascivious farce that aims at pure shock value in its attack against the age's moral depravity. The Sparkish–Alithea–Harcourt triangle is, however, central to the play's commentary on love and honour in a society dedicated to mendacity, selfishness, deception and cruelty, and these three characters who embody some of the negative influences of the town's ethos likewise point to prescription for a happy and lasting marital relationship.

Sparkish is a vain, affected fop who has deluded himself that he has earned the reputation of a gentleman of breeding, elegance and wit when, in fact, his acquaintances regard him as a fool and a nuisance. Just prior to his first entrance, Dorilant's description of him as one who 'can no more think that men laugh at him than that women jilt him, his opinion of himself is so good' (I,i,273–5) and Horner's estimation that he is 'the greatest fop, dullest ass, and the worst company' (I,i,314–6) primes the audience to read this pretentious character as a familiar and satiric portrait of the many actual would-be wits of the town who tried to emulate the fashionable libertines of the age by espousing their sentiments and aping their behaviour, and whose very lack of all the inherent and requisite qualities – the wit, aplomb, and spirit – to succeed in their masquerade rendered them sources of amusement and ridicule. Sparkish's comical absurdity rests especially with his continual and deliberate attempts to bring everyone's attention to his self-deluded status as a revered gentleman of culture and wit (i.e., his 'parts') by boasting of his attendance at the king's supper, lauding his ostensible popularity among the wits at the playhouse, proudly dismissing any desire for knighthood lest he be ridiculed by bourgeois playwrights, and, most tellingly, repeatedly praising his own witticisms. His ineptness at imitating the rakes with whom he consorts provokes audience laughter, but it also brings to the foreground those libertine tenets that sought to undermine conventional social values, holding them up for constant scrutiny and reflection within the context of this fool who tries to embody them. Most notably, because rakes denigrate the value of women and decry marriage as an impediment to male companionship, Sparkish likewise echoes these sentiments and denounces 'matrimonial love' as not the 'best and truest love in the world' (III,ii,352) but as inferior and unequal to the friendships formed between men. Not without deliberate irony, of course, Wycherley shows that neither Sparkish nor any male in the play actually possesses the type of strong bonds with one another which they habitually toast and for which they express their preference. By valuing a bond that exists only in this play's libertine rhetoric, Sparkish adheres unwittingly to an empty illusion – one that actually helps to foster the subordination of women in patriarchy's discourse and, by extension, its accepted and revered practices, as demonstrated primarily by the husbands in this play.

Believing he enjoys the superior bonds of a fraternal community to sustain him and propped up by his libertine code of conduct, Sparkish feels no compunction about entering into a marriage with a woman for whom he has no affection and from whom he can acquire an estate – after all, other rakes did just that routinely, as Sparkish himself takes care to note when he breaks his engagement to Alithea. His only interest in Alithea – apart from money – rests with the ways in which she can serve his vanity by posing as his property, an attractive and desirous possession to flaunt in front of his acquaintances in order to garner their admiration and envy of him: he proudly informs Pinchwife, who questions the soundness of his judgement in encouraging Alithea to forge a friendship with Harcourt, 'I love to be envied and would not marry a wife that I alone could love' (III,ii,413–5), and he echoes his desire to show off Alithea by way of an analogy that likens her to nothing more than a chattel, 'It may be I have a pleasure in't, as I have to show fine clothes at a playhouse the first day and count money before poor rogues' (III,ii,408–10). His complete self-centredness prevents him from experiencing the slightest feelings for anyone but himself, and thus his want of jealousy springs neither from his adherence to the libertine imperative of total self-possession nor from his trust in Alithea's virtue (as he would have everyone believe) but from his emotional void: 'we wits rail and make love often but to show our parts; as we have no affections, so we have no malice' (II,i,312–14). This admission to Alithea, though intended to explain Harcourt's advances as harmless and characteristic of men of wit like himself, reveals, of course, that he feels nothing for her and shows that he woefully

misunderstands the libertine's emotional self-restraint and com-
posure as the complete want of any emotion or affection whatsoever. And his overall treatment of her (including trying to avoid
her at the Exchange and happily abandoning her on two occasions – to sit with the wits at the playhouse and to attend the
king's supper at Whitehall) coupled with his singular pursuit of a
hollow reputation denote a selfish nature fed by infinite vanity.
And the centrality of Sparkish's vanity is nowhere more evident
than in his angry rebuttal to Alithea's alleged betrayal of him with
Horner: 'Could you find out no easy country fool to abuse? None
but me, a gentleman of wit and pleasure about the town?'
(V,iii,36–8). His vitriol derives not from jealousy but from injured
pride and disbelief that a gallant of his distinction could be
rejected by any female. His earlier lack of affection and his indifference for Alithea have transformed into a very real emotion that
points to his vanity and self-absorption: hatred for this woman
who has irreparably damaged his cherished reputation among
the men whose admiration and envy he had worked so diligently
to procure. He has now become what he has most feared in the
eyes of his acquaintances – that is, what he was all along but was
too stupid to perceive – the fool whom playwrights ridicule on
the stage, and he didn't even receive a knighthood into the
bargain.

Harcourt represents the typical libertine of manners comedy,
though he exhibits none of the Hobbesian drive for power and
supremacy over others, particularly women, that such characters
as Horner or Dorimant display. He is a gallant drawn with a light
touch: a benign, gentleman-libertine like Etherege's Courtall and
Freeman who possess wit and sophistication without the sexual
debauchery, vicious cunning, and insatiable ego that characterise
many later Carolean rakes. Like all the town wits, Harcourt has
internalised the ideals of the libertine ethos, especially privileging
male companionship with the obligatory devaluing of female
worth: 'Mistresses are like books. If you pore upon them too
much, they doze you, and make you unfit for company'
(I,i,243–5), he quips with Horner and Dorimant as they banter the
benefits of wine over women, though he does admit to his companions that between the two alternatives, 'love will still be
uppermost' (I,i,266). When he first meets Alithea, he falls in love
with her immediately, but his attempts to convince her of his

incipient affection and to persuade her to break off her engagement with Sparkish and marry him ('But if you take marriage for a sign of love, take it from me immediately' [II,i,271–2]) are met with Alithea's cool rebuff; she has charged him with membership in 'the society of wits and railleurs' (II,i,191–2) and thus clearly perceives his flirtation as the habitual and notorious posturing of a town rake. Despite her rejection, he takes every opportunity to court her, most often forced to do so in Sparkish's presence, which allows Harcourt the advantage of pointing out to Alithea his rival's self-centredness, pretence to wit, and lack of affection for her. In their lengthy and humorous exchange in Act III, scene ii, Harcourt openly mocks Sparkish's sheer stupidity with a series of double entendres and calculated gestures which elude the fool's comprehension, thus proving his point and ultimately driving Alithea to complete frustration over Sparkish's denseness:

> HARCOURT: No, no, madam, e'en take him for heaven's sake –
> SPARKISH: Look you there, madam.
> HARCOURT: Who should in all justice be yours, he that loves
> you most. (*Claps his hand on his breast*)
> ALITHEA: Look you there, Mr Sparkish, who's that?
> SPARKISH: Who should it be? – Go on, Harcourt.
> HARCOURT: Who loves you more than women titles or fortune
> fools. (*Points at Sparkish*)
> SPARKISH: Look you there, he means me still, for he points at
> me.
> ALITHEA: Ridiculous!
>
> (III,ii,357–66)

Through his wit and cleverness, Harcourt reveals to Alithea the depth of Sparkish's inanity – most especially in his disguise as his alleged twin brother, Ned, who will serve as the chaplain officiating at Sparkish's and Alithea's marriage ceremony, an impersonation which completely fools Sparkish and solidifies Alithea's perception of her fiancé's 'invincible stupidity' (IV,ii,182). To win Alithea, however, Harcourt must possess qualities that extend well beyond the fashionable ideals of wit and urbanity that he, as a gallant, believes are sufficient attributes to court town ladies and even induce Alithea to reject Sparkish and marry him. While Harcourt's gallantry and wit may attract

Alithea's attention and even her affection, they prove ineffective in convincing her to compromise her honour by breaking her contract with Sparkish. Harcourt's opportunity to demonstrate that he values those qualities of virtue and honour that Alithea most reveres and to show her that he is a man of substance rather than surfaces occurs in the final scene when both the misunderstanding over Margery's disguise as Alithea and the letter to Horner that Margery had attributed to her sister-in-law cause Alithea to be wrongly accused of losing her honour to Horner – a false accusation that Horner does not correct in order to protect his new lover, the country wife, from discovery. Facing a room populated with literally everyone in the play, Alithea tries to clear her reputation, but none will believe her in the face of such damning evidence – no one except Harcourt, who goes to Alithea and displays a level of devotion and trust absent in all the other male characters:

> ALITHEA: O unfortunate woman! A combination against my honour, which most concerns me now, because you share in my disgrace, sir, and it is your censure, which I must now suffer, that troubles me, not theirs.
>
> HARCOURT: Madam, then have no trouble, you shall now see 'tis possible for me to love too, without being jealous; I will not only believe your innocence myself, but will make the world believe it.
>
> (V,iv,290–8)

Harcourt has moved physically and ideologically from Horner's libertinism and the town's ethos to Alithea's idealism which embraces faith in the possibility of honour and fidelity in human relationships.

Alithea, whose name signifies 'truth', is a young and virtuous lady of the town who enjoys 'the innocent liberty' and pleasures it offers – the drawing room at Whitehall, the Exchange, the parks and the playhouses – but as a product of the town, she has blindly conformed to some of its social conventions and expectations without questioning their actual inherent validity and worth. Although she possesses the social acumen to navigate through the pitfalls presented by all the town's temptations – particularly those that would compromise her virtue – she deludes herself that she knows the town well enough and behaves with sufficient propriety and intelligence to insulate her from any injury to a lady's most guarded possessions: her honour and reputation. She is wrong, and she will learn from her folly.

Valuing the *beau monde*'s requisites of sophistication and wit, Alithea agrees to the arranged marriage that her brother-guardian has negotiated for her with Sparkish because, at the very least, he is from the same social class and he ostensibly possesses the necessary attributes of a town gallant – both of which social convention deemed mandatory. However, Alithea, like all the town held captive by appearances over reality, fails to discern the difference between surface and substance, and thus she woefully misreads Sparkish's external posturing as signs of his inner worth and nature. She misinterprets his treatment of her – that is, his indifference toward her and his willingness to allow Harcourt access to her (especially those private moments alone with Harcourt, first in the corner at Pinchwife's lodgings and later at the playhouse) – as evidence that he lacks jealousy, a trait which indicates that he trusts in her honour: 'that I am not jealous is a sign you are virtuous' (III,ii,248–9), he tells her, and she believes him in large part because she values her honour and reputation above all else. And because Sparkish seems to revere the inner qualities of others rather than superficies, Alithea believes he possesses a depth of character that separates him from the other town wits who merely wish to satisfy their egos. Although she learns through Harcourt's intervention that she has mistaken Sparkish for a man of wit and substance, she nonetheless refuses to break off her engagement and marry Harcourt because she remains foolishly slavish to other social conventions that dictate her life.

Alithea's rationale for holding to her contractual obligations to Sparkish – 'the writings are drawn, sir, settlements made; 'tis too late, sir, and past all revocation' (II,i,253–4), she explains to Harcourt during their first encounter – is, at face value, commendable, and Wycherley intends audiences to take it as such. In a world where verbal oaths and written contracts are broken as readily as ladies' fans and concepts like honour and virtue are but words to be twisted to suit one's personal self-interest, Alithea's adherence to her contract with Sparkish puts her in direct contrast to the other characters who betray their marital vows and opt for personal pleasure at every available opportunity. At stake, Alithea insists, are her reputation and honour if she reneges on the agreement: 'I must marry him', she informs Harcourt, because 'my reputation would suffer in the world else' (II,i,273–4). Equally important, her strong convictions about honour preclude her betrayal of a man whom she believes loves her: 'he loves me, or he would not marry me' (II,i,265), she insists to Harcourt, and thus for these reasons she will 'not be unjust to him' (II,i,256), a sentiment she repeatedly echoes up until the last minute when her maid Lucy, helping her dress for the ceremony, presses her to stop the wedding: 'my justice will not suffer me to deceive or injure him' (IV,i,19–20). Honour and reputation, the two most prized commodities possessed by females in this society, must be protected at all costs, and Alithea is willing to pay the highest possible price for them. She has already acknowledged to Lucy that she loves Harcourt ('I would see him no more because I love him' [IV,i,13–14]), but she will sacrifice love for a code of honour that very few in her society actually adhere to in practice. That Alithea holds noble sentiments is clear, but that she misplaces her ideals on a man whom she does not love and who lacks her virtue and substance is patently foolish, and even more foolish is her tenacious hold onto an ideal strictly for the sake of appearances. Just as Lady Fidget and her companions carefully safeguard their reputations so that the world will believe they possess virtue, so, too, does Alithea place her highest regard on the *appearance* of her virtue above the virtue itself. Indeed, as Lucy tells her, little honour is gained in marrying a man one does not love – 'Can there be a greater cheat or wrong done to a man than to give him your person without your heart?' (IV,i,21–2) – and her mockery of Alithea's 'rigid honour' (IV,i,34) points to the hypocrisy and duplicity in Althea's willingness to engage in a marital contract under false pretences (she, after all, believes Sparkish is marrying her out of love) in order to keep her reputation as a lady of honour intact. Although she embodies the virtue that none, save Harcourt, possess, Alithea values appearances and social convention just like the rest of the *beau monde*, and she will remain intransigent in her self-sacrifice to these 'ideals', even if doing so means forgoing personal happiness.

In her conversation with Lucy, Alithea reveals that behind her code of ethics vis-à-vis her marriage contract with Sparkish lurk other motives equally tied to social custom and convention, motives that get to the core of Wycherley's indictment of the deleterious practices and presumptions condoned by his society that led to women's marital unhappiness and unfaithfulness. After some prodding by Lucy, Alithea admits that by marrying a man like Sparkish who lacks jealousy, she will be spared the tyrannical control of a possessive and domineering spouse whose abusive treatment of a wife typically causes 'the loss of her honour, her quiet, nay, her life sometimes, and what's as bad almost, the loss of this town; that is, sent into the country, which is the last ill usage of a husband to a wife, I think' (IV,i,66–70). While Alithea does not want to lose the innocent pleasures of the town to which she is accustomed, she also wishes to escape the fate of women like Margery, whose maltreatment and confinement she has witnessed firsthand, and thus she most desires to retain a level of independence which society requires women to capitulate upon marriage to their husbands. To avoid such torment caused by a spouse who will disrespect, nag, and even cause the death of his wife or drag her to the country, Alithea prefers to relinquish marital bliss by accepting a man she does not love so that she can retain some rights to the personal freedom which marriage annuls for women. Her strategy, then, is not so much self-sacrifice as it is self-survival: to eschew right from the start the sovereign–subject relationship that led to lifelong subjugation and misery. Equally unsettling, albeit equally revealing of the realities women faced in prearranged marriages, is Alithea's rationalisation for entering into a loveless marriage at all: she parrots the firmly established, insidious myth which women in this society (and no doubt all of them in this play) routinely accepted as truth when, in response to Lucy's admonition about a union without love, she retorts, 'I'll retrieve it for him after I am married a while' (IV,i,24–5). During the seventeenth century, as women were customarily forced to wed according to parental dictates and against their inclination, they were likewise instructed that if they made the best of their lives by appreciating and caring for their spouses then love for their husbands would develop in the fullness of time.[21] Wycherley demonstrates the actual consequences of such a specious myth through the Fidgets' and Pinchwifes' failed marriages. Loveless unions do not breed affection – they breed contempt and rebellion.

At the end of the play, Alithea's folly unravels before her. Sparkish shows her his true colours: he reveals he had no trust in her virtue and admits he did not love her but only wanted her dowry, and after his angry tirade, he severs their engagement, leaving Alithea relieved that the marriage ceremony was invalid and vocalising self-condemnation for her thorough lack of judgement in which she had prided herself for keeping well insulated from the town's potential treachery: 'How was I deceived in a man!' (V,iv,84). And in the final moments of the play, Alithea, surrounded ironically by a room full of hypocrites who would quickly condemn her with secret pleasure, finds herself facing the primary fear that she believed her virtuous behaviour had guarded her against: her prized honour and reputation have been impugned, and with seemingly incontrovertible evidence. Here, Alithea makes a stunning *volte-face*: she tells Harcourt that she does not care about the censure of others, only about his regard for her (V,iv,290–4, quoted above). Having learned from Sparkish that external appearances do not always convey inner reality, Alithea applies this lesson to herself as well, and she no longer regards her most important possessions to be her reputation and appearance in the outside world, but rather puts the highest value on the trust from the only person whose opinion of her truly matters: Harcourt. In her education of the real world, Alithea recognises her blind subscription to the false values of the town, and her advice to 'any over-wise woman of the town, who, like me, would marry a fool for fortune, liberty or title' (V,iii,92–3) is that she will face a life of unhappiness if she weds for any reasons other than mutual love, respect and trust. With Harcourt, Alithea will secure the marriage which she envisaged, one in which 'love proceeds from esteem' (II,i,263), and their respect and affection for each other forecast a happy union in which both will remain faithful, trustful, independent, loving, and, equally important, free of the emotional decay and rancour eventually endured by others who marry for such personal motives as carnal pleasure, financial gain, or social position.

At the centre of all the chicanery stands Horner, poised to capitalise on the foibles and follies of human nature and sexuality: specifically, the personal unhappiness and sexual dissatisfaction of married women who must retain their honourable reputations, and the fear of cuckoldry and sexual anxiety of their husbands.

With his clever ruse as a eunuch giving him access to the former while securing him sanction from the latter, Horner serves as Wycherley's percipient, dramatic catalyst who puts in motion a set of conditions that proves his hypothesis of society's baseness and hypocrisy, and, by extension, illustrates the playwright's satiric critique of male–female relationships within marriage. More than just a dramatic device, however, Horner – the nominal hero who opens and concludes the play – serves as a self-appointed moralist, a master of ceremonies who initiates the game and lets the audience enjoy watching the sport he has devised for his own amusement. The moment he walks on stage with his self-assured swagger and delivers his initial aside, he immediately takes spectators into his confidence as witnesses to his clever scheme to unmask social pretensions, thereby tacitly enlisting their collusion with his moralisation on the corruptness of his well-deserved victims as he positions himself as the super-ior observer and detached commentator on the depravity and mendacity of others without holding himself accountable to the same moral standards he applies to his dupes. Horner is, how-ever, like those he victimises, deceptive and lewd – feigning impotence to satisfy his aggressive instincts – and it is, after all, his plot that instigates the very behaviour he indicts, just as his sexual exploits mirror the offences against moral decency that he likewise flays. Yet Wycherley withholds such judgements against Horner, and although he neither condones nor solicits audiences' approval of his character's sexual excesses, he does expect theatregoers to applaud Horner's wit, intelligence, and ingenuity as the ultimate satirist who exposes hypocrisy and corruption.

As one of the most notorious rakes in all of Restoration comedy, Horner – so obsessed with power and sexual debauch-ery as to promulgate the false rumour that he is impotent, thereby losing his revered reputation as a virile male – has been the sub-ject of much literary criticism, all of which, unsurprisingly, focuses solely on his profligate behaviour, a logical point of attack not merely because his sexual antics emblematise the moral decay at the heart of this comedy but also – and far more significantly – because he does nothing with his intelligence and knowledge to affect the slightest transformation in any of those fools who have afforded him so much amusement. Characterising himself as pos-sessing superior insight into human psychology and nature,

Horner orchestrates his plot allegedly to expose the town's rampant affectations and pretensions, but the only witness he allows to observe the truth of his theory is the inconsequential quack; he shares his scheme with none of his male companions (who would delight in his cleverness but surely betray a confidence), preferring to operate in isolation as the lone seducer of society's upperclass women.[22] And at the end of the play, Horner will continue his imposture for his own entertainment and sexual fulfilment, and thus his actions convey a self-centred egoist bent on his own pleasure gained from the social evils he excoriates rather than a hero who somehow, even inadvertently, helps to remedy them. Consequently, Horner's failure as the putative hero to bring about any collective harmony or change at the play's closure perforce directs critical attention to what motivates him in the first place to initiate a scheme that, dramatically and thematically speaking, comes to naught.

Although Horner's pretence as a eunuch is a foolproof plan – so much so that within the span of a very short time, as indicated in the 'china scene', he has acquired more lovers than he can physically satisfy – his reasons for taking such drastic measures that will destroy his rakish reputation, bring mockery from the entire town, and remove him from male homosocial bonding and sexual competitiveness just to ferret out sexually compliant women continue to baffle most commentators on this play, each of whom takes a different perspective on Horner's motivation. His self-characterisation as a 'Machiavel in love' (IV,iii,75) suggests to some that Horner is simply a despicable villain with a lack of conscience and overriding desire for power, which must necessarily manifest itself sexually in a libertine. But actually Horner is no villain in the true sense, for, unlike Dorimant, he does not victimise young and naïve virgins nor does he molest unwilling participants, but rather he seduces only those women who possess a bold enthusiasm equal to his own. Similarly, Horner's myriad, savage tirades against women in which he likens them to dogs (II,i,537–43), expresses his deep hatred for them (III,ii,17–20), and vows 'to laugh at 'em and use 'em ill' (III,ii,21–2) have been cited as proof of a deep-seated misogyny that motivates his primary goal of using women sexually while proving his sexist premise that all females are whores. Yet, his incessant railing against women is no doubt a clever tactic for bolstering his mask as a eunuch whose only option in light of his sexual nullity is loathing the object of sexual desire, a ploy that enables him to deflect any suspicions away from his true sexual appetite and nefarious plot. Other than his rhetorical strategies, which include the hackneyed railing against women and valorising of male friendship, Horner's behaviour demonstrates that he seems to prefer the company of women to that of men. In the banquet scene that parallels the male-drinking segment in Act I, Horner finally drops the ceremonious libertine pose he strikes habitually with his male cohorts and, for the first time in the play, engages in an honest, straightforward conversation that approaches something akin to genuine bonding in a way never achieved among the male characters, who are all compelled to compete with each other on every level of masculine behaviour.

Neither a pure villain corrupting innocents nor a baleful misogynist abusing women, Horner does possess a high dose of Hobbesian aggression and lust for power that his scheme ultimately satisfies, and that he obtains this superior control over everyone he chooses without any force, without their knowledge, and with their wholesale volition due to their secret fears and weaknesses provides him his greatest sources of extreme delight and amusement. He derives ultimate pleasure from the game itself, procuring what he desires – uncomplicated affairs with willing partners, ridicule of those whom he dupes, and power over his cuckolded victims – with very little effort. And the nature of his trysts indicates clearly that he lusts for power not sex: like Dorimant, he feels no affection toward the women he beds (though, of course, Horner expects no affection from them in return) and he garners no joy from sexual congress. The infamous china scene tells it all: it demonstrates that Horner's greatest satisfaction stems from his ability to dupe the inane Sir Jaspar right under his nose and to prove Lady Fidget's complete hypocrisy and venal nature, and, furthermore, that Horner, like Dorimant, views sexual liaisons as raw concupiscence, animalistic acts in which he will enter 'the back way' (IV,iii,145) and will copulate until exhausted and depleted of all the 'china' he can produce, ironically becoming the eunuch he purports to be. Horner represents the darker side of the hardcore libertine: isolated and without close friends or confidants, sexually competitive and aggressive, undesirous of emotional attachment, and selfishly motivated. More especially, he also signifies the ironies inherent in libertinism by showing himself not as the romantic and satisfying lover he imagines himself to be but as nothing more than a sexual automaton that his doxies will use period-ically as needed. The greatest irony, of course, is that in his dis-guise as a eunuch, Horner has unwittingly feminised himself in more ways than one: not only is he suitable solely for such female pastimes as theatregoing, card playing and gossiping (as Sir Jaspar implies), he has also become a mechanical phallus, redu-cing himself to what is typically the feminine role of sexual object only, an anatomical part that is the sum of his entire worth.

Quite fittingly, Wycherley concludes his satire with Horner, the sign of male impotence, standing surrounded by the women who have had him and the husbands who prefer to believe otherwise for an ensemble 'dance of cuckolds', a grotesque celebration of debauchery and deceit in lieu of the traditional Restoration denouement featuring the betrothal dance heralding the imminent nuptials of the young and loving gay couple. While Alithea and Harcourt signal the potential for a happy marriage, Wycherley's grand finale fails to establish moral equilibrium and harmony. Rather, the finale suggests – with everyone remaining unchanged and glued to their masks of self-delusion or hypocrisy – the impossibility of concord in an ossified system ruled by eunuchs and cuckolds who believe the phallus empowers them to dom-inate, mistreat, and devalue women in order to maintain what are nothing more than the fragile and fallacious, though necessary, illusions that male homosocial bonds are sacred and reign supreme, and that sovereign rights in and of themselves will guar-antee them loyalty, deference and affection from their wives in a union calculated solely to deploy women as faithful subjects who help them sustain and ratify the very male privilege, dominance, and lineage on which their divine right to rule wholly depends.

The Country Wife remained popular throughout the Restoration and well into the first half of the eighteenth century when it enjoyed some 150 performances,[23] but it could not survive the radical shift in audience makeup and the attendant changes in tastes that consigned many Carolean and Restoration comedies to theatrical obscurity until the early twentieth century. By the middle of the eighteenth century, the mercantile class had rapidly ascended as England's new source of power and wealth. This rich and influential middle class, which was far more conservative than the leisure class of seventeenth-century London and was allied less with a Carolean disposition and more with Puritan attitudes, preferred the sentimental comedies of Richard Steele and George Farquhar with their depictions of middle-class characters adhering to more conventionally moral behaviour, and, during the later decades of the eighteenth century, opted for the 'laughing' comedies of Oliver Goldsmith and the sophisticated and benign wit-comedies of Richard Brinsley Sheridan. Although Wycherley's play did not resurface until the 1920s, it did survive in bowdlerised forms that appealed to the new middle class's comparatively delicate sensibilities. In John Lee's 1765 version of *The Country Wife*, Wycherley's original was whittled down to a two-act afterpiece that jettisoned all offensive dialogue and omitted major characters, including Sir Jaspar, Lady Fidget, Quack, and Horner, whose dialogue in the condensed version was assigned to Dorimant. Although Margery, Pinchwife, Harcourt, and Alithea survived the cutting, they barely resembled their originals (e.g., Pinchwife sees the error of his ways and reconciles with Margery, promising to release his stronghold over her). The following year, David Garrick, London's leading actor-director in the late eighteenth century, completely overhauled Wycherley's comedy, rewriting considerable portions, renaming characters, retitling it *The Country Girl*, expurgating all sexual references, and justifying his sterilisation by claiming that the celebrated comedies of the previous age required purging, for 'no kind of Wit ought to be received as an Excuse for Immorality'.[24] Garrick's five-act version replaces Horner with a new character, Young Belville, whose non-sexual, gentlemanly pursuit of the unwed Peggy Thrift (previously Margery) is thwarted by her guardian, Jack Moody (Pinchwife's replacement). This saccharine version, which ends happily with two marriages (Harcourt–Alithea and Peggy–Belville), held the stage throughout the eighteenth and nineteenth centuries, and it even continued to receive sporadic revivals during the twentieth century long after Wycherley's original comedy had reclaimed its place in the repertoire of commercial theatres.

In the 1920s, after a century-and-a-half since its last public performance, *The Country Wife* finally reappeared on the English stage thanks first to the efforts of an amateur company dedicated to reviving neglected works by early British dramatists, such as Fletcher, Ford, Heywood, Dryden, and Otway. This 1924 production staged by the Phoenix Society at the Regent Theatre was followed two years later by another brief revival at the Everyman Theatre. Although these productions were staged for coterie audiences and had limited runs of only a handful of performances, thus receiving little press coverage, the efforts of both companies proved pivotal in re-establishing Wycherley's reputation as a major comic playwright and attesting to the stage viability of this long-forgotten comedy. With its reintroduction to theatregoers in the early twentieth century, *The Country Wife* held the stage throughout the remainder of the century as the most produced Restoration comedy, enjoying countless revivals by both amateur and commercial companies.

The brief and abridged stage history of *The Country Wife* on the professional stage that follows below reveals that early directors of this newly rediscovered comedy interpreted it incorrectly as comedy of manners, an historic genre that ostensibly centres on the era's reputed elegance and grace, and they focused all artistic and creative energies on replicating the style of the period through set design, costumes, line delivery, and actorial gestures: that is, they produced 'museum pieces' that purportedly offered a close approximation to the original performances. While it is a fallacy that such period revivals can actually recreate historical productions for modern spectators, directors are often enamoured of such approaches while audiences likewise enjoy dramatisations of eras past, but typically such revivals that attempt solely to recapture the style of a period do so at the expense of thematic focus and contemporary relevance. In the case of *The Country Wife*, directors could combat critics' attacks on the play's licentiousness by deflecting attention away from its bawdiness and cruelty and redirecting audience focus to the style of the piece, transforming it into pure comedy or farce rather than the satire Wycherley intended; in sum, they removed the soul of the play, leaving only its outer and elegant shell. Not until the latter part of the twentieth century did directors downplay or forgo the museum approach and resurrect Wycherley's play as a satirical commentary on the world of love, sex and marriage that still reverberates with a familiar ring some 300 years after its première.

The first production of *The Country Wife* in London's commercial West End took place in 1934 at the Ambassadors Theatre under the management of Sydney Carroll. To assuage potential audience shock and to ameliorate its receptivity to the play, Carroll crafted a shrewd programme note that not only recognised the Phoenix Society's revival as an indication that contemporary audiences possessed the sophistication required to appreciate Restoration comedy, but also described his production as one that aimed primarily at affording young actors the rare opportunity to perfect their talents in such seldom performed, highly stylised period plays. Carroll's tactic of predisposing spectators and critics to regard his revival as testimony to their finely cultivated tastes worked, for most reviewers focused their comments on the actors' consummate skill at conveying the wit, manners and elegance of the period and lauded Carroll for 'deliberately giving opportunities to the young players of to-day to cultivate a quality of mannered acting and formal speech for which our more usual theatre offers few opportunities'.[25] Baliol Holloway, a popular, classical actor well trained in the physical and vocal requirements of such comedies, directed the play as a traditional museum piece, one replete with all the fluttering fans, gracious bows, and elegant poses thought to be the essence of Restoration comedy. As one critic noted, 'fine feathers, gallant manners, and that style which is the essence of true "costume comedy", cover a multitude of sins, and here we laugh at that which, in another manner, would provoke indignant outcry'[26] – that is, the theme and contents of *The Country Wife*, if presented as a new play in a contemporary setting with naturalistic acting, would not, as the *Daily Telegraph* reviewer (3 March 1934) noted, 'be passed by the Lord Chamberlain, if it were necessary to submit it to him'.

Even though Carroll cut the original, eliminating 'a good deal of its grossness' and 'most of its coarse expressions'[27] – as had been done at both the Phoenix and Everyman revivals – a few critics did find the subject matter distasteful. Most, however, agreed with *The Times* critic (3 March 1934) that 'it is remarkable considering what subject [Wycherley] has to discuss, how little gross his language is; it is not decorous, but neither is it brutal or corrupt'. That critics used such tepid adjectives as 'naughty' in their descriptions of Wycherley's characters, remarked that 'the play is not nasty' (*Evening News*, 3 April 1934), and thought the notorious china scene 'went for nothing by sheer lack of interest'[28] with Horner and Lady Fidget merely talking through the locked door to Sir Jaspar on the other side, indicates the extent to which the play's sexual, bawdy energy was excised and replaced by the 'sparkle, verve, gusto'[29] that ostensibly constituted the gist of Restoration comedy. In the main, this first West End revival of *The Country Wife* – the first in almost 200 years – was 'pushed along with admirable artificial force without any attempt at modern "natural" acting' so as to allow spectators to believe, as did *Illustrated Sporting and Dramatic News* (17 March 1934), that with this costume version of the comedy 'you get your real Wycherley thrown at you'. Actually, the *real* Wycherley was decades away.

The 1930s also witnessed one of the most historic productions of *The Country Wife*. Regarded as the theatrical event of the season with a star cast that included Ruth Gordon as Margery, Edith Evans as Mrs Fidget, and Michael Redgrave as Horner, the Old Vic's revival, directed by Tyrone Guthrie, played to packed houses during its five-week run and broke all attendance records for this relatively conservative theatre's 1936-7 production season. Guthrie, like Holloway two years prior, cut portions of the original and recast the remaining dialogue into a three-act structure, and he commissioned Oliver Messel to design period costumes and scenery (the latter cleverly simulated the seventeenth-century locales by drops painted in perspective). Peppered throughout the reviews are familiar remarks about the play's thematic coarseness, but once again the directorial approach of 'costume comedy' – coupled no doubt with the judicious pruning and de-emphasised prurience in the actors' stage business and line delivery – garnered the Old Vic kudos for its 'light, sparkling, and gaily decorated' performance.[30] Although Guthrie was a creative and experimental director known for his fresh approaches to classical drama (e.g., a modern-dress *Hamlet*), he took no such artistic liberties with Wycherley's play and chose to direct it as fast-paced, high-spirited farce that focused on the witty aphorisms and stylised elegance that had now become commonplace in revivals of Restoration comedy: 'the costumes are brilliant, the scenes perfect period pictures, and the players strike just the right note of elaborate artifice', noted Stephen Williams (*Evening Standard*, 6 October 1936). By staging it as a 'blazing farce'[31] that revealed the depravity of characters from an age very much removed in time, Guthrie enabled spectators to remain emotionally detached from the characters without engaging their moral judgements: 'The appeal is continually to the mind', remarked Herbert Farjeon (*The Bystander*, 21 October 1936), 'never to the feelings.' Critics singled out for praise the performances of Michael Redgrave, new to the Old Vic, as a 'wickedly virile' Horner with a 'charming frankness which would deceive wiser husbands than any he encounters'[32] but without any indication that he delights in those machinations which should be a source of pride or pleasure to him, a delight in sexual conquests that 1930s audiences would have no doubt found distasteful. And Edith Evans, a popular actress of Restoration comedy, received encomiums for providing a Lady Fidget that was 'a constant source of sophisticated gaiety' (*The Times*, 7 October 1936) and apparently one without any evidence of an over-active libido.

The bulk of critical praise went to Ruth Gordon, a well-known American actress with a lilting voice and halting delivery that lent Margery a particular air of timidity and innocence not captured by previous actresses. Gordon avoided the usual interpretation by her predecessors of Margery as a sly, young girl ripe for the enjoyment of the town's pleasures, and rather showed 'with admirable subtlety a mind so virginal that the monstrous could grow in it as easily as the blameless'.[33] While Gordon's American accent proved helpful in approximating a seventeenth-century rustic, her 'innocence so subtly overdone as to be incredible, her shy confidences to the audiences, her gawky movements which are so well controlled that they have a sort of negative grace' made for 'an entirely delicious performance'[34] that attracted throngs of theatregoers not only at the Old Vic, but also those in New York, where Gordon starred in a Broadway production of *The Country Wife* that opened in December 1936. Unlike their English counterparts, American theatregoers, still suffering the aftershocks of the Depression, gleaned from the performance an analogue of their own society's moral dissolution – an analogy which escaped notice by London's critics, who read Guthrie's handling of the play as a romping farce which invites the audiences to take nothing seriously and to view all characters as objects of well-deserved laughter. This interpretation, intended or not by Guthrie, would influence numerous future directors.

The English Stage Company, one of England's most revered theatrical organisations, produced *The Country Wife* during its first year of operation. Committed primarily to encouraging young dramatists and producing plays ignored by the commercial West End theatres, ESC opened the Royal Court Theatre on 2 April 1956 with Angus Wilson's long-forgotten play, *The Mulberry Bush*, and after experiencing a slow start that seemed to forecast failure within the first month, the company won critical acclaim for its production of John Osborne's *Look Back in Anger* and it solidified its reputation for fostering new and promising talent with its revival of *The Country Wife*. Among the novice actors still to prove their mettle was Joan Plowright, a recent addition to the corps of actors, whose superb performance as Margery garnered her lead roles at the Royal Court for subsequent seasons and secured the success of Wycherley's comedy. Playing Margery initially as a 'bundle of bucolic naïvety' with just the right 'note of comically distorted rustic simplicity' and an 'open delight at the queer things that happen to her in the wicked world', Plowright imbued the character with an increasingly 'knowing slyness' that hinted at her gradual savvy of the way of the world, displaying in particular 'some truly hilarious effects in her discovery of the delights of infidelity'.[35] With 'an accent that flips around the shires', Plowright made Margery 'a gorgeous little goof' with 'rustic candour and simplicity enlivened by a mischievous instinct for the pleasures of the town as, one by one, they are brought within her understanding'.[36] Laurence Harvey focused his interpretation of Horner on the character's moral decadence and less on his exuberance at debauching the town's willing women and proving his theory about their eager compliance, but the 'satanic, decadent beauty about his looks' and the 'rasp in his voice'[37] served him well in capturing the sardonic nature of Wycherley's master manipulator.

By underscoring the darker side of Horner's character and accentuating Margery's transformation from country innocence to knowledge and enjoyment of the town, director George Devine no doubt sought to convey the deeper themes residing in Wycherley's comedy, and his avoidance of period costumes and scenery, as well as the absence of reviewers' references to any actorial focus given solely to the artifice and elegance of the period, suggests further that Devine decided to avoid the strictly museum-like approach and steered his production by a directorial concept that, by placing the action in a non-representational, unspecified locale and era rather than the seventeenth century, allowed audiences to draw contemporary parallels. Unfortunately, neither critics nor audiences made such analogies, but subsequent directors, those bent on foregrounding past– present connections suitable to Wycherley's comedy, would improve on Devine's concept by using scenographic and performance strategies that made their analogues more easily – and, in some cases, obtrusively – discernible.

The 1960s offered audiences two notable revivals intended to showcase the talents of two recognised, though not yet famous, young actresses in the role of Margery: Judi Dench and Maggie Smith. The 1966 production by the Nottingham Playhouse Company – founded in 1963 on the principle of producing quality performances that matched London's West-End offerings – took the concept of museum theatre to an extreme: while the historically accurate costumes and period music were not particularly anomalous, Stephen Doncaster's scenery replicated the spectatorial experience of the Carolean theatregoer – that is, flats that actually slid along grooves with the aid of the authentic-looking stage-hands positioned in the wings and periodically visible to the audience during the scene changes. In a production that aimed all its energies at convincing spectators that they had entered a time warp and arrived at Drury Lane in 1675, Judi Dench's Margery was, fortunately, not eclipsed by the scenographic tricks. Compared to previous Margerys, Dench, an actress with a powerful stage presence, made the character visually cynosural, and her every calculated bit of character business and subtle physicalisation of Margery proved riveting to watch: her scurrying about the stage as she sidesteps every danger from Pinchwife, scampering with delight as her husband leads her to Horner's lodgings, as well as her remarkably protean face that telegraphed a range of subtle emotions to the audience, in particular Margery's unbounded joy and wonder at each of the town's evils that Pinchwife limns to her. Despite Dench's masterful performance, the revival received tepid reviews faulting the production for its failure to make the play accessible and meaningful to mid-1960s audiences.

Likewise, The Chichester Festival Theatre's 1969 staging aimed at no specific thematic message for its contemporary audience,

but to his credit, director Robert Chetwyn did reject the customary approach to the comedy as a 'sombre social documentary of a
bygone permissive society'[38] that typically leaves spectators
detached and bored when no topical connections are made for
them. Capitalising on the late-1960s theatrical taste for shocking
and radical performance approaches that included comparatively
high doses of sexuality, profanity and promiscuity (witness *Hair*
and *Paradise Now*, for example), Chetwyn responded to his era's
nascent permissiveness by shaping his revival into one that
would attract patrons by its lubricity, using a performance concept that some critics contend is the sole import of Wycherley's
comedy: a playful and 'sprightly dramatisation of a dirty joke'.[39]

In some respects, Chetwyn did sterilise the revival: he downplayed the misogyny, expunged any scent of moral decay or
physical sordidness, and directed the actors to play for broad
farce that included a wealth of physical pranks, but he did
explore the play's sexuality – specifically, male heterosexuality –
doing so in an unconventional manner that would have startled
and possibly offended the most jaded theatregoers, especially the
men. No doubt taking his cue from not only the historical fact that
seventeenth-century males kissed one another in public as a form
of greeting but also from the play's libertine rhetoric espoused
repeatedly by the males who boast of their companionship and
denigrate women, Chetwyn calls the question as to precisely how
much 'hetero' figures into the sexuality of those men who
devalue love and affection with women and privilege their bonds
with one another. In this production, the male characters
exchanged kisses with one another at each greeting and departure, and on occasion, recalled critic Harold Hobson, they 'even
interrupt their conversations to leap at each other, gluing themselves mouth to mouth. My heart bled for the neglected women,
frightened though most of them looked, as the men, in full sight
of their despised charms, pursued with enthusiasm their
amorous goings-on' (*Sunday Times*, 13 July 1969). Though problematising male heterosexuality within the context of misogyny,
Chetwyn's homosexual critique of this play's libertines eluded
most observers for two reasons: within the farcical handling
(pratfalls and visual jokes) of the characters, the full-mouth oscul-
ations between the men could be easily dismissed as yet another
ocular joke among many; and the production's overall lack of

focus, each actor given free reign to develop and embellish character details that failed to add up to a concrete directorial vision, resulted in a performance that seemed something like a collision of the two 'unrelated worlds of sanctimonious bourgeois comedy and camp revue' (*The Times*, 26 July 1969) in which audiences were not asked to consider any serious social commentary that may have guided Chetwyn's directorial decisions.

Working within the framework of the revival's robust visual comedy, Maggie Smith incorporated risible character business throughout her performance as Margery that reinforced the prevalent sexually farcical tone: at Pinchwife's references to the town's pleasures, Margery, kneeling at his feet, falls back 'like a startled puppy, dropping the slipper she held for him' and then 'beams at the audience sudden, joyous knowledge where the forbidden fruit hangs', and in the letter-writing scene she sits 'panting, hanging her tongue almost to her chin, climbing half on to the writing-table with anxiety' and accidently snagging 'the quill in her hair, her eye, her inkwell' (*Observer*, 27 July 199) in a provocative display of acute sexual attraction and anticipation. From Pinchwife's 'ribald gait on bent knees' to Lady Fidget's 'tottering walk' and Horner's 'lightning recovery as he staggers out of the bedroom in the china scene' (*Times*, 10 July 1969), the Chichester production turned Wycherley's satirical comedy into a bedroom farce in which sex – hetero or otherwise – seemed to be everyone's walk of life.

London's prestigious National Theatre produced the play in 1977 under the direction of Peter Hall, who sought to elevate Wycherley to the status of other early-English dramatists, such as Ben Jonson, for his moral skewering of society, and to achieve this end, he packed the programme with historical minutiae that included a short biography on Wycherley and a diagram of Wren's playhouse, the latter inserted so as to explain his set design's antiquarian details such as the proscenium doors and forestage. Unfortunately, Hall erred in grafting 'historical pedantry' (*The Times*, 1 December 1977) to his production in the hope that it would raise public estimation of Wycherley as a classical playwright, for it hampered the performance's overall rhythm: specifically, the oblique positioning of the proscenium doors to the upstage wall (which could revolve and reveal a new locale) made for protracted movements to and from the central

acting area and the forestage, resulting in a dilatory pace in blocking that impeded the effect of the dialogue's quicker tempo. Hall,
known for his exhaustive training and rehearsing of actors in all
aspects of stylised acting, avoided the stereotypical mannerisms
used in most revivals of manners comedy, but his search for the
accurate pace congenial to Wycherley's satire – something he had
accomplished superbly with other dramatists' plays – proved less
successful. Like previous directors, Hall settled for a hackneyed
and uninspired production concept of this play – the 'downright
unequivocal lust' (*Guardian*, 1 December 1977) of the seventeenth
century's leisure class, and although the audience was spared the
snapping fans and formal poses from the characters, it was left 'to
deduce what instruction it likes' (*Financial Times*, 1 December
1977) from a revival that incorporated prurient visual business
(actors pointing to their crotches, china the size of a lighthouse)
just for quick and easy laughter. Other than Ben Kingsley's entertaining Sparkish, 'a brilliantly inventive and entirely traditional
portrait of a Restoration fop, bubbling with piglike snorts of
laughter at his own jokes, and nervous balletic lunges' (*The Times*,
1 December 1977) that vivified the character's perpetual nervous
energy, the cast failed to sparkle. Most disappointing was Albert
Finney's Horner, for in trying to convey the character's detachment toward his victims, Finney seemed 'so determined not to
allow the rake to show any feelings that he seems to be hardly
interested in the proceedings at all' (*Sunday Times*, 4 December
1977). In sum, Hall's revival made for a 'ponderous evening' (*The
Times*, 1 December 1977), perhaps warning future directors that
antiquarian revivals of Wycherley's comedy are reductive and
irrelevant to contemporary spectators and that production concepts that focus on lust and farce alone fail to capture the
profundity of Wycherley's mordant satire.

   The first truly innovative interpretation of *The Country Wife*
that conveyed the brutality and venality of an acquisitive society
bent on self-interest and personal pleasure and that made those
themes accessible to a contemporary audience was staged by
Manchester's Royal Exchange (1986). Nicholas Hytner's revival,
'so energetic and up-to-date it's bursting at the seams' (*Sunday
Times*, 28 December 1986), used Wycherley's comedy as an analogue to the 1980s Reagan–Thatcher years characterised by an
obsession with conspicuous consumption, materialism, sexual

excess, corporate greed and capitalism. Recalling the revival years later, critic Martin Hoyle (*Financial Times*, 14 July 1994), lauded Hytner's 'strutting, rapping production' which depicted 'a predatory jungle where people are commodities, where the innocent survive only by learning duplicity, and where the clowns in authority are not only buffoons but can be brutes as well'. Hytner's production combined 'the sleazy cocksureness of the Restoration decades with the unashamed chutzpah of the 1980s' (*Sunday Times*, 28 December 1986), and he drove his topical commentary home by using musical compositions that wedded baroque strains with the sound of rock and by conflating the two analogous periods through costume design, blending seventeenth-century silks with punk fashion that included evening dresses worn over Bermuda shorts, wigs and spiked hair, and servants sporting sunglasses and a Walkman.

In his politically charged production, Hytner populated the stage with 'slick, preening entrepreneurial types, overdressed and underemployed' (*Sunday Times*, 28 December 1986), obvious allusions to the new crop of callous and cagey business investors, like the parvenu Sir Jaspar, who, with their smug glee over their obscenely high profits made through Thatcher's covertly corrupt entrepreneurial initiatives – ones that aimed at making the rich even richer – created a new disenfranchised 'underclass' (a neologism of the 1980s) composed of legions of unemployed and homeless. Similarly, Gary Oldman's Horner, 'a lean fitness fanatic, tough and slightly androgynous, upwardly mobile and downwardly coarse' (*Sunday Times*, 28 December 1986), magnificently captured Wycherley's rake through a 1980s perspective: completely self-absorbed with his physical appearance, oblivious to the privation around him, seeking status via sexual liaisons with society women, and wanting any of the polish and charm of those gentlemen of bygone days, Horner is a rapacious individual who gladly capitalises on either the acquisitiveness or bankruptcy (sexually speaking) of others.

Hytner's directorial concept also stressed the spectatorial nature that underlies Wycherley's comedy, the implication that one seeks commodities (material goods, people, sex) not for their own sake but for their status as trophies to display for others to envy – that is, conspicuous consumption: the production 'catches perfectly the tone of rapacity which drives people, not so much to possess but to be seen to possess' (*Sunday Times*, 28 December 1986). In a revival that underscored sex as a commodity in a world now driven by the corporate mantra that greed is good, Hytner called for a particularly repugnant Pinchwife (Ian McDiarmid), a 'rat-like scavenger, unshaven and dishevelled among the preening gang' (*The Times*, 23 December 1986), an old, irascible vermin who scurried about the countryside to find a young virgin who could satisfy his greedy lust. Hytner orchestrated his revival as an assault on the spectators, and intending to shake them up and make them recognise the predatory and dispassionate tendencies in contemporary society, he directed Pinchwife to hector the audience by periodically 'flinging himself down in house seats to address his asides to the nearest spectator' (*The Times*, 23 December 1986), carrying his vitriol right into the auditorium and enlisting spectators' reactions to the perversity and self-centredness of this decadent society. The entire production concept worked exceeding well, for Martin Hoyle, faulting a 1993 RSC production for its lack of *zeitgeist*, remembered Hytner's revival fondly as one of the few that worked, and one that 'above all, though it disturbed' spectators, offered an energy, style and vision that he found 'exhilarating'.

For the most part, the 1990s witnessed a few lustreless museum revivals of *The Country Wife*, but in 1993, as Britain watched one scandal after another unfold to reveal the hypocrisy and corruption within both the government and the royal family, Wycherley's satire about promiscuous sex, greed, class privilege, and upper-class morality seemed the obvious choice as a dramatic analogue to Britain's current political, economic, and moral landscape. Three productions – two revivals and one musical adaptation – premièred almost concurrently, and although each director took a unique and different approach to the original comedy, all three sought to drive home the connexion between the conditions during Charles's reign and the current state of British affairs. The sudden popularity of Wycherley's play was axiomatic to most spectators and critics, but for any who missed the obvious, reviewer Georgina Brown (*Independent*, 11 August 1993) offered a concise summary:

> Wycherley's play is set in London of 1675, when England was wallowing in the after-effects of two lost wars, the Plague and

the Great Fire; society is cynical and despairing, with a debt crisis as desperate as its moral crisis. In some ways, then, not unlike Britain 1993.

By 1993, the failed economic policies of Thatcherism had come home to roost with a vengeance. The national economic plan of the 1980s that was propagandised as a panacea for the country's financial condition and was forecast to yield economic benefits to everyone including members of the working and lower classes proved to be patent lies. (In America, President Ronald Reagan called it 'trickle-down-economics', that is, wealth at the top would 'trickle down' to the masses by way of increased employment and investment opportunities.) From the privatisation of the country's utilities to the investment schemes at Lloyds, the new entrepreneurial initiatives lined only the pockets of the wealthy and left Britain with a staggering national debt of nearly £50 billion, soaring inflation that could not be halted, imminent recession that could not be staved off, plunging employment figures that created untold homeless victims, and a failing welfare system that left the elderly and infirm without adequate financial and medical assistance. The country was, as Georgina Brown described, despairing, and its collective disillusionment over the deplorable state of the country's economic condition was understandably intensified greatly as the public learned during John Major's administration of the fraud and greed – rather than the ostensibly singular concern for national economic welfare – that actually fuelled Thatcher's economic plan. On a daily basis, newspapers featured articles detailing the obscene profits made by the chosen few, the unconscionable frauds perpetrated on the unwitting public, and the pervasive damage done by a group of immoral leaders and businessmen who profited most from a series of economic strategies that left the average Briton holding the price tag. If Britons hoped to find a thread of morality left in the country by turning to the last bastion of decency – the royal family – its hopes were quickly dashed as the scandal of Prince Charles's long-term, adulterous affair with Camilla Parker Bowles hit the news-stands and dominated tabloid and television news for countless months. Across the board, the morality preached to the public by various government officials and members of the royal family was all a sham, a well-groomed image

created for the media to project to a trusting audience, but this
façade of decency and virtue that was intended to garner wholesale reverence and emulation shattered with every new scandal
that exposed the lies and duplicity of those entrusted to uphold
the conventional values and morals they so hypocritically and
continually espoused.

The Heather brothers' musical adaptation took its cue from the
royal family's sex scandal, as director Bob Carlton implies in his
opinion of the original play's current appeal:

> It's a play about the ruling classes and sexual hypocrisy –
> people of quality defending the morals of the nation. And it
> speaks directly to today's audience. You only have to look at
> the tabloid press to see the Government calling for a return to
> Victorian values and the rogering in high places that goes
> on.[40]

Appositely retitled *Lust* and staged at the West-End's Haymarket,
Wycherley's dark comedy was transformed into a light-hearted,
sing-along sex romp that incorporated a musical pastiche of folk,
rock and rococo strains, introduced lewd dance routines,
removed most of the original's dialogue, and interpolated a
wealth of humorous byplay and one-liners like the following
exchange between Alithea and Pinchwife: 'If you were my husband, I'd poison your food.' 'If you were my wife, I'd eat it.'[41]
Obviously, neither the Heather brothers nor Carlton sought to use
Wycherley's play as a springboard for a serious interrogation of
the source of Britain's pervasive disillusionment; in fact, the
play's inherent cynicism was avoided completely by the deliberate antedating of the musical to 1661 – one year after the
Restoration when most people were still celebrating their liberation from Puritanism and sanguine about their future under
Charles's new regime. *Lust* was one of those 'naughty-but-nice'
(*Daily Mail*, 13 August 1993) musicals, offending no one except
those who preferred that some semblance to Wycherley's text –
other than just Horner's sexual escapades – had remained intact.

At the Harrogate Theatre, Andrew Manley directed a multi-
media version of *The Country Wife*, a Brechtian approach that
interlaced Wycherley's play with video recordings from contemporary British life that included clippings of Prince Charles and

Lady Diana from their royal wedding and other candid shots in
order to highlight the past–past analogue of the declining monarchy caught up in sexual excess. The juxtaposition of these selected
video shots intermixed with the play's action strongly suggested
that Princess Diana 'may not, like the country wife, have been the
naïve she appeared to be. And as for Horner's harem of Fidget,
Dainty and Squeamish, one could only think of Camilla Parker
Bowles.'[42] This directorial concept that focused on the current
moral decay required cutting the original text to rid it of any hint
of possible virtue and redemption: hence, Manley deleted the
Alithea–Harcourt subplot because he believed that 'Wycherley
created this "dull" couple to take the hard edge off the play and
give it a moral setting' (*Independent*, 11 August 1993). Manley also
put the play's rampant promiscuity into a fitting context for his
1993 spectators who were facing a sobering reality that sexual
debauchery came at a very high price indeed: taking advantage of
the play's various references to the 'pox', Manley renders Horner
'vicious and without humour', a fornicating Grim Reaper with
'the Aids plague writ large'.[43] Overall, critics responded
favourably to Manley's blunt and cheeky revival, deeming it a
'brilliant and mischievous' interpretation that 'captures the moral
climate of Majorland – all tight-lipped morality and uninhibited
greed'.[44]

Max Stafford-Clark's revival of *The Country Wife*, the first
revival of this play by the Royal Shakespeare Company, offered
the most intellectual and illuminating directorial approach to
Wycherley's comedy to date. Reading the play's contemporary
relevance on a less topical and more transhistorical level,
Stafford-Clark focused his 1993 production not on the current
political and moral climate but rather on the universal verities of
sexual politics that inform male–female relationships in all patriarchal and patrilineal cultures. The inspiration for this interpretation derived clearly from Stafford-Clark's study of recent
scholarly works that interrogate exogamy and the 'trafficking of
women' by men as primarily motivated to strengthen their
homosocial bonds with one another rather than solidifying their
ties with women. In his programme note, Stafford-Clark sums
The Country Wife as 'a comprehensive range of responses to a
social situation in which the routing of homosocial desire through
women is clearly presented as compulsory' – a quote taken

directly from Eve Kosofsky Sedgwick's 1985 seminal study *Between Men: English Literature and Male Homosocial Desire* (p. 49) in which a chapter on Wycherley's play (*The Country Wife*: 'Anatomies of Male Homosocial Desire') investigates the extent to which 'the men's heterosexual relationships in the play have as their raison d'être an ultimate bonding between men; and that this bonding, if successfully achieved, is not detrimental to "masculinity" but definitive of it'.[45]

Sedgwick's anatomisation of masculinity, male desire for bonding as a collective sex, and men's drive for superiority over other males, reveals the role that patriarchal society maps out for women as singular facilitators of these three male imperatives which, without the women's collusion, would not be possible. In sum, women have no inherent value other than enhancing a man's status among other men, which is the male's primary motive in his possession and circulation of them. In this play that focuses so singularly on fear of cuckoldry – which is, after all, an act men perpetrate against other men – and rhapsodises so continually on the superiority of male friendship over heterosexual relationships, *The Country Wife*, notwithstanding its comic moments, affords a less-than-droll portrait of male anxiety and hatred toward women whom they have empowered to control their status within the homosocial community and who can, by their potential to betray them and negate their masculinity, render them symbolic eunuchs through their acts of adultery. Max Stafford-Clark's revival underscored this masculine anxiety rooted in misogyny as it concomitantly revealed the unavoidable contempt that women feel for the men who use them for their own homosocial purposes: 'We get a savage portrait of a corrupt society', noted the *Guardian* (12 August 1993), 'in which male promiscuity hides hatred of women and female coyness is a mask for vengeful rapacity', a 'vivid and aggressive revival' showing 'the bleak, mutual dislike which simmers at the heart of all the sexual skirmishings' (*Daily Mail*, 13 August 1993).

Glaringly absent from Stafford-Clark's interpretation were those conventional farcical touches deployed by directors to render the action a mindless, innocuous sex romp in which both men and women merely seek out sexual pleasure devoid of any emotional attachment. Stafford-Clark ferreted out the motives for such rapacious behaviour, liberating these characters from the previous one-dimensional portrayals of over-sexed and under-satisfied individuals and charging them with deep-seated reasons for their vicious attitudes and behaviour toward the opposite sex. Gone was 'the stale old Restoration business – the fans, the exaggerated fancies and fops', allowing for 'none of the artificiality'[46] that pinions the characters in a fictional world removed from reality. This RSC revival demanded that the audience take the play seriously, and thus, quite expectedly, audience laughter was at a minimum (as this author, who attended a performance at the Swan, can attest), but 'the muffling of comic impact', as John Gross (*Telegraph*, 15 August 1993) suggested, was 'a matter of design, or at any rate a price the director thinks worth paying'. For those spectators and critics who had either visited the concurrently running productions at the Haymarket and the Harrogate or who adhered to the conventional reading of Wycherley's comedy as a bawdy satire that focuses on only the innocuous and outward displays of sexual vices, the RSC's more profound reading of the impetus for the battle of the sexes proved startling and unsettling, especially in its critique of the male characters as something more sinister, fragile and malevolent than previous productions had allowed.

From Horner to Sparkish, Stafford-Clark shocked the audience with his radical depiction of the men as the weaker sex, one riddled with loathing, fear and apprehension, using the play's entire action 'to expose an unexpected world of male vulnerability' and an overall 'unlovely masculine' society where 'sex is both an ultimate goal and a source of insecurity and terror' for the male.[47] Horner – removed from his typical position at the centre of the action and reduced to just another character in the ensemble – showed the stereotypical libertine as anything but the Don Juan of male myths for whom women pine. Jeremy Northam's 'cold, unsmiling performance as Horner makes the flesh creep', while his 'rampaging libido seems more like a disease than pleasure'.[48] From the moment he entered, recalled John Peter (*Sunday Times*, 15 August 1993), 'you sense that for him women are a commodity: necessary, briefly pleasurable and utterly tedious, to be used and speedily discarded'.

Just as Northam's Horner showed all of the rake's contempt for the women he seduces with none of the physical attraction and sexual charm of the romanticised, mythic libertine, Robin

Soans's Pinchwife was firmly grounded in the real world rather than one of caricature or stereotype: his characterisation was 'no joke-cuckold but a man whose self-doubt turns to venom' (*Guardian*, 12 August 1993). Pinchwife showed no love for Margery, made his threats against her disturbingly real and frightening (holding the penknife to her face in his threat to poke out her eyes), and howled like a wounded animal at each thought of being rendered a cuckold – grabbing his crotch or falling on a phallic cane when his suspicions seem realised, bits of business that garnered some audience laughter but more significantly pointed to the source of his fear of emasculation, a fear that Soans projected at every turn with his pained facial expressions and wildly bulging eyes. Providing 'a compulsive study of paranoia: stooped by jealousy, confiding his misogynistic fears to the world with deadpan pithiness' (*Time Out*, 18 August 1993), Soans's performance left no one in doubt as to Pinchwife's real loathing of women and his potential for cruelty toward them.

In every instance, the male characters showed contempt for women – Sparkish spitting viciously on Alithea when he severs their betrothal, Pinchwife twisting Margery's arm behind her back to bend her to his will – and even in those scenes typically hailed as examples of clever libertine banter, this revival stressed that male power and possession over women stemmed from their hatred toward them: the 'laddish conversations between Wycherley's young bucks, usually passed off as wit, gain a grinding, misogynistic edge' (*Evening Standard*, 13 July 1994). And if any spectator should have missed this point 'that inside every libertine is a man who fears and hates women' (*The Times*, 14 July 1994), interpolated lyrics sung at the end of the performance by a chorus of the play's male characters summed it up with a bold crassness that included the following verse: 'At heart we hate 'em, curse and berate 'em, mount and mate 'em.'[49]

As for the females in this savage reading of Wycherley's comedy, they 'unexpectedly steal the production's satiric thunder' (*Time Out*, 18 August 1993) and eclipse the men at every turn. Lady Fidget (Abigail McKern) and her rapacious 'virtuous gang' overpowered the males in each scene, and in the banquet sequence, they proved so formidable that one forgot Horner's presence until they mocked him as their ersatz husband and made familiar with him: 'he might as well be a pile of doomed sausagemeat' (*Time Out*, 18 Aug 1993). Debra Gillett's Margery provided the revival's bulk of comic relief. Her performance of a country girl was brilliantly sketched in her slow and deliberate speech, as if searching for the right words to express the ideas that leapt to her mind. Margery was a mercurial, child-like creature, 'as unpredictable as the weather, one minute sinking to the ground in her exaggerated respect for Pinchwife, the next crumpling into a paroxysm of grief at his first criticism', and her face, 'a souring milk-churn of agitated emotions' (*Observer*, 17 July 1994), provided a constant visual sign by which to read her ever-changing emotional state. Wide-eyed and innocent at the beginning of the play, with 'rebellious twitches of the mouth' (*The Times*, 14 July 1994) betraying her desire for freedom, Gillett's Margery left no uncertainty at the denouement that she has learned to tell lies like the best of them.

Stafford-Clark described Wycherley's comedy as 'a message from the past to the present' (*Independent*, 11 August 1993), a play charged with male–female hostility that manifests in a state of perpetual war brought on by the sexual politics that remain operative in contemporary society. And to make this past–present analogue clear to the audience at the outset, Stafford-Clark substituted Wycherley's original prologue with one newly written that prepared the audience to read the play's action as applicable to 1993 *zeitgeist* as well. Although many critics longed for a lighter take on Wycherley's satire, most agreed that Stafford-Clark had, as John Peter (*Sunday Times*, 15 August 1994) opined, 'grasped the central point about this play, which is that these men do not really like women at all', and that 'the way men value women reflects their secret value of themselves'. Most critics tacitly implied that a production of *The Country Wife* in the later twentieth century requires a directorial approach that revisions the action in a way that makes it meaningful to a more sophisticated audience sensitised to misogyny. Nick Curtis (*Evening Standard*, 13 July 1994), who attended the revival after its transfer to the Barbican's Pit Theatre, summed the general feeling among most spectators who saw the RSC's bold and daring version of *The Country Wife*:

> Stafford-Clark rises above the uncritical buffoonery that can make *The Country Wife* a palatable romp, but his shrewd anatomising of the play's sexual politics robs it of some

humour. An unequal mixture of full-fledged comedy and a rediscovery of the play's dark side, his version is ultimately more satisfying than either of those poles would have been alone.

Stafford-Clark may not have reconciled the play's dark tone within a wholly comedic atmosphere – that is, presuming such a mixture is stylistically possible and compatible – but his interpretation will hopefully encourage other directors of this satire to find new and viable performance concepts rather than borrow from the hackneyed, stock approaches that neither tax the creative energies of the director nor challenge the intellectual acuity of contemporary spectators.

8
The Plain Dealer:
Honour, Courage and Heroism

Although *The Country Wife* is Wycherley's most studied and performed comedy, many of his contemporaries regarded *The Plain
Dealer* as his finest play, praising Wycherley, as did John Dryden,
for having 'obliged all honest and virtuous men, and enrich'd our
stage by one of the most bold, most general, and most useful
satires, which has ever been presented on the English theatre'.[1]
However, Wycherley's last comedy is not merely his harshest and
most comprehensive satire by virtue of its attack against the
world at large, as Dryden suggests, it is also one of the most
ambiguous and contradictory plays in all of Restoration drama,
and while a number of critics today echo Dryden's overall praise
of the play, most find themselves in a position similar to that of
the première's audience on 11 December 1676 who, as John
Dennis reported, 'appeared doubtful what judgement to form of
it'.[2] Saving the play from oblivion in its own day were
Wycherley's fellow Court Wits whose 'loud approbation of it',
Dennis further noted, 'gave it both a sudden and a lasting reputation' among theatregoers, thereby helping to secure its place in
the permanent repertory well into the eighteenth century. But

neither Dryden's nor the Court Wits' strong endorsement of *The Plain Dealer* helps to clarify the mystery of exactly what Wycherley intended to convey in this play that not only flagellates everyone in society – parents, friends, lovers, and lawyers, to name just a few of his targets – as corrupt, disloyal, selfish and hypocritical liars, none of whom alters his behaviour by the end of the play, but also, and more significantly, that features a nominal hero, Manly the plain-dealer, who proves no better, and in some instances worse, than the hypocrites he so self-righteously and vociferously flays. Compounding the interpretative problem is the fact that at the comedy's conclusion, Manly – a humourless and hostile malcontent whose sombre and unrelenting invectives against society give the play a dark and heavy atmosphere – wins the virtuous and devoted heroine, a traditional comic denouement at odds with the play's overall negative and bleak tone and a reward strikingly inappropriate for a character whose positive qualities remain negligible. These inconsistencies not only confounded Carolean spectators – except, it seems, Dryden and the Court Wits – they also continue to plague modern readers and theatregoers who find great difficulty in reconciling Wycherley's abrasive hero with the fifth-act emoluments he scarcely deserves.

Wycherley's atypical use of such a contrived comic ending – Manly's astonishing *volte-face* in accepting Freeman's friendship and Fidelia's love – greatly affects spectators' interpretation of the play, for it creates a radical and unexpected shift in focus from what audiences had been assuming was Wycherley's main satiric target throughout the bulk of the play – that is, the pervasive hypocrisy and mendacity that Manly rails against – to Manly himself, suggesting that it is his journey from blind intransigence to enlightenment and not the vices of the age that is the comedy's real main thrust. The denouement redirects audience attention solely to Manly since he is the only character who undergoes any transformation whatsoever, and it rewrites Wycherley's thematic message into a satiric indictment not necessarily only against the world that Manly abhors but rather also against the misanthrope himself who, in turning his back on society and believing he can exist without others, is dangerously antisocial and patently self-deluded, and who must, Wycherley seems to imply, make some accommodation by both relinquishing his unrealistic fantasy as to how the world should ideally operate and accepting society as it truly is: imperfect and flawed though offering the occasional opportunity for true friendship and selfless love.

The Plain Dealer's denouement clearly indicates that Wycherley intends to highlight Manly over society's evils, but his overall purpose may well have extended considerably beyond the trite message that man needs human companionship regardless of the risks, for it foregrounds Manly in a far more pertinent way, one that calls the question about the nature of the hero himself, this self-professed man of honour and courage who does nothing to remedy the ills of society other than to rail against them, who contributes to the moral decay of the world he damns so freely, and who, for all his intentional lack of positive intervention, nonetheless ends up with the spoils from a war that he himself initiates against society. Wycherley was indeed writing about the dishonour, hypocrisy and disloyalty rampant in a world inured to such evils, as Dryden implies, but his primary focus was not merely on such easy and axiomatic targets as fops, fools and cheats, for he also aimed his satire toward the one individual to whom society looks for curative and emulative actions: the hero. Indeed, while some scholars maintain that Wycherley was simply reworking one of his sources (Molière's The Misanthrope [1666]) to posit his own solution to the age-old dichotomy of self-versus-society,[3] Wycherley, in fact, borrowed some of the details from the French comedy's plot and character but not necessarily its central theme, for a closer look at the deliberate contradictions wrought by Wycherley in delineating his main character brings the play into sharp focus as a disquisition about the qualities of heroism. In fact, viewing the play within this context of heroic action allows all those disparate characterisations of Manly suggested by critics who find him a comic dupe, a moralist, a psychopath or an idealist likewise to fall into place not as a result of unfortunate solecisms in Wycherley's writing that ostensibly signal the dramatist's confusion as to his own specific aims with this play and its main character (as some scholars suggest[4]) but as intentional contradictions and ambiguities intended to call attention to the attributes lacking in this flawed hero who symbolised an age wanting altogether in heroism.

That Wycherley would problematise the nature of the hero and heroic action is wholly consistent with the era's almost singular preoccupation with the qualities of heroism, a preoccupation born out of a disturbing truism that the author Samuel Butler (1612–80), known best for his social and political satires, lamented in his *Prose Observations*: 'No Age abounded more with Heroical Poetry then the present, and yet there was never any wherein fewer Heroical Actions were performed.'[5] From the beginning of the Restoration, writers grappled with depictions of heroism, turning first to epic poetry, the most revered literary form, in their attempts to apply heroic virtue to the leaders of their newly restored English society, ascribing to them those classical qualities that had inspired awe and admiration since the ancient Greek writers fashioned the first epic poems: selflessness, courage, loyalty, honour, and most especially magnanimity – that is, a greatness of the soul, spirit and mind – which manifested itself in a fearlessness against death and valour on the battlefield.[6] From the days of Homer, such laudable and uncommon attributes were deemed inherent in kings and others of rank and title who by nature ostensibly possessed such superhuman qualities that made them god-like, as Thomas Hobbes averred in his exegesis of poetic genre that appropriated the court as the only fitting subject of epic poetry: 'For there is in Princes, and men of conspicuous power (anciently called *Heroes*) a lustre and influence upon the rest of men, resembling that of the Heavens.'[7] As poets were crafting their epics to correspond with these conventional notions that conflated nobility with honour and heroism, playwrights offered heroic dramas that featured valiant and commendable leaders who risked their lives against powerful adversaries to protect the sacred values of love and honour (see Chapter 2). By the 1670s, however, when Wycherley wrote *The Plain Dealer*, the epic poem had fizzled out, replaced by mock-epics and satires such as those penned by Butler, and at the playhouses, heroic drama likewise became obsolete, a genre laughable for its unrealistic depiction of superhuman heroes who traversed the fictional worlds on stage but were nowhere to be found on the streets of London or in the corridors of Whitehall.

During the second decade of Charles's reign, poets and playwrights, for the most part, gave up on heroism in the classical sense because it had become devalued, denigrated by Charles's unheroic lechery and transparent duplicity, by the failure of the English navy either to win its wars against the Dutch or to secure military successes that equalled those during

Cromwell's regime, and by the disarray at court where government officials and others in power put self-interest and private motives above the nation's well-being. The ideals of heroism had become especially corrupted by a new breed of men of rank and title whose libertine escapades – public drunkenness, flagrant debauchery, vandalism – provided fodder not only for tavern gossip but also for poems and plays written by authors whose seeming romanticisation and valorisation of their iconoclasm and profligacy transformed them into ersatz heroes. Men like Lord Rochester, who understandably would later denounce his dissipation while dying of syphilis at 33, represented the new, young hero, wealthy and titled anarchists who waged their wars not against formidable foes threatening national security but against conventional values at home, spending their leisure time in drunken brawls, smashing sundials and windows, seducing then abandoning gullible young women whom they often impregnated, disrobing in public for their own amusement at shocking onlookers, and a wealth of other equally puerile and pathetic activities that constituted the bulk of their valiant conduct. While some of these aristocrats fought in the two failed Dutch Wars, few earned any distinction in battle worthy of poetic eulogies or panegyrics, and the notoriety they earned in the popular press centred on their private lives and peccadilloes. These new heroes – or antiheroes – captured the imagination, though not always the widespread approval, of the public, and they significantly influenced the younger generation who found their antics not only befitting a gentleman but also requisite for such a distinction, youthful and impressionable men who also sought to emulate these aristocrats in large part because their scandalous behaviour brought them fame, however dubious, and reputations as men of 'wit'. During the Carolean era, 'the English had lost their bearings as to what counted as heroic',[8] observes John Spurr, and the literature of the period mirrors this loss through its displacement of the classical hero and its substitution with a figure that proved a more accurate reflection of the adulterated, contemporary 'hero' as Butler and many others saw him.

In *The Plain Dealer*, Wycherley anatomises the current state of heroism, presenting audiences with a problematic character quite atypical from those in his other plays and one that audiences had perforce to view within the context of heroic action: a captain who

commands a ship that escorts a convoy of merchant vessels to the
Indies during one of England's wars with the Dutch. Wycherley
himself had been directly involved in combat during the Second
Dutch War (1664–7) and surely witnessed at firsthand the degree
of bravery and courage exhibited by sailors who met their deaths
or withstood severe injury fighting in what would ultimately
become a losing battle. During the Dutch War, as in any period,
courage in combat was a barometer by which to measure true
heroism, and those brave soldiers who had lost their lives or body
parts demonstrated a level of fortitude and fearlessness that
inspired poets: the Earl of Sandwich, dressed in his naval uni-
form, went down with his burning ship in the battle of Sole Bay
(1672) during the Third Dutch War, prompting elegists to write
graphic and inspiring descriptions of his heroic demise – 'Had
you but seen how unconcern'd he stood, / Flames over's head,
his feet dabbling in blood; / In what a fearless and compos'd
estate / He braved the approach of the severest fate' and 'Blest
Sandwich! Earth's envy! Heaven's delight! / Whom the Gods
honoured to die in fight!'⁹ Even those sailors who endured anaes-
thetic-free amputations during the heat of battle earned glory for
their personal sacrifices: Captain Haddock who continued to
command his ship at Sole Bay while a surgeon sliced through the
torn ligaments and muscle of his toe, as well as others who withstood amputations of limbs without the slightest flinch, symbolised admirable heroes willing to risk their lives to honour their
country.¹⁰ Wycherley's Captain Manly would have immediately
sparked audiences' recollections of the most recent Dutch War
(1672–4) and its uncommon heroes like Sandwich, and the
marked disparity in Manly's behaviour between the classic hero
and the contemporary version emblematised the wide gulf that
currently existed between heroic ideals of the past ages and the
human reality of seventeenth-century England.

Within the course of *The Plain Dealer*'s lengthy, single-scene
first act, Wycherley immediately establishes issues of heroism,
beginning first with Manly and his questionable nature as a hero,
one whose vacillation between heroic virtue and sham heroism
forces spectators to alter their sympathies for him repeatedly, ini-
tiating at the outset a constant shift in their approval of him as
well as their interrogation of his definition of heroic action that
they will grapple with throughout the course of the play as Manly

behaves in ways glaringly inconsistent with his rhetoric and reveals a disturbing, antiheroic strain. At Manly's first entrance, audiences identify him instantaneously as a hero and interpret his sentiments within a positive context of heroic behaviour: dressed in his simple captain's garb and pursued by the lavishly outfitted Lord Plausible, a 'ceremonious, supple, commending coxcomb' as described by Wycherley in the *dramatis personae*, Manly's opening, vitriolic attack against hypocrites like Plausible who readily conform to the age's 'slavish ceremonies', 'little tricks', and 'supercilious forms' (I,i,2–3) that bespeak society's pretence, perfidy, and duplicity establishes him as a plain-speaking, salty sailor whose rugged individualism, naked honesty, unshakable principles, and nonconformity smack of heroic virtue. Plausible's specious attempts to defend the pervasive disloyalty, gossiping and back-biting among false friends and acquaintances as an acceptable, normative custom ('But if I did say or do an ill thing to anybody, it should be sure to be behind their backs out of pure good manners' [I,i,50–2]) serve only to fuel Manly's positive position as a plain-dealer fully justified in his condemnation of a dishonourable society of which he wants no part. Within only a few minutes, however, Manly diminishes his stature by his unprovoked assault on Plausible: *'thrusting out my Lord Plausible,'* as the stage direction indicates, through the front door. Although audiences would have laughed at the cowardly flatterer being flung out of the room by force, Manly's aggressiveness, thus far exhibited only in diatribes and curses, has transcended mere rhetoric and now manifests itself in a surprising exhibition of physical force, a show of violence against an innocuous and effeminate foe that warns of an unchecked hostility capable of lashing out in retaliation. The hero's physical prowess that ensures his victory in battle is shown in Manly to be nothing more than outright bullying, a troubling display of physical dominance that erupts quickly in this character when frustration against those who disagree with his ideals or challenge his position and beliefs knows no other recourse but violence, a propensity for assault that will manifest again in the scene at Westminster Hall and in his base, physical 'revenge' on Olivia.

The picture of Manly the plain-dealing hero as less a reclusive pacifist and more an habitual pugilist is reinforced moments later when the two sailors discuss their adventures with Manly at sea prior to the opening of the play: 'I never saw him pleased but in the fight', remarks Sailor 1, an observation Sailor 2 confirms immediately, 'A pox, he's like the Bay of Biscay, rough and angry, let the wind blow where 'twill' (I,i,150–5). Manly, enamoured of battles and confrontations regardless of where they take place and with whom they occur, has a strain of antagonism and defiance that accounts for his deliberate sinking of his ship damaged in battle. Although the sailors note Manly's courage fighting against the Dutch, they disagree as to whether Manly's decision to destroy the ship (which he apparently justified as a means of keeping it from falling into the hands of the enemy or those mercenary courtiers who seize damaged vessels for profit) was a prudent tactic. With their debate left unresolved – neither sailor viewing the incident as an especial display of their captain's valour – spectators grapple with the exact extent of Manly's heroism, reflecting back on his rash treatment of Plausible a few seconds earlier, questioning Manly's judgement overall, and positioning his act of intentional sabotage (which caused Manly to lose half of his fortune stowed aboard the ship as well as the investments of others) within the context of those Dutch-War heroes who battled foes to the bitter end and went down with their ships. For a hero who so loves to fight – that is, fight and win – and inveighs against cowardice, Manly's capitulation, born out of spite, impetuousness, or perhaps fear of humiliation in defeat, came relatively easily. Having destroyed his vessel for motives that ring equally valid and hollow, Manly does circumvent the possibility of disgrace in battle and preserves his own illusion of his masculine (manly) bravery and unimpeachable heroic stature, but confidence in his brand of heroism is challenged again.

Following this exchange, Wycherley's disquisition on heroism in general as well as its implications vis-à-vis Manly gains a new perspective with the entrance of Freeman, Manly's lieutenant and foil. Described by Wycherley as 'a complier with the Age', Freeman is a clever rake, witty and self-possessed, who manoeuvres his way through the world by his charm and will, and, unlike Manly, nonchalantly accepts the flaws in others in large part because he can capitalise on them. Freeman's unruffled, easygoing tolerance of society and its rogues and villains accentuates the full force of Manly's fanaticism, for while Manly's railing against Plausible seemed an appropriate attack against an overly mannered society, his sustained rage over the hypocrisy and disloyalty of the entire civilised world next to Freeman's carefree, rational defence of compliance with social forms renders him something of a monomaniac whose raving appears obsessive, brutish and myopic. Manly, dedicated to the heroic concept of a 'singular' friendship, as he tells Freeman (I,i,233–5) – one and only one true friend, like Damon and Pythias, notes Peter Holland[11] – shows himself an extremist warring against everyone, accosting all with his debate about society's evils, caring only about promulgating his opinion, dismissing out-of-hand any possible alternatives or compromise, and believing his bullish ranting should induce others to adopt his philosophy. Although Manly offers cogent reasons for his idealistic philosophy of life, Freeman's crafty chastising of Manly and his argument's defects when applied to the real world (I,i,284–319) shows Manly as blinded by his feelings of moral righteousness and supremacy above all others, a superiority that he believes empowers him to assault others at will and without just cause or provocation. The hero who fails to discriminate between real foes or threats and who attacks others for the sheer pleasure of showing his force and asserting his righteousness over them may make a formidable warrior willing to rush blindly into combat for its own sake, but it also makes for a loose cannon, and more importantly it signifies a fanatic, one who is equally eager to battle any cause personal to him though perhaps inimical to social amity without questioning its validity and soundness or its effect on others, as Freeman tries to explain to him.

The juxtaposition of Manly and Freeman, however, serves an equally significant purpose in furthering Wycherley's anatomisation of heroic virtue, for by introducing the latter very early in the play, Wycherley quickly adds to the mix a character whom audiences would have identified as the conventional hero of manners comedy: the libertine. In fact, his status as the play's sole rake has encouraged some to read him as the golden mean and the real plain-dealer,[12] though such characterisations are actually procrustean fits and at odds with Wycherley's strategy in presenting him as Manly's foil and his only true friend. Freeman is intended to represent the other polarity of heroism: just as Manly (an older, veteran sailor) is meant to call to mind the embodiment of the classical hero – courageous, honourable, principled – so is

Freeman (a young gallant) used to symbolise the ersatz hero of
seventeenth-century England. As with Manly, however,
Wycherley puts an unflattering and realistic spin on this typical
hero of Carolean comedies and the popular press: while Manly
symbolises the classical hero besmirched by indiscriminate
aggression and delusions of singular greatness and superiority
that render him necessary during a war crisis but dangerous and
anachronistic in the modern world, Freeman is a far cry from the
charming and irresistible rakes romanticised on the stage or in the
public's imagination and is a more thoroughly accurate depiction
of the contemporary libertine contaminated by self-interest and
pleasure and concerned solely with personal gain. Although he is
a plain-dealer in the sense that he is forthright about his mercenary motives for pursuing the wealthy Widow Blackacre, his willingness to marry this older, litigious harridan solely out of greed
in return for his sexual favours is unsavoury. Having squandered
his own fortune, Freeman will sell himself to the highest female
bidder in order to rob her of her own estate so that he can continue his life of pleasure, as the Widow Blackacre makes unequivocally clear:

> I mean, you would have me keep you that you might turn
> keeper, for poor widows are only used like bawds by you;
> you go to church with us but to get other women to lie with.
> In fine, you are a cheating, chousing spendthrift and, having
> sold your own annuity, would waste my jointure.
>
> (II,i,1077–82)

Prostituting himself with his only commodity that he believes
is in great demand, blatantly offering to gratify the Widow's sexual desires if she will take care of his financial wants in a scene
that makes him look ridiculous as he struts his stuff in front of
Blackacre while she shoos him away, completely uninterested in
his sexual offerings, Freeman is for the most part unprincipled,
equally willing to prostitute himself around town, feigning sincere friendship to everyone who could potentially help or harm
him and whom he admits he has 'hugged, kissed, flattered and
bowed to' (I,i,274–80) though he despises them all. Quite fittingly, Manly distrusts Freeman's offer of friendship, and spectators
likewise recoil from this young libertine who, like Rochester and

other rakes of the town, enjoys assaulting inanimate objects as a display of the 'new' heroism ('I am an old scourer and can naturally beat up a wench's quarters that won't be civil. Shan't we break her windows too?' [V,ii,424–5]), and who upholds no values and draws no line in his selfish pursuits.

With the introduction of Fidelia toward the end of this lengthy first scene, Wycherley brings on one final character who invokes the concept of heroism, a young lady lifted out of heroic drama and placed in the middle of seventeenth-century London as the spokesperson for honour, purity, and loyalty (which her name signifies). The striking incongruity of her presence there – espousing virtue and valour while periodically speaking blank verse along the way – within the contemporary world of hypocrites and knaves works by contrast to foreground the glaring absence around her of those ideals she embodies, and it underscores as well the unlikelihood of such ideals existing in this society, save, that is, for such similarly fantastical transplants as she. Having mustered the bravery to abandon her family and fortune in order to disguise herself as a cabin boy and follow Manly, Fidelia – like all heroines in heroic drama – would sacrifice her life for the man she loves, willing and courageous enough even to trek after him to the remote Indies where, 'among the sooty Indians' and their barbaric customs, she would gladly 'live his wife, where wives are forced / To live no longer when their husbands die' (I,i,637–8). She is the physical embodiment of the masculine ideal of heroic virtue, fittingly and ironically encased in the outward disguise of a man but in reality, underneath the fake appearance of maleness, a feminine force, the very force that Manly equates with cowardice, the opposite of heroism. Fidelia will challenge Manly's notions of honour and courage during the course of the play – 'cruelty and courage never dwelt together' (I,i,440), she tells him in their first exchange, an apposite retort to the man who accuses her of cowardice (and thus of a lack of honour and heroism) and then later rationalises his rape of Olivia as a means of vindicating his 'honour'.

While Manly and Freeman represent the antipodes of heroism, Novel, Plausible and men of their ilk, 'the gaudy, fluttering parrots of the town, and apes and echoes of men only' (I,i,656–7), as Manly describes them,[13] embody the acute absence of any masculine, heroic virtue. In the opening scene of the second act,

Wycherley deliberately establishes a marked contrast with the preceding one that showed the tough and masculine world of Manly with its Spartan quarters and rough edges by giving audiences a sobering glimpse into one of the various unheroic quarters of the society that Manly has been inveighing against – the cowardly fops who, as Manly's sailors alluded to earlier, capitalise on the war by retrieving salvage ships for profit but lack the courage and fortitude to engage in battle (I,i,110–15).[14] Lounging in an intimate circle in Olivia's lavishly appointed drawing-room and wearing their fashionable periwigs, luxuriously embroidered coats and silk hose while sipping their afternoon tea are a group of effeminate emulators of Charles's court who sport swords as a fashion statement and while away the hours in their cabals, amusing themselves at the expense of others whom they malign and ridicule for their own entertainment. Their back-biting and gossiping denote their frivolous priorities and self-appointed superiority in a society composed of vain, superficial and competitive animals who preen, strut and snipe in an effort to assert their dominance in their vacuous and pathetic lives filled with treachery and cupidity. In his indictment against this artificial and affected society, Wycherley also widens his circle of reference to include the entire fashionable peerage at large. Using Lord Plausible's references to Sir John Current and Sir Richard Court-Title, two aristocratic fops who successfully pretend to attributes they lack – that is, courage, wit, wealth – and who, by their very titles as well as their sheer skill in deceiving others, have gained themselves reputations as the 'patterns of heroic virtue', and 'the honour of our nation, the glory of our age' (II,i,358, 361–2), Wycherley depicts the entire aristocracy as a self-absorbed and hollow group that has conveniently redefined ideals such as honour and valour to mirror their own vapid lifestyles and empty values.

Within the context of heroism, these individuals represent to spectators the effete, mannered and self-interested society that the Earl of Sandwich, Captain Haddock, and other sailors – as well as the fictional Manly – fought to honour and protect, a privileged corps of enervated aristocrats and upper-class individuals who certainly gave not the slightest thought to the numerous appeals made to them by politicians and poets to renounce their idleness and prove their mettle, as in the poem *Honour's*

Invitation, or a Call to the Camp (1673), written on the occasion of
the Third Dutch War, which featured Charles II entreating young
profligates to throw off 'all the luxuries of wanton peace' and join
forces against the enemy in a lofty cause:

> Then rouse at last from this lethargic dream,
> And let heroic actions be thy theme.
> No more to base effeminate follies yield,
> Thy country's genius calls thee to the field.[15]

Men such as Novel and Plausible, 'two pulvillio boxes' and
'musk-cats' (II,i,616–7) concerned more with the cut of their
clothes (which Novel believes shows a man's 'wit and judgement,
nay, and his courage too' [II,i,666–7]), prefer to remain on the
sidelines of battle while finding entertainment in their malicious
derision of heroes, mocking them for their foolish aspirations to
heroism and laughing hysterically at their own distasteful jokes
about wooden legs or the amputated arms that made the wounded look like 'a pair of compasses' (I,i,588–99). With their callous
quips and howling laughter, Novel, Plausible and Olivia serve as
a chorus in their collective jocularity toward heroism: they call to
mind for Carolean theatregoers the prevailing amusement they
similarly displayed toward the ideals depicted either in the performances of heroic dramas or in the verses of the mock epics and
satires of the day, a reaction that bespoke their overall crisis in
confidence in the possibility of heroism at all. The humour here
for the audience, of course, loses a good deal of its punch as
Wycherley intentionally has spectators observe these cruel and
vacuous individuals mock heroism while Manly, Freeman and
Fidelia eavesdrop and react silently with shock and offence.

Carefully orchestrating each snide quip from this group at
Manly's expense, Wycherley manipulates audience sympathy for
him once again as the play's hero. And when Manly steps forward from behind the screen that has hidden him and his companions to denounce Olivia for her deceit only to have her turn
on her heels and brutally ridicule him as a fool and an egoist,
spectators' compassion for him increases exponentially. This
woman, whom Manly had believed 'never knew artifice' and
'hates the lying, masking, daubing world' (I,i,651–4), is a beautiful, alluring, vain, coarse, libidinous, and greedy hypocrite who

has stolen his fortune, married his only friend, and duped more than one man out of his valuable possessions by her crafty manipulation of his ego: 'she stands in the drawing room like the glass, ready for all comers to set their gallantry before her, and, like the glass too, lets no man go from her unsatisfied with himself' (IV,ii,112–15), remarks Novel after he realises Olivia has finagled jewels from both him and Plausible by pandering to their male vanity, a stratagem that worked on Manly as well (IV,ii,250–3). Notwithstanding Olivia's cruelty toward Manly and the sympathy she evokes for him here, however, Wycherley shifts the audience's perspective toward Manly yet again by giving to Olivia the role of a mock-panegyrist whose description of his fanatical behaviour chimes in with what spectators have so far observed for themselves. Her ridicule of his heroic, masculine demeanour and posturing has the ring of truth, most notably when she describes his courage, 'which most of all appears in your spirit of contradiction, for you dare give all mankind the lie and your opinion is your only mistress, for you renounce that too when it becomes another man's' (II,i,720–6). Manly's courage, Olivia implies, rests with his passion for being contrary and railing, as she states later, 'at all mankind' (IV,ii,269), foolishly believing in only his own opinion and trusting that opinion so long as it is held by no one else but him. Simply put, Olivia's mockery of Manly deconstructs his masculine behaviour and appearance (e.g., his 'lion-like mein', the 'manly roughness' of his voice, his masculine unkemptness [II,i,688–760]) as purely a role he enacts to disguise his complete want of such manly heroism, a charge she will level against him once again and which audiences will have to judge as well.[16]

Manly's escalating rage in this scene – thrusting Plausible and Novel out of the room to be rid of their snickering – is excusable given Olivia's reprehensible treatment of him, but Olivia's cool detachment accentuates his fury and redirects theatregoers' attention to his unchecked emotionalism, an emotionalism exhibited in the first scene which spectators suspect they have not seen the last of here. Ironically, for all his ceremonious rhetoric about plain-dealing, Manly, it would seem, actually cannot tolerate a little plain-dealing when it is aimed his way, for Olivia has been forthright with him in this scene about her true feelings for him and what she thinks of his heroic demeanour. But her harsh candour with him, not very unlike his toward others, only engenders his fury, and it calls to mind the hypocrisy in his earlier response to Freeman when the lieutenant asked him how he would respond if he admitted to him that 'the world thinks you a madman, a brutal'. Manly's reply, 'I, instead of hating thee, should love thee for thy plain-dealing' (I,i,316, 332–3), is now seen as nothing short of an outright lie. Olivia has in so many words told Manly what Freeman did not have the courage or inclination to do, and having thrown a little plain-dealing his way, Olivia actually believes she will finally be rid of him ('I think I have given him enough of me now never to be troubled with him again' [II,i,863–4]). Olivia is wrong, however, for with Manly, plain-dealing flows only in one direction.

Having been the victim of Olivia's treachery, as well as her plain-dealing which challenged his image of himself as a true and singular hero, Manly – emotionally stung by her rejection, candour and cruelty – must retaliate, but in so doing, of course, he proves Olivia's allegations: his heroism is a façade that hides his own hypocrisy and cowardice. Blaming Olivia for his own uncontrollable emotionalism, which he defines as love (lust? revenge?), Manly takes a precipitous fall from his heroic ideal which fittingly begins in Westminster Hall, the ostensible temple of truth and justice but actually the locus of society's pervasive corruption and lies. Speaking in blank verse as if his emotions possess epic and heroic proportions, Manly reveals his altered inner state, which he intends to hide from Freeman out of masculine necessity:

> How hard it is to be an hypocrite!
> At least to me, who am but newly so.
> I thought it once a kind of knavery,
> Nay, cowardice, to hide one's faults; but now
> The common frailty, love, becomes my shame.
> He must not know I love th' ungrateful still,
> Lest he contemn me more than she, for I,
> It seems, can undergo a woman's scorn
> But not a man's –
>
> (III,i,30–88)

Needing to maintain his guise of masculine self-control and to avoid Freeman's contempt for his feminine frailty, Manly decides that plain-dealing (as it applies to him at least) is no longer in his best interest and he will forgo it so that no one – save Fidelia, whom he knows he can trust to remain discreet and whom he now needs to help him secure his revenge – will discern that he is anything less than the complete embodiment of manhood and heroic stoicism. Clearly, in turning the 'hypocrite', as he calls it, Manly, never having been challenged before by any who dared to cross his path, reveals that he has all along possessed those base characteristics which he believed set him apart and above everyone else, though he will deploy linguistic strategies here and elsewhere to rationalise his contemptuous behaviour and thus keep his self-image intact. More than eager now to enlist the aid of another, this hero previously so singular in his needs and friendships, presses Fidelia to 'pimp' (III,i,104) for him with Olivia by using any duplicitous and false means necessary: 'Go flatter, lie, kneel, promise anything to get her for me' so that he can 'lie with her, out of revenge' (III,i,119–20, 133). By referring to his lust and sexual aggression as revenge, Manly can compartmentalise his plot against Olivia as something akin to heroic action, nothing more than a fitting retaliation against a formidable foe who has injured him, though Fidelia – the symbol of honour – tries to convince him otherwise.

Following the scene in Westminster Hall – where Manly continues his assaults on everyone, boxing the ear of a lawyer, grabbing the nose of an alderman, and informing a stranger that he had slept with his fiancée (unsolicited information that can only cause this couple emotional havoc) – Manly digresses from a mere hypocrite like everyone else in society to something far more despicable. With Olivia having rejected all of Fidelia's pleas on Manly's behalf and encouraging Fidelia to visit her once again, Manly, unconcerned with Olivia's repulsion toward him (as reported by Fidelia) and her unwillingness to see him, let alone 'lie with him', as he had foolishly hoped, will extract his sexual revenge by raping Olivia: Fidelia will meet Olivia that evening and after she 'talks' love to her, then Manly will secretly substitute himself in the darkened room and 'act love' to Olivia without her knowledge (IV,i,167–8). When Fidelia challenges him, Manly, previously so precise about the words he wielded and faulting others for their corrupted use of language to suit their own ends, resorts to sophistry:

FIDELIA: You act love, sir! You must but act it indeed after all I
    have said to you. Think of your honour sir. Love –
MANLY: Well, call it revenge and that is honourable. I'll be
    revenged on her and thou shalt be my second.
FIDELIA: Not in a base action, sir, when you are your own
    enemy.

(IV,i,170–5)

Manly's earlier insistence to Freeman that 'counterfeit honour
will not be current with me; I weigh the man, not his title'
(I,i,207–9) is pure bunk and rhetoric born out of his subscription
to heroic ideals to which he is neither constitutionally nor morally suited, but he will twist and distort words and concepts so that
they conform to his own perverse needs while protecting his
sham heroism. Honour – a word manipulated repeatedly by
many of Wycherley's amoral characters, particularly in *The
Country Wife* – is not an absolute and inviolable concept but rather
a fluid ideal open to casuistic tweaking. As in Olivia's drawing-
room where Novel and Plausible define honour according to the
beau monde's perverted needs, or in Westminster Hall where
lawyers and judges falsify truth for personal advantage and
where the law is divorced from morality, logic and ethics, Manly
likewise sets himself up as the sole definer of ideals, diviner of
truth and dispenser of justice, all of which he conveniently severs
from any judgement or reasoning other than his own. Regardless
of Manly's manipulation of words, his rape of Olivia is neither
just nor honourable, as Fidelia notes – it is the ultimate act of cruelty, brutality and cowardice, a point that Wycherley takes care to
drive home for spectators, who are fully aware of Manly's nefarious plot: in a conversation just minutes before the rape, Olivia
counters Fidelia's reference to Manly's 'undoubted courage' with
a simile that the audience knows will momentarily be proven
unnervingly accurate: 'Like the hangman's, can murder a man
when his hands are tied. He has cruelty indeed, which is no more
courage than his railing is wit' (IV,i,271–4).[17] Throughout the
action, Many has revealed a disturbing propensity for physical
aggression – at first humorous, though disquieting, as he flings
Plausible out of his room – but in his rape of Olivia, he shows his
masculine (manly?) aggression at its basest, the most unheroic act
perpetrated by any character in the play and one which

demonstrates an arbitrary use of power that he believes he can appropriate to himself as society's only judge and exemplar of honour, courage and heroism.

In the closing moments of the play, Wycherley rewards this flawed embodiment of the classical hero in a highly implausible *deus ex machina* in which Manly gains a beautiful and wealthy young woman who has no sooner revealed her identity and professed her love than he immediately offers her both his heart and his retrieved fortune. Manly, it would seem, has been wholly vindicated by Wycherley, and yet despite Manly's quick and unexpected readiness to embrace Fidelia's love and Freeman's friendship, Wycherley intentionally withholds any further transformations in this character: Manly does not capitulate to a more moderate position regarding tolerance of society's mendacity and hypocrisy, with which he has, of course, been in collusion, but rather remains intransigent in his opinion that the world is still quite 'odious' (V,iii,189), though he will reside in it for Fidelia's sake. Having arrived at no epiphany about his own defects, Manly remains the egotistical, self-righteous individual who misdefines the classical hero as a man fuelled and characterised only by aggressive action and physical dominance void of any feminine qualities (such as those possessed by Fidelia) that would mitigate or impair masculine heroism. Given these tendencies, Manly naturally prefers to live in Hobbes's pre-social world where natural instincts have full reign, where war against all others is a way of life, where justice is an individual and subjective matter, where no sovereign force or social laws will interfere with unchecked and belligerent quests for power and supremacy, and, more importantly, where such aggression is revered and practised on a daily basis: 'I rather choose to go where honest, downright barbarity is professed, where men devour one another like generous hungry lions and tigers' (II,i,699–702). Virtually shipwrecked in a world that denounces such animalistic warfare readily available in the remote Indies, Manly will impose his pugnacity on its inhabitants because, as he demonstrates repeatedly, he loves a good fight no matter the place or the opponent. It is unsurprising, then, that Manly does not care to change the world: he needs it precisely the way it is so that he can provoke a few battles wherever he goes – from the halls of Westminster to the bedrooms of his unsuspecting enemies – a pattern of behaviour that shows no signs of attenuation in the denouement. If Manly has gained any honour whatsoever, it is only grafted to him through Wycherley's deliberate design of having him accept Fidelia, the only character in this play who signifies an heroic ideal once revered by society but now corrupted by its cavalier acceptance of (and in some cases reverence for) base behaviour and amoral self-interest, qualities that Manly, previously a well-known libertine around town, has assimilated into his definition of classical heroism.

While the blustering and bearish Manly gains a beautiful heiress, so does the unscrupulous ersatz hero, Freeman, get his own reward – a hefty annuity garnered through his blackmail scheme against the Widow. Like Manly, Freeman has done nothing to earn such a fortune: he is another man of 'inaction' willing to let the world operate as it chooses so long as he can benefit from its evil. A predator cornering his prey and not releasing his grasp until he gets what he wants, Freeman embodies all the negative attributes of the rapacious libertine celebrated by his age's poetry, plays and press. That Wycherley viewed Freeman as a despicable knave is evident from his intentional omission of what audiences would have anticipated as his fitting and final reward as libertine: a suitable mate. Although Wycherley provides such a woman in Eliza, he allows them no dialogue together, thus foreclosing any chance for a traditional happy ending for this rogue. Freeman, far from the golden mean that Eliza perhaps represents, lacks the capacity to care about anything beyond his own desires, which are limited strictly to financial gain, and to marry him off to Eliza would have suggested that he symbolises the regenerative and recuperative effects of a true hero when, in fact, as Wycherley shows us, Freeman, as a representative of his era's selfish and acquisitive rakes, is nothing of the sort.

Wycherley handles his would-be heroes and denouement with considerable irony: the die-hard, irascible misanthrope who threatens violence at every turn and should be exiled to a remote island, remains among a society he loathes, and the wily, young libertine who uses the system for his own financial advancement and should be reformed by love never displays a desire for such affection or the capacity for such redemption. Neither potential hero offers a modicum of hope for a better world, but the society Wycherley depicts seems to imply that it wants no heroes – classical or otherwise – to intervene and set things right. If heroism is a laughable and outdated ideal, a relic from the past that cannot live amicably in the modern world, and if the young, new world cannot cultivate a viable heroic ideal of its own to fill the void, then society's only hope, Wycherley implies facetiously, rests with the occasional, chimerical transplant from a foreign land or genre who reminds everyone of those lost heroic virtues such as honour, courage, fidelity, and selflessness that went down with the ship.

Following its première on 11 December 1676, the *The Plain Dealer* enjoyed frequent revivals during the remainder of the seventeenth century, most notably the performance at Whitehall on 14 December 1685 that prompted James II to secure Wycherley's release from debtors' prison (see Chapter 6). The play retained its popularity throughout the eighteenth century as well, receiving 66 performances until 1743, and after a 22-year hiatus, *The Plain Dealer* resurfaced again, albeit in a revised form, when in 1765 Isaac Bickerstaffe adapted it for David Garrick at Drury Lane.[18] Altered and expurgated to suit the sensibilities of eighteenth-century audiences, Bickerstaffe's adaptation proved quite successful, encouraging others, like Garrick (who would adapt Wycherley's *The Country Wife* the following year), to follow suit with other Restoration plays that had been similarly neglected because of their putative indecencies in action and language. Toward the end of the century, John Philip Kemble, the leading actor-manager of his day, tried his hand at revising Wycherley's comedy, but after only three performances that played to decreasing audiences, Kemble shelved his adaptation, making his 6 April 1796 production the last performance of Wycherley's comedy until the twentieth century.

Wycherley's original play – though certainly expurgated and sanitised – resurfaced in November 1925 when the Renaissance Theatre Company revived it at the Scala Theatre for one performance only during its Sunday-evening programme. Although the Renaissance Theatre Company, devoted to staging neglected plays by early English dramatists, had been successful, like other amateur British theatre companies (e.g., The Phoenix Society), in securing a place for such dramas in the repertory of London's commercial theatres, such was not the case for *The Plain Dealer*. Hampered by under-rehearsing and an inordinate amount of prompting from the wings, the performance did not impress the few critics in attendance, who found the play 'all patches' with radical shifts in tone and a lack of coherence.[19] Despite the efforts of the Renaissance Theatre to rekindle audience interest in Wycherley's long-forgotten play – as the Phoenix Society had done successfully the year before with *The Country Wife* – *The Plain Dealer* would remain unproduced until the Royal Shakespeare Company resurrected it toward the end of the twentieth century.

After a 245-year absence from the commercial theatre, *The Plain Dealer* finally had its first professional revival on 27 April 1988, staged initially at the Royal Shakespeare Company's Swan Theatre in Stratford-upon-Avon and transferred the following year to The Pit in London. Director Ron Daniels succeeded in capturing the play's various clashing tones and moods (e.g., the satire, the comedy, the villainy, the violence), striking the necessary delicate balance between the comedy's savagery and its inherent vitality: 'it catches Wycherley's exhilaration in the face of so much corruption, without losing sight of his underlying moral outrage'.[20] Interpreting the play as 'a severe and poignant moral satire' that underscored the brutality and viciousness of Wycherley's characters (save, of course, Fidelia), Daniels allowed the play's dark tone to take centre stage, encouraging the actors 'to unravel the glittering, poisonous conversations with a most purposeful emphasis',[21] revealing the human baseness and perfidy that lurked behind even those most comic moments. Even the epicene fops, Plausible (Tom Fahy) and Novel (Mark Hadfield) – both 'so plastered with white make-up they seem to be growing their own berouged death masks' and costumed, respectively, like a 'garish wedding cake' and 'as a Restoration punk, hair standing literally on end, a walking candy stick of shocking pink, blue and yellow'[22] – though played over-the-top as risible exemplars of the extremes of artifice, provided unmistakable glimpses of the cruelty that resides even in ostensibly refined and cultured socialites, locating the 'moral grime under the paint and powder'[23] of these coxcombs and the countless others like them. From the preening fops who 'snigger over the teacups at their hosts of the night before', the 'silky purrings' of Olivia (Joanne Pearce) – all 'porcelain prettiness on the outside, all rampant itchiness underneath' with 'her close-set drilling eyes betraying not a flicker of humanity' and 'oozing poison like some fragrant perfume' – to the fanatical Widow (Marjorie Yates), a 'grim, hatchet-faced cross between Andromache and Goneril' with her 'truculent and quick-thinking' deviousness and spite, this was a world plagued by unrelenting menace.[24]

Daniels subscribed to the interpretation that Wycherley neither posited a viable solution to the moral decay posed by the play nor presented an ideal hero worth emulating. Freeman (Oliver Cotton), a possible contender as the golden mean, was 'an unctuous smoothie'[25] who deftly negotiated his noncommittal way through every situation and was neither to be trusted nor revered, while Geraldine Alexander portrayed Fidelia not as Manly's moral redeemer but as a 'vapid refugee from a romantic Arcadian world' who, having stumbled into a nightmare-world of conniving and vicious knaves, 'is out of her genre and out of her depth, and – as an authority on moral values – about as useful as Tinkerbell'.[26] Nor was David Calder's Manly an heroic idealist but rather as much an object of satire and attack as the other depraved characters, a performance that made it quite clear that Wycherley intended to criticise the character's ferocious bearishness and misanthropic invectives. Although some critics faulted Calder for making Manly too cross and strident throughout – an understandable error given the character's incessant railing – without revealing the 'dark sub-text of discontent, psychological alienation and sexual self-destruction'[27] underneath his irascibility, others found traces of humanity that rendered Manly more sympathetic and less a one-dimensional monomaniac. With each startling revelation of the treachery surrounding him at every turn and with shock at his own fall 'as he watches himself stoop to rape, in an ignominious mania for Olivia', Manly's 'eyes bulge with wronged outrage, but hint also – and just to the right degree – that he may be squinting into a tragic abyss'.[28] By the time the revival transferred to The Pit, Calder had added other touches that underscored the vulnerability under all of Manly's rancour, a glimpse at his fallibility and humanness that evoked pathos without suggesting a modicum of heroism.

Lacking a clear-cut hero and an uplifting, optimistic denouement, Daniels's production illuminated Wycherley's society 'of twisted values and double dealing festooned with silks, where love turns to revenge, straightforwardness to hypocrisy, openness to bitterness and gossip to malice', and where 'even the highly improbable ending seems fragile, making one suspect that pus still lurks in the wounds waiting to erupt'.[29] Understandably, this world without heroes or hope 'leaves an acrid taste behind', noted Eric Shorter (*Daily Telegraph*, 29 April 1988), a bitter taste that Dryden and the Court Wits may well have experienced also.

Notes

1 Carolean Context

1. Restoration drama has been appropriated various inceptive and terminal dates; on the various possible periodisations of Restoration theatre and drama, see Robert D. Hume, *The Development of English Drama in the Late Seventeenth Century* (Oxford: Clarendon, 1976), pp. 3–10.

2. Numerous celebrations occurred in shires as well; see Richard Hutton, *The Restoration* (Oxford: Clarendon Press, 1985), p. 126.

3. Those afflicted were later given gold pendants and assurance that they would miraculously recover; see Hutton, *Restoration*, p. 128.

4. A solid overview of the various political panegyrics written on the occasion of Charles's restoration is found in Nicholas Jose, *Ideas of the Restoration in English Literature, 1660–1771* (Cambridge, MA: Harvard University Press, 1984), chs 1–4.

5. Maurice Ashley, *Charles II: Man and Statesman* (New York: Praeger, 1971), p. 112.

6. Such repressive legislation included the Test Acts that required all Catholics to attend Anglican services and swear oaths of allegiance to the Church of England, and the Conventicle Act which punished anyone worshipping outside the Anglican Church; see Hutton, *Restoration*, ch. 8.

7. A history of the Court Wits can be found in John Harold Wilson, *The Court Wits of the Restoration* (Princeton, NJ: Princeton University Press, 1948).

8. Hobbesian theory applied to Restoration comedy is found in Thomas H. Fujimura's seminal study *The Restoration Comedy of Wit* (Princeton, NJ: Princeton University Press, 1952).

9. Henry B. Wheatley (ed.), *The Diary of Samuel Pepys* (London: Bell, 1893), VII, p. 39.

10. Cabal was an acronym for the five ministers to whom Charles turned for advice after Clarendon's fall: Clifford, Arlington, Buckingham, Ashley Cooper, and Lauderdale. These men, none Anglican, supported Charles's secret bid for religious toleration, which Parliament strongly opposed, as well as the end of the Anglican monopoly.

2 Carolean Theatre and Drama

1. For a history of theatre and drama during the Interregnum, see Leslie Hotson, *The Commonwealth and Restoration Stage* (Cambridge, MA: Harvard University Press, 1928).

2. For a detailed account of the patentees' three-month struggle to assert their control over London's actors and theatre activity, see John Frehafer, 'The Formation of the London Patent Companies in 1660', *Theatre Notebook*, 20 (1965): 6–30.

3. Henry B. Wheatley (ed.), *The Diary of Samuel Pepys* (London: Bell, 1893), I, p. 288.

4. Both Killigrew's and Davenant's tennis-court theatres were remodelled into viable playhouses by dividing the court along the net line into two areas: half of the space for the audience and the other half for the performance area. Photographs of a model reconstruction of Davenant's theatre can be found in Elizabeth G. Scanlan, 'Reconstruction of the Duke's Playhouse in Lincoln's Inn Fields, 1661–1671', *Theatre Notebook*, 10 (1956): 48–50, and reconstructions of both tennis-court theatres are available in Edward Langhans, 'The Theatres' in Robert D. Hume (ed.), *London Theatre World, 1660–1800* (Carbondale, IL: Southern Illinois University Press, 1980), pp. 37–8.

5. Henry B. Wheatley (ed.), *The Diary of Samuel Pepys* (London: Bell, 1893), II, p. 63.

6. For a discussion of the Bridges Street Theatre's components, see D. C. Mullin, 'The Theatre Royal, Bridges Street: A Conjectural Restoration', *Educational Theatre Journal*, 19 (1967): 17–29 and E. A. Langhans, 'Pictorial Material on the Bridges Street and Drury Lane Theatres', *Theatre Survey*, 7 (1966): 80–100.

7. The absence of definitive documentation on the Dorset Garden Theatre has led to a debate over its configuration; see, for example, Edward Langhans, 'A Conjectural Reconstruction of the Dorset Garden Theatre', *Theatre Survey*, 13 (1972): 74–93; John R. Spring, 'Platforms and Picture Frames: A Conjectural Reconstruction of the Duke of York's Theatre, Dorset Garden, 1669–1709', *Theatre Notebook*, 31 (1977), 6–19; Robert Hume, 'The Dorset Garden Theatre: A Review of Facts and Problems', *Theatre Notebook*, 33 (1979): 4–17; John R. Spring, 'The Dorset Garden Theatre: Playhouse or Opera House?' *Theatre Notebook*, 34 (1980): 60–9; Robert Hume, 'The Nature of the Dorset Garden Theatre', *Theatre Notebook*, 36 (1982): 99–109. For conjectural reconstructions of this playhouse, see Spring (1997) and (1980), as well as Langhans (1972) and 'The Theatres', *London Theatre World, 1660–1800* (1980), 40. For a sketch of the

theatre's exterior, see John Palmer, *The Comedy of Manners* (London: G. Bell, 1913), p. 74, and Edward Langhans, 'The Dorset Garden Theatre in Pictures', *Theatre Survey*, 6, 2 (November 1965): 134–46.

8. In his prologue for *A Beggar's Bush*, the inaugural performance at Drury Lane, Dryden referred to the new playhouse as a 'a plain built house' with a 'mean ungilded stage' in contrast to the resplendent decorations at Dorset Garden. For an excellent reconstruction and isometric drawing of the 1674 Drury Lane, see Edward Langhans, 'Wren's Restoration Playhouse', *Theatre Notebook*, 18 (1964): 91–100.

9. A more detailed discussion of the scenic area and its use (including special effects) can be found in Montague Summers, *The Restoration Theatre* (New York: Humanities Press, 1964), chs 4 & 6; Colin Visser's 'Scenery and Technical Design', in Hume (ed.), *London Theatre World*, pp. 66–118; Richard Southern, *Changeable Scenery* (London: Faber and Faber, 1952) ch. 8; J. L. Styan, *Restoration Comedy in Performance* (Cambridge University Press, 1986), ch. 2; Peter Holland, *The Ornament of Action* (Cambridge: Cambridge University Press, 1979), pp. 21–48; E. L. Avery and A. H. Scouten, *The London Stage, 1660–1700* (Carbondale, IL: Southern Illinois University Press, 1968), pp. lxxxiv–xc; Lee J. Martin, 'From Forestage to Proscenium: A Study of Restoration Staging Techniques', *Theatre Survey*, 4 (1963): 3–28; Jocelyn Powell, *Restoration Theatre Production* (London: Routledge and Kegan Paul, 1984), ch. 3.

10. The word 'scene' had various meanings in Restoration drama: when it appeared in the stage directions, it meant the shutters and scenic area behind them; thus, stage directions such as 'the scene opens' or 'the scene closes' meant literally the changing of the wings and shutters and not the beginning or conclusion of the action.

11. Southern, *Changeable Scenery*, pp. 114–15; Styan, *Restoration Comedy*, p. 27.

12. For a discussion of the various ways in which doors and balconies could be used in conjunction with the scenery, see Visser, 'Scenery and Technical Design', pp. 68–72 and Summers, *Restoration Theatre*, ch. 4, especially pp. 126–44. The curtain was not used to indicate the end of acts; it was raised following the prologue and not closed until after the epilogue. To indicate the end of an act, the stage was probably left bare (wings and shutters moved off).

13. Powell, *Restoration Theatre Production*, p. 87.

14. Holland, *Ornament of Action*, ch. 2 ('Performance: Theatres and Scenery'), especially the discussion of Etherege's use of specific locales in *She Would If She Could*, pp. 48–54.

15. Managers' sexual exploitation of actresses occurred throughout the Carolean period, but it was especially prevalent in the 1670s with the rise of 'sex comedies' and 'horror' plays that featured torture and rape. For a detailed study of the actresses' sexual exploitation both on and off the stage, see Elizabeth Howe, *The First English Actress: Women and Drama, 1660–1700* (Cambridge: Cambridge University Press, 1992). Jacqueline Pearson, *The Prostituted Muse: Images of Women & Women Dramatists, 1642–1737* (New York: St. Martin's Press, 1988) also discusses

female characters in the plays as well as the plight of female playwrights. For a different reading on the exploitation of actresses, see Deborah Payne, "Reified Object or Emergent Professional? Retheorizing the Restoration Actress', *Cultural Readings of Restoration and Eighteenth-Century English Theatre*, ed. Douglas Canfield and Deborah Payne (Athens, GA: University of Georgia Press, 1995), pp. 13–38.

16. David Roberts, *The Ladies: Female Patronage of Restoration Drama, 1660–1700* (Oxford: Clarendon Press, 1989), p. 94.

17. Powell, *Restoration Theatre Production*, pp. 12–13. In the seventeenth century, an English pound equalled 20 shillings or 240 old pennies; modern decimal currency has 100 pence to the pound, therefore 18 old pennies equal 15 pence, two shillings and sixpence equal 25 pence in today's money.

18. Compare, for example, 1600 when Elizabethan London, with a population of perhaps as many as 200,000 people (half that of the Restoration), supported five or six established theatre companies.

19. A detailed discussion of audiences can be found in Emmett L. Avery, 'The Restoration Audience', *Philological Quarterly*, 45 (1966): 16–88, and Harold Love, 'Who Were the Restoration Audience?' *Yearbook of English Studies*, 10 (1980): 21–44. For a discussion of the audience's composition and its shifting tastes for dramas during the Restoration and eighteenth century, see Robert D. Hume, '"Restoration Comedy" and its Audiences', *The Rakish Stage*, ed. Robert D. Hume (Carbondale, IL: Southern Illinois University Press, 1983), pp. 46–81.

20. Dale B. J. Randall's *Winter Fruit: English Drama, 1642–1660* (Lexington: University Press of Kentucky, 1995) discusses the closet dramas written during the Interregnum; though not produced, these plays depicted political themes for or against the Commonwealth.

21. J. Douglas Canfield suggests various subgenres in 'The Ideology of Restoration Tragicomedy', *ELH*, 51 (1984): 447–64. An excellent overview of Carolean tragicomedy which includes its genesis with Giovanni Battista Guarini's *Il Pastor Fido* (1590) is found in Nancy Klein Macguire, 'Tragicomedy', *The Cambridge Companion to English Restoration Theatre*, ed. Deborah Payne Fisk (Cambridge: Cambridge University Press, 2000), pp. 86–106.

22. John Harrington Smith, *The Gay Couple in Restoration Comedy* (New York: Octagon, 1971), p. 3, passim.

23. See David S. Berkeley, 'Préciosité and the Restoration Comedy of Manners', *Huntington Library Quarterly*, 18 (1955): 109–28.

24. Harold Weber, *The Restoration Rake-Hero* (Madison, WI: University of Wisconsin Press, 1986) discusses the various types of libertines during this period, as does Robert D. Hume, 'The Myth of the Rake in "Restoration" Comedy', *Studies in the Literary Imagination*, 10, 1 (Spring 1977): 25–55 and Robert Jordan, 'The Extravagant Rake in Restoration Comedy', *Restoration Literature*, ed. Harold Love (London: Methuen, 1972), pp. 69–90.

25. Jean Elisabeth Gagen provides a comprehensive study of the Restoration heroine in *The New Woman: Her Emergence in English Drama,*

1660–1730 (New York: Twayne, 1954); see also Margaret Lamb McDonald, *The Independent Woman in the Restoration Comedy of Manners* (Salzburg: University of Salzburg, 1976), and Douglas M. Young, *The Feminist Voices in Restoration Comedy: The Virtuous Women in the Play-worlds of Etherege, Wycherley and Congreve* (Lanham, MD: University Press of America, 1997).

26. Thomas H. Fujimura offers the most thorough analysis of these plays as wit comedies in his *Restoration Comedy of Wit* (Princeton, NJ: Princeton University Press, 1952), which uses Hobbesian philosophy as its critical base and offers a detailed discussion of the era's definition of wit.

27. Some of these recent historicist studies include Susan Staves, *Players' Scepters: Fictions of Authority in the Restoration* (Lincoln: University of Nebraska Press, 1979), especially ch. 2; Nancy Klein Maguire, *Regicide and Restoration: English Tragicomedy, 1660–1671* (Cambridge: Cambridge University Press, 1992); J. Douglas Canfield's two-volume study, *Tricksters and Estates: On the Ideology of Restoration Comedy* (Lexington: University of Kentucky Press, 1997) and *Heroes and States: On the Ideology of Restoration Tragedy* (Lexington: University of Kentucky Press, 2000); Susan Owen, *Restoration Theatre and Crisis* (Oxford: Clarendon, 1996); and Bridget Orr, *Empire on the English Stage, 1660–1714* (Cambridge: Cambridge University Press, 2001).

28. Michael Neill, 'Heroic Heads and Humble Tails: Sex, Politics, and the Restoration Comic Rake', *The Eighteenth Century: Theory and Interpretation*, 24, 2 (Spring 1983): 116.

3   Etherege and the Carolean Theatre

1. The exact date and location of Etherege's birth are unknown, though the spring of 1636 and Berkshire seem most probable. Biographical details here are indebted to Arthur Huseboe's comprehensive account (*Sir George Etherege* [Boston: Twayne, 1987], pp. 1–50) and H. F. B. Brett-Smith's commentary in his edition of Etherege's plays: *The Dramatic Works of Sir George Etherege*, I (Oxford: Blackwell, 1927).

2. Also, many of his letters written years later from Ratisbon display fluency in French.

3. Edmund Gosse, *Seventeenth Century Studies* (New York: Dodd, Mead, 1897), p. 262; William Oldys, 'Sir George Etherege', *Biographia Britannica* (rpt. Hildesheim, Germany: Georg Olms, 1969) III, 1841.

4. Etherege was regarded as one of the finest songwriters of his day, his songs set to music by numerous composers, including Henry Purcell. For a discussion of Etherege's dramatic use of songs in his plays, see Purvis E. Boyette, 'Songs of George Etherege', *Studies in English Literature, 1500–1900*, 7, 3 (1966): 409–19. For an account and text of Etherege's poems and songs, see James Thorpe (ed.), *The Poems of Sir George Etherege* (Princeton, NJ: Princeton University Press, 1963).

5. Gildon (*The Lives of Characters of the English Dramatick Poets* [London, 1698]) quoted in Brett-Smith, *Dramatic Works*, p. xxii; John

Downes, *Roscius Anglicanus*, ed. Judith Milhous and Robert D. Hume (London: Society for Theatre Research, 1987), p. 77.

6. Oldys, 'Sir George Etherege', p. 1844.

7. See Brett-Smith, *Dramatic Works* (pp. xxviii–xxix) for a number of these verses.

8. Etherege's Ratisbon correspondence has been reprinted with commentaries in: Sybil Rosenfeld (ed.), *The Letterbook of Sir George Etherege* (1928, rpt. New York: Blom, 1971) and Frederick Bracher (ed.), *The Letters of Sir George Etherege* (Berkeley, CA: University California Press, 1974).

9. Bracher, *Letters*, p. 266.

10. Rosenfeld, *Letterbook*, p. 413.

11. Etherege also received a £100 annual pension which the king granted him in 1682.

12. In a letter to Jepson (27 February 1687), Etherege alludes to personal reasons for accepting the appointment: 'Nature, you know, intended me for an idle fellow, and gave me passions and qualities fit for that blessed calling, but fortune has made a changeling of me, and necessity now forces me to set up for a fop of business' (Rosenfeld, *Letterbook*, p. 336).

13. Rosenfeld, *Letterbook*, p. 305.

14. Oldys, 'Sir George Etherege', p. 1848.

15. Quoted in Huseboe, *Sir George Etherege*, p. 36.

16. Bracher, *Letters*, p. 170.

17. Rosenfeld, *Letterbook*, pp. 139, 167.

18. For a discussion of *The Comical Revenge* as a political play, see Richard Braverman, *Plots and Counterplots: Sexual Politics and the Body Politic in English Literature, 1660–1730* (Cambridge: Cambridge University Press, 1993), pp. 64–82.

19. 'George Etherege and the Form of a Comedy', John Russell Brown and Bernard Harris (eds), *Restoration Theatre*, Stratford-upon-Avon Studies, 6 (London: Edward Arnold, 1965), p. 44.

4 *She Would If She Could*: Comedy of Manners

1. Henry B. Wheatley (ed.), *The Diary of Samuel Pepys* (London: Bell, 1893), VII, pp. 307–8.

2. Performances at court were held on 28 May 1668 and 27 February 1679 (Emmett L. Avery and Arthur H. Scouten, *The London Stage: 1660–1700* [Carbondale, IL: Southern Illinois University Press, 1968]), pp. 137, 285.

3. For discussions of other modes and scenes that influenced *She Would*, see Kathleen Lynch, *The Social Mode of Restoration Comedy* (New York: Octagon, 1965), pp. 49–50 and Robert D. Hume, *Development of English Drama* (Oxford: Clarendon, 1976), pp. 265–7.

4. For example, Courtall and Freeman encounter two masked women in the park to whom they promise not to consort with other females until their next rendezvous; of course, these ladies turn out to be

Gatty and Ariana, the nieces whom they meet later that day. But Courtall's and Freeman's discomfiture at meeting Gatty and Ariana at Sir Oliver's home springs not from the coincidence but rather from their duplicity and dishonesty: their appetite for more than one woman at a time has placed them in this embarrassing dilemma.

5. Laura Brown, *English Dramatic Form, 1660–1760* (New Haven, CT: Yale University Press, 1981), p. 30.

6. William Oldys, 'Sir George Etherege', *Biographia Britannica* (rpt. Hildesheim, Germany: Georg Olms, 1969), III, 1842.

7. In his magisterial and exhaustive survey of extant Carolean comedies prior to *She Would*, Hume discovered that this comedy proved both 'unique' and 'unparalleled' in its emphasis on wit; for his discussion of the play's novelties see *Development of English Drama*, pp. 266–7. For more detailed discussions of Etherege's use of wit in this play, see in particular Robert Markeley, *Two-Edg'd Weapons: Style and Ideology in the Comedies of Etherege, Wycherley and Congreve* (Oxford: Clarendon Press, 1988); Dale Underwood, *Etherege and Seventeenth Century Comedy of Manners* (New Haven, CT: Yale University Press, 1957); Thomas H. Fujimura, *Restoration Comedy of Wit* (Princeton, NJ: Princeton University Press, 1952); and David R. Wilkinson, *The Comedy of Habit* (Leiden: Universitare Pers, 1964).

8. The most exhaustive and comprehensive explanation of the types of wit found in Carolean and Restoration comedy is available in Wilkinson's study above.

9. Hume, *Development*, p. 337; Hume also posits that Betterton's *The Amorous Widow* (*c.* 1670) served as the most likely prototype for 1670s manners comedies, though his focus is on plot devices such as farcical action, sources in Molière, and satire on cits (all of which appear sporadically in the sex comedies of the 1670s and none of which exist in *She Would*). For a contrary reading of Betterton's play, see Brian Corman, *Genre and Generic Change in English Comedy, 1660–1710* (Toronto: University of Toronto Press, 1993), pp. 43–5.

10. Susan Staves, 'The Secrets of Genteel Identity in *The Man of Mode*: Comedy of Manners vs. the Courtesy Book', *Studies in Eighteenth Century Culture*, 19 (1989): 117.

11. Norman Holland, for example, insists that the young lovers are 'completely aware of the line where social pretense leaves off and plain dealing begins' and describes them as 'aware of their double selves as an actor in a part' (*The First Modern Comedies: The Significance of Etherege, Wycherley and Congrave* [Cambridge, MA: Harvard University Press, 1959], pp. 33–4) while most recently Rothstein and Kavenick (*The Designs of Carolean Comedy* [Carbondale, IL: Southern Illinois University Press, 1988], p. 81) echo that the lovers 'never mistake their own motives or confuse role with reality'. For a different reading on the libertines, one that argues critics perforce attribute such self-awareness to the lead male characters because canonical readings of Carolean and Restoration comedy privilege male cognitive mastery, see B. A. Kachur, 'Etherege's *She Would If She Could*: Rereading the Libertines', *Restoration and 18th-Century Theatre Research*, 12, 2 (Winter 1997): 40–60.

12. Lynch, *The Social Mode*, p. 150.

13. On the play's treatment of the double standard, see B. A. Kachur, 'Etherege's *She Would*' and Michael Cordner, 'Etherege's *She Would If She Could*: Comedy, Complaisance and Anti-Climax', *English Comedy*, Michael Cordner et al. (eds), (Cambridge: Cambridge University Press, 1994), pp. 158–79.

14. Robert Wess, 'Utopian Rhetoric in *The Man of Mode*', *The Eighteenth Century: Theory and Interpretation*, 27, 2 (Spring 1986): 147.

15. Charlene Taylor (ed.), *She Would If She Could* (Lincoln: University of Nebraska Press, 1971), p. xxv.

16. Peter Holland, *The Ornament of Action: Text and Performance in Restoration Comedy* (Cambridge: Cambridge University Press), p. 52. Holland suggests also that in the Mulberry scene, the ladies' quick and repeated entrances indicate their control of the forestage area and by extension the garden itself, thereby indicating their control of this world's demand for disguise and repartee (p. 53).

17. Ironically, these characters never actually enjoy the anonymity they hope to find in London because they repeatedly and unexpectedly meet one another in the same public and private locales; see Cordner ('Comedy, Complaisance and Anti-Climax', pp. 161–2) on the town's ostensible liberty and the play's ironic treatment of this freedom.

18. Virginia Birdsall and Jocelyn Powell view Sir Joslin as the Dionysian spirit incarnate; see Birdsall, *Wild Civility: The English Comic Spirit on the Restoration Stage* (Bloomington, IN: Indiana University Press, 1970) pp. 70–1 and Powell, 'George Etherege and the Form of Comedy', *Restoration Theatre*, Stratford-upon-Avon Studies, 6, John Russell Brown and Bernard Harris (eds), (London: Edward Arnold, 1965), pp. 54–5.

19. Edward Burns, *Restoration Comedy: Crises of Desire and Identity* (New York: St. Martin's Press, 1987), p. 34.

20. *Country Life*, 10 May 1979; *Guardian*, 16 April 1979.

5 *The Man of Mode*: Comedy and the Masquerade

1. See Michael Cordner (ed.), *The Plays of Sir George Etherege* (Cambridge: Cambridge University Press, 1982), p. 211. In a letter dated 7 December 1685, the Earl of Middleton wrote to Etherege in Ratisbon to inform him of both the successful recent production of *The Man of Mode* at Court and the king's remark to Middleton that he expected Etherege to write another comedy (see Frederick Bracher (ed.), *The Letters of Sir George Etherege* (Berkeley, CA: University of California Press, 1974), p. 269.

2. Gerard Langbaine, *An Account of the English Stage* (Oxford, 1691), p. 187.

3. For a detailed discussion of Etherege's real-life sources for his characters, see Brett-Smith (ed.), *The Dramatic Works of Sir George Etherege* (Oxford: Blackwell, 1927), I, xxiv–xxv; also see William Oldys, 'Sir George Etherege', *Biographia Britannica* (rpt. Hildesheim, Germany: Georg Olms, 1969), III, 1843.

4. John Dennis, 'A Defense of Sir Fopling Flutter', *The Critical Works of John Dennis*, ed. Edward Niles Hooker (Baltimore, MD: Johns Hopkins University Press, 1939), II, 241–5. Dennis also furthers the speculation that Etherege had specific contemporary models in mind for characters in the comedy. For a lucid summary of Steele's and Dennis's debate, see Brian Corman, 'Interpreting and Misinterpreting *The Man of Mode*', *Papers on Language and Literature*, 13 (Winter 1977): 35–40.

5. Norman Holland, *The First Modern Comedies: The Significance of Etherege, Wycherley and Congreve* (Cambridge, MA: Harvard University Press, 1967), p. 95.

6. David Wilkinson, *The Comedy of Habit* (Leiden: Universitaire Pers, 1964), p. 81.

7. On the rise of sex comedies during the 1670s, see John Harrington Smith, *The Gay Couple in Restoration Drama* (New York: Octagon, 1971), ch. 4, and for an elaborate discussion of sex comedies as well as those other genres of the 1670s that featured such extreme sexual behaviour, see Robert Hume, *The Development of English Drama in the Late Seventeenth Century*, ch. 7. See Maximillian E. Novak, 'Margery Pinchwife's "London Disease": Restoration Comedy and the Libertine Offensive of the 1670s', *Studies in Restoration and Eighteenth-Century Drama*, 10 (Spring 1977): 1–23, and Harold Weber, *The Restoration Rake Hero* (Madison, WI: University of Wisconsin Press, 1986) for a discussion of the new libertine in the 1670s.

8. For such binary readings of the characters, see for example Thomas Fujimura's seminal study, *Restoration Comedy of Wit* (Princeton, NJ: Princeton University Press, 1952), pp. 104–16.

9. Bishop Gilbert Burnet (1643–1715) reported as early as 1668 that 'the court fell into much extravagance in masquerading; both the king and queen and all the court went about masked, and came into houses unknown, and danced there, with a good deal of wild frolic. People were so disguised that, without being in the secret, none could distinguish them.' *History of His Own Time*, ed. Osmund Airy (Oxford, 1897), I, p. 473.

10. John Spurr's *England in the 1670s: 'This Masquerading Age'* (London: Blackwell, 2000) provides a splendid historical, political, and cultural overview of this decade.

11. Terry Castle, *Masquerade and Civilization: The Carnivalesque in Eighteenth-Century English Culture and Fiction* (Stanford, CA: Stanford University Press, 1986), p. 38.

12. An elaboration on the play's game motif can be found in Derek Hughes, 'Play and Passion in *The Man of Mode*', *Comparative Drama*, 15, 3 (1981): 231–57.

13. *Guardian*, 31 March 1986.

14. *Financial Times*, 15 July 1988; *Time Out*, 20 July 1988; *Guardian*, 15 July 1988. The following year, Hynes and the RSC transferred the production from the Swan (Stratford) to London, and a significant change was made to the set in order to highlight the 'game' motif: a merry-go-round.

15. *Daily Telegraph*, 15 July 1988.

16. *Time Out*, 20 July 1988; *Guardian*, 15 July 1988.

17. *Guardian*, 15 July 1988; *Independent*, 15 July 1988.

18. For an excellent discussion of Dorimant's varied roles, most especially as they manifest through his use of language, see Robert Markley, *Two-Edg'd Weapons: Style and Ideology in the Comedies of Etherege, Wycherley and Congreve* (Oxford: Clarendon, 1988), pp. 121–37.

19. Edward Burns, *Restoration Comedy: Crises of Desire and Identity* (London: Macmillan, 1987), p. 42

20. *Evening Standard*, 14 September 1971.

21. Markley, *Two-Edg'd Weapons*, p. 126.

22. Weber, *Restoration Rake-Hero*, p. 70.

23. *Guardian*, 15 July 1988.

24. Judith W. Fisher, 'The Power of Performance: Sir George Etherege's *The Man of Mode*', *Restoration and Eighteenth-Century Theatre Research*, 10, 1 (Summer 1995): 17.

25. Weber, *Restoration Rake-Hero*, p. 84.

26. *Sunday Times*, 17 July 1988.

27. Robert Waterhouse, Terry Hands and Timothy O'Brien, 'A Case of Restoration', *Plays and Players*, 19 (November 1971): 15.

28. Robert Hume, 'Reading and Misreading *The Man of Mode*', *Criticism*, 14, 1 (Winter 1972): 5, 2.

29. John Barnard, 'Point of View in *The Man of Mode*', *Essays in Criticism*, 34, 4 (October 1984): 302. On this point of Fopling's importance to the structure and tone of the play, see also Wandalie Henshaw, 'Sir Fopling Flutter, or The Key to *The Man of Mode*', *Essays in Theatre*, 3, 2 (May 1985): 98–107.

30. A more detailed list of the similarities between Fopling and Dorimant can be found in Henshaw, 'Sir Fopling Flutter', p. 104 and Fisher, 'The Power of Performance', p. 23.

6 Wycherley and the Carolean Theatre

1. Biographical details given here have been culled from Willard Connely, *Brawny Wycherley* (New York: Scribners, 1969); B. Eugene McCarthy, *William Wycherley: A Biography* (Athens, OH: Ohio University Press, 1979); and Katherine M. Rogers, *William Wycherley* (New York: Twayne, 1972), pp. 19–56.

2. There is some discrepancy over the exact dates when Wycherley wrote his four plays. In the last years of his life, he told Alexander Pope that he had written *Love in a Wood* when he was 19, *The Gentleman Dancing Master* at 21, *The Plain Dealer* at 25, and *The Country Wife* at 31. Internal evidence from the plays (e.g., topical allusions) suggests, however, that Wycherley wrote the plays close to their premières. See William Chadwick, *The Four Plays of William Wycherley* (Hague: Mouton, 1975), pp. 193–5, and McCarthy, *William Wycherley*, pp. 47–8, including the lengthy expository footnote on this subject.

3. For a summary of Calderón's play and Wycherley's indebtedness to it, see James Urvin Rundle, 'Wycherley and Calderón: A Source

for *Love in a Wood'*, *Publications of the Modern Language Association*, 64 (1949): 701–7, and for a brief comparison between the two plots, see Kenneth Muir, *Comedy of Manners* (London: Hutchinson, 1970), pp. 70–1.

4.   Lord Lansdowne, 'A Letter with a Character of Mr. Wycherley', *The Genuine Works in Verse and Prose of the Honourable George Granville, Lord Landsdowne* (London: 1732), I, pp. 435.

5.   A discussion of Wycherley's numerous sources is found in Peter Holland (ed.), *The Plays of William Wycherley* (Cambridge: Cambridge University Press, 1981), pp. 345–6.

6.   On Wycherley's use of language, see Robert Markley, *Two-Edged Weapons: Style and Ideology in the Comedies of Etherege, Wycherley and Congreve* (Oxford: Clarendon, 1988), pp. 138–94, and James Thompson, *Language in Wycherley's Plays* (University, AL: University of Alabama Press, 1984).

7.   Landsdowne, 'A Letter with a Character of Mr Wycherley,' p. 436.

8.   Charles Gildon, *Memoirs of the Life of William Wycherley, Esq; with a Character of his Writing by the Right Honourable George, Lord Landsdowne* (London: 1718), p. 22.

7   *The Country Wife*: Love, Marriage and Sovereignty

1.   William Archer, *The Old Drama and the New* (New York: Dodd and Mead, 1926), p. 193.

2.   See for example Thomas Fujimura, *Restoration Comedy of Wit* (Princeton, NJ: Princeton University Press, 1952), Norman Holland, *The First Modern Comedies: The Significance of Etherege, Wycherley and Congreve* (Cambridge, MA: Harvard University Press, 1967), Rose Zimbardo, *Wycherley's Drama: A Link in the Development of English Satire* (New Haven, CT: Yale University Press, 1965), Eve Kosofsky Sedgwick, *Between Men: English Literature and Male Homosocial Desire* (New York: Columbia University Press, 1985), and David M. Vieth, '*The Country Wife*: Anatomy of Masculinity', *Papers on Language and Literature*, 2, 4 (Fall 1966): 335–50 for some of these various interpretations of the play.

3.   Eric Rothstein and Frances M. Kavenik, *The Designs of Carolean Comedy* (Carbondale, IL: Southern Illinois University Press, 1988), ch. 2.

4.   Smith attributes the label 'cynical' to those comedies written between 1675 and 1687; see *The Gay Couple in Restoration Comedy* (New York: Octagon, 1971), pp. 82–107.

5.   See Susan Staves, *Players' Scepters: Fictions of Authority in the Restoration* (Lincoln, NE: University of Nebraska Press, 1979), ch. 3; and for a discussion of libertines' attitudes about marriage as evidenced in pamphlets and plays, see Maximillian E. Novak, 'Margery Pinchwife's "London Disease": Restoration Comedy and the Libertine Offensive of the 1670s', *Studies in Restoration and Eighteenth-Century Drama*, 10, 1 (Spring 1977): 1–23. Prior to Mary Astell's writings, John Locke's *Two Treatises of Government* (1689) likewise argued for shared familial power between mother and father. For a discussion of the relationship between

marriage and sovereignty, see Lawrence Stone, *The Family, Sex and Marriage in England, 1500–1800* (New York: Harper and Row, 1977), chs 2 and 5.

6. Staves, *Players' Scepters*, pp. 166–9.

7. For discussions of Carolean plays as reflections of myths of 'restoration', see Staves, *Players' Scepters* and also Richard Braverman, *Plots and Counterplots: Sexual Politics and the Body Politic in English Literature, 1660–1730* (Cambridge: Cambridge University Press, 1993).

8. For an opposing view that argues Wycherley 'rejects the traditional sexual morality of Christian society, which attempts to deny free play to the erotic drive, to channel it into the one acceptable outlet of marriage', see Gorman Beauchamp, 'The Amorous Machiavellism of *The Country Wife*', 11, 4 (Winter 1977–8): 316–30.

9. P. F. Vernon, 'Marriage of Convenience and The Moral Code of Restoration Comedy', *Essays in Criticism*, 12, 4 (October 1962): 373.

10. Jon Lance Bacon, 'Wives, Widows, and Writings in Restoration Comedy', *Studies in English Literature, 1500–1900*, 31, 3 (Summer 1991): 432.

11. For a discussion of women as sexual commodities, see Sedgwick, *Between Men*, especially the introduction and ch. 3 on *The Country Wife*.

12. Derek Cohen offers an excellent and detailed study of the play's depiction of the threat to patriarchy in '*The Country Wife* and Social Danger', *Restoration and Eighteenth Century Theatre Research*, 10, 1 (1995): 1–14.

13. Ronald Berman, 'The Ethic of *The Country Wife*', *Texas Studies in Literature and Language*, 9, 1 (Spring 1967): 54.

14. All the men use metaphors of hunting to describe their pursuit of women as animals and prey, or liken women to food meant for consumption and property that they can 'dwell in' at leisure; see, for example, Act I, scene i.

15. Holland, *The First Modern Comedies*, p. 74.

16. Helen Burke, 'Wycherley's "Tendentious Joke": The Discourse of Alterity in *The Country Wife*', *The Eighteenth Century*, 29, 3 (1988): 231.

17. For detailed discussions of this point, see David M. Vieth and W. Freedman, 'Impotence and Self-Destruction in *The Country Wife*', *English Studies*, 53, 5 (October 1972): 421–3, and John A. Vance, *William Wycherley and the Comedy of Fear* (London: Associated University Press, 2000), ch. 3 *passim*.

18. See, for example, William R. Chadwick, *The Four Plays of William Wycherley* (The Hague: Mouton, 1975), p. 114 and Katharine M. Rogers, *William Wycherley* (New York: Twayne, 1972), p. 71.

19. For a detailed description of such an interpretation, see Vance, *William Wycherley*, pp. 108–11, 119.

20. On Harcourt's and Alithea's use of figurative language that does not, like that of the other characters, debase sex with imagery of disease and war but rather with romantic sentiments, see Holland, *The First Modern Comedies*, p. 78.

21. George Savile, the Marquis of Halifax (1633–95), offers his daughter advice on husbands and marriage by way of an admonition that will help better direct her 'in the part of your Life upon which your *Happiness* most dependeth'; Savile warns: 'It is one of the *Disadvantages* belonging to your *Sex*, that young Women are seldom permitted to make their own *Choice*; ... In this case there remaineth nothing for them to do, but to endeavour to make that easie which falleth to their *Lot*, and by a wise use of every thing they may dislike in a *Husband*, turn that by degrees to be very supportable, which, if neglected, might in time beget an *Aversion*.' To temper his daughter's rebuke, Savile goes on to explain that men are the lawgivers, but that nature has afforded women some advantages, such as 'strength in your *Looks* ... and power by your *Tears*'. *The Complete Works of George Savile, First Marquess of Halifax*, ed. Walter Raleigh, (1912; rpt. New York: A.M. Kelley, 1970), pp. 7–8. The relationship between Halifax's parental warning and Alithea's plight is noted by Chadwick, *The Four Plays*, pp. 109–110.

22. H.W. Matalene ('What Happens in *The Country Wife*', *Studies in English Literature, 1500–1900*, 22, 3 [Summer 1982]: 395–411) argues convincingly that Horner, who habitually seduced common women, is nothing more than a social climber wanting access to society's more fashionable ladies who have previously snubbed him.

23. The last performance of *The Country Wife* took place in 1753. For a stage history of the play during the eighteenth century, see Emmett L. Avery, '*The Country Wife* in the Eighteenth Century', *Research Studies of the State College of Washington*, 10 (1942): 141–72.

24. Preface to *The Country Girl* (London: 1766), quoted in Avery, '*The Country Wife*', p. 156.

25. Unidentified and undated review, Production File, Theatre Museum (London).

26. 'An Unsavoury Play Without Blushes', unidentified and undated review, Production File, Theatre Museum (London).

27. *Daily Telegraph*, 3 March 1934.

28. 'Wycherley Play Revived: An Instructive Satire', unidentified and undated review, Production File, Theatre Museum (London).

29. *Sunday Times*, 4 March 1934.

30. *The Times*, 7 October 1936.

31. *Evening Standard*, 6 October 1936.

32. *The Times*, 7 October 1936.

33. *Sunday Times*, 11 October 1936.

34. *Daily Telegraph*, 7 October 1936.

35. *Evening Standard*, 13 December 1956; *Tatler*, 9 January 1957; *Observer*, 16 December 1956; *Daily Telegraph*, 13 December 1956.

36. Unidentified, undated review, Theatre Museum (London); *Observer*, 16 December 1956; *The Times*, 13 December 1956.

37. Unidentified, undated review, Production File, Theatre Museum (London).

38. *Sunday Telegraph*, 13 July 1969.

39. *Sunday Telegraph*, 13 July 1969.

40. *Independent*, 11 August 1993.

41. *The Times*, 21 July 1993.

42. *Independent*, 11 August 1993.

43. *Independent*, 11 August 1993.

44. *Independent*, 11 August 1993.

45. Sedgwick, *Between Men*, p. 50.

46. *Evening Standard*, 11 August 1993; *Telegraph*, undated, Production File, Theatre Museum (London).

47. *Evening Standard*, 11 August 1993; *Guardian*, 12 August 1993.

48. *Daily Telegraph*, undated, Production File, Theatre Museum (London).

49. *Guardian*, 12 August 1993.

8 *The Plain Dealer*: Honour, Courage and Heroism

1. *Essays of John Dryden*, ed. William Paton Ker (Oxford: Clarendon, 1926), I, 182.

2. *The Critical Works of John Dennis*, ed. Edward Niles Hooker (Baltimore, MD: Johns Hopkins University Press, 1939), II, 277.

3. Wycherley's borrowing from Molière's *The Misanthrope* has steered critics in the wrong direction, viewing Wycherley's play as a satire against the entire society or an attack against Manly (Alceste) for his uncompromising nature; this critical approach, moreover, typically leads critics to regard Wycherley's play as inferior to its model; see, for example, Norman Holland, *The First Modern Comedies: The Significance of Etherege, Wycherley and Congreve* (Cambridge, MA: Harvard University Press, 1959), p. 109.

4. See for example, K. M. Rogers, 'Fatal Inconsistency: Wycherley and *The Plain-Dealer'*, *ELH*, 28 (1961): 158, and William Chadwick, *The Four Plays of William Wycherley* (Hague: Mouton, 1975), p. 179.

5. Samuel Butler, *Prose Observations*, ed. Hugh De Quehen (Oxford: Clarendon, 1979), p. 175.

6. See John Spurr, *England in the 1670s: 'This Masquerading Age'* (London: Blackwell, 2000), pp. 93–5.

7. 'The Answer of Mr Hobbes to Sir William Davenant's Preface Before Gondibert' in William D'Avenant, *Gondibert: An Heroick Poem* (1651; rpt. Menston: Scolar Press, 1970), p. 72.

8. Spurr, *England*, p. 85.

9. 'The Glory of Dying in War' (1672), quoted from Spurr, *England*, p. 85.

10. On the battle of Sole Bay and its heroes, see *ibid.*, pp. 29–32 and 85–6.

11. Peter Holland, *The Ornament of Action: Text and Performance in Restoration Comedy* (Cambridge: Cambridge University Press, 1979), p. 188.

12. For example, see Holland, *First Modern Comedies*, pp. 96–113; Thomas H. Fujimura, *Restoration Comedy of Wit* (Princeton, NJ: Princeton

238 *Notes*

University Press, 1952), p. 149; and Katherine M. Rogers, *William Wycherley* (Boston: Twayne, 1972), p. 80.

13. Freeman will mockingly echo Manly's description of these fops whom Olivia allegedly loathes when she reveals her true colours (II,i,563–4).

14. Charles II allowed mercenaries (often men of rank) to seize damaged or disused ships and sell them as salvage for profit.

15. *Honour's Invitation* in *The Harleian Miscellany*, I, p. 347 (quoted from Spurr, *England*, pp. 87–8).

16. On the issue of masculinity and gender, which includes the Widow's sexual non-availability, see A. Velissariou, 'Gender and the Circulation of Money and Desire in Wycherley's *The Plain Dealer*', *Restoration: Studies in English Literary Culture, 1660–1700*, 18, 1 (Spring 1994): 27–36, and Sandra Sherman, 'Manly, Manliness, and Friendship in *The Plain Dealer*', *Restoration: Studies in English Literary Culture, 1660–1700*, 20, 1 (Spring 1996): 18–30.

17. Critics disagree as to whether Manly had sufficient time to consummate his lust and perpetrate his crime; of course, his failure to do so does not diminish his unheroic stature. See Percy G. Adams, 'What Happened in Olivia's Bedroom? or, Ambiguity in *The Plain Dealer*', *Essays in Honor of Esmond Linworth Marilla*, ed. Thomas Austin Kirby and William John Olive (Baton Rouge: Louisiana State University Press, 1970), pp. 174–87 and Robert F. Bode, 'A Rape and No Rape: Olivia's Bedroom Revisited', *Restoration: Studies in English Literary Culture, 1660–1700*, 12, 2 (Fall 1988): 80–6.

18. *The Plain Dealer*'s history on the eighteenth-century English stage is detailed by Emmett L. Avery, 'The Plain Dealer in the Eighteenth Century', *Research Studies of the State College of Washington*, 2 (1943): 234–56.

19. 'The Renaissance Theatre', *The Times*, 16 November 1925; 'The Plain Dealer', unidentified, undated review, Production File, Theatre Museum (London).

20. *The Spectator*, 3 June 1989.

21. *Financial Times*, 29 April 1989.

22. *Independent*, 2 May 1988; *Guardian*, 29 April 1988.

23. *Jewish Chronicle*, 26 May 1989.

24. *Punch*, 2 June 1989; *Independent*, 24 May 1989; *Guardian*, 24 May 1989; *Independent*, 2 May 1988; *The Times*, 28 April 1988; *Financial Times*, 29 April 1988.

25. *Independent*, 2 May 1988.

26. *Independent*, 2 May 1988.

27. *The Times*, 1 May 1988.

28. *Independent*, 2 May 1988.

29. *City Limits*, 19 May 1988.

Select Bibliography

History – Cultural, Political, Social

Ashley, Maurice, *Charles II: The Man and the Statesman* (New York: Praeger, 1971).

Clark, J. C. D., *Revolution and Rebellion: State and Society in England in the Seventeenth and Eighteenth Centuries* (Cambridge: Cambridge University Press, 1986).

Fraser, Antonia, *Charles II: His Life and Times* (London: Weidenfeld and Nicolson, 1993).

_____, *Royal Charles: Charles II and the Restoration* (New York: Delta, 1979).

Hutton, Ronald, *The Restoration: A Political and Religious History of England and Wales, 1658–1667* (Oxford: Clarendon Press, 1985).

_____, *Charles the Second: King of England, Scotland and Ireland* (Oxford: Clarendon Press, 1989).

Jones, J. R., *Country and Court: England, 1658–1714* (London: Edward Arnold, 1978).

Morrah, Patrick, *Restoration England* (London: Constable, 1979).

Spurr, John, *England in the 1670s: 'This Masquerading Age'* (London: Blackwell, 2000).

Stone, Lawrence, *The Family, Sex and Marriage in England, 1500–1800* (New York: Harper and Row, 1977).

Wilson, John Harold, *The Court Wits of the Restoration* (Princeton, NJ: Princeton University Press, 1948).

Literary Criticism and Theatre History

Avery, Emmett L. and Arthur H. Scouten, *The London Stage: 1660–1700* (Carbondale, IL: Southern Illinois University Press, 1968).

239

Bevis, Richard W., *English Drama: Restoration and Eighteenth Century, 1660–1798* (London: Longmans, 1988).
Birdsall, Virginia, *Wild Civility: The English Comic Spirit on the Restoration Stage* (Bloomington, IN: Indiana University Press, 1970).
Braverman, Richard, *Plots and Counterplots: Sexual Politics and the Body Politic in English Literature, 1660–1730* (Cambridge: Cambridge University Press, 1993).
Brown, John Russell and Bernard Harris (eds), *Restoration Theatre*, Stratford-upon-Avon Studies, 6 (London: Edward Arnold, 1965).
Brown, Laura, *English Dramatic Form, 1660–1760* (New Haven, CT: Yale University Press, 1981).
Bruce, Donald, *Topics of Restoration Comedy* (London: Victor Gollancz, 1974).
Burns, Edward, *Restoration Comedy: Crises of Desire and Identity* (New York: St. Martin's Press, 1987).
Canfield, J. Douglas, *Tricksters and Estates: On the Ideology of Restoration Comedy* (Lexington, KY: University of Kentucky Press, 1997).
_____ and Deborah C. Payne (eds), *Cultural Readings of Restoration and Eighteenth-Century English Theater* (Athens, GA: University of Georgia Press, 1995).
Chadwick, William R., *The Four Plays of William Wycherley* (Hague: Mouton, 1975).
Connely, Willard, *Brawny Wycherley* (New York: Scribners, 1930).
Corman, Brian, *Genre and Generic Change in English Comedy, 1660–1710* (Toronto: University of Toronto Press, 1993).
Donaldson, Ian, *The World Upside-Down* (Oxford: Clarendon, 1970).
Fisk, Deborah Payne, *The Cambridge Companion to English Restoration Theatre* (Cambridge: Cambridge University Press, 2000).
Fujimura, Thomas H, *Restoration Comedy of Wit* (Princeton, NJ: Princeton University Press, 1952).
Harwood, John T., *Critics, Values, and Restoration Comedy* (Carbondale, IL: Southern Illinois University Press, 1982).
Hawkins, Harriet, *Likeness of Truth in Elizabethan and Restoration Drama* (Oxford: Clarendon, 1972).
Holland, Norman, *The First Modern Comedies: The Significance of Etherege, Wycherley and Congreve* (Cambridge, MA: Harvard University Press, 1959).
Holland, Peter, *The Ornament of Action: Text and Performance in Restoration Comedy* (Cambridge: Cambridge University Press, 1979).
Howe, Elizabeth, *The First English Actresses: Women and Drama, 1660–1700* (Cambridge: Cambridge University Press, 1992).
Hughes, Derek, *English Drama, 1660–1700* (Oxford: Clarendon, 1996).
Hume, Robert D., *Rakish Stage* (Carbondale, IL: Southern Illinois University Press, 1983).
_____, *Development of English Drama* (Oxford: Clarendon, 1976).
Huseboe, Arthur, *Sir George Etherege* (Boston: Twayne, 1987).
Kavenik, Frances M., *British Drama, 1660–1779: A Critical Survey* (New York: Twayne, 1995).

Lynch, Kathleen, *The Social Mode of Restoration Comedy* (New York: Octagon, 1965).

McCarthy, B. Eugene, *William Wycherley: A Biography* (Athens, OH: Ohio University Press, 1979).

Markley, Robert, *Two-Edg'd Weapons: Style and Ideology in the Comedies of Etherege, Wycherley and Congreve* (Oxford: Clarendon, 1988).

Milhous, Judith and Robert D. Hume, *Producible Interpretation: Eight English Plays, 1675–1707* (Carbondale, IL: Southern Illinois University Press, 1985).

Muir, Kenneth, *The Comedy of Manners* (London: Hutchinson, 1970).

Orr, Bridget, *Empire on the English Stage, 1660–1714* (Cambridge: Cambridge University Press, 2001).

Owen, Susan J., *Perspectives on Restoration Drama* (Manchester: Manchester University Press, 2002).

_____ (ed.), *A Companion to Restoration Drama* (London: Blackwell, 2001).

Palmer, John, *The Comedy of Manners* (London: G. Bell, 1913).

Powell, Jocelyn, *Restoration Theatre Production* (London: Routledge and Kegan Paul, 1984).

Roberts, David, *The Ladies: Female Patronage of Restoration Drama, 1660–1700* (Oxford: Clarendon, 1989).

Rogers, Katharine M., *William Wycherley* (Boston: Twayne, 1972).

Rothstein, Eric and Frances M. Kavenik, *The Designs of Carolean Comedy* (Carbondale, IL: Southern Illinois University Press, 1988).

Smith, John Harrington, *The Gay Couple in Restoration Comedy* (New York: Octagon, 1971).

Southern, Richard, *Changeable Scenery: Its Origin and Development in the British Theatre* (London: Faber and Faber, 1952).

Staves, Susan, *Players' Scepters: Fictions of Authority in the Restoration* (Lincoln, NE: University of Nebraska Press, 1979).

Styan, J. L., *Restoration Comedy in Performance* (Cambridge: Cambridge University Press, 1986).

Taney, Retta M., *Restoration Revivals on the British Stage: 1944–1979* (Lanham, MD: University Press of America, 1985).

Thompson, James, *Language in Wycherley's Plays: Seventeenth-Century Language Theory and Drama* (University, AL: University of Alabama Press, 1984).

Underwood, Dale, *Etherege and Seventeenth Century Comedy of Manners* (New Haven, CT: Yale University Press, 1957).

Vance, John A., *William Wycherley and the Comedy of Fear* (London: Associated University Presses, 2000).

Vernon, Paul F., *William Wycherley* (London: Longmans, 1965).

Weber, Harold, *The Restoration Rake-Hero* (Madison, WI: University of Wisconsin Press, 1986).

Wilkinson, David R., *The Comedy of Habit* (Leiden: Universitare Pers, 1964).

Zimbardo, Rose, *Wycherley's Drama: A Link in the Development of English Satire* (New Haven, CT: Yale University Press, 1965).

Index

242

Printed in the United States
32940LVS00001B/78